Priya Bala is a writer specializing in food. She is a restaurant critic of repute and the author of *Foodprints – A Trail of Meals & Memories*. She has forayed into cooking in professional settings and runs Yo Colombo, a Sri Lankan food brand based on the principles of sustainability. As a chef and writer, she is uniquely placed to understand the food industry.

Jayanth Narayanan began his career in the corporate world and was later drawn to the restaurant industry, with all its challenges and thrills. An enterprising restaurateur, he runs Mani's Dum Biryani, the popular quick-service restaurant brand. Jayanth is an alumnus of BITS, Pilani, and holds an MBA from XLRI, Jamshedpur.

Together, Priya and Jayanth have co-authored *Start Up Your Restaurant* and *Secret Sauce – Inspiring Stories of Great Indian Restaurants*.

Priya Bala and Jayanth Narayanan

Published by
Rupa Publications India Pvt. Ltd 2024
7/16, Ansari Road, Daryaganj
New Delhi 110002

Sales centres:
Bengaluru Chennai
Hyderabad Jaipur Kathmandu
Kolkata Mumbai Prayagraj

Copyright © Priya Bala and Jayanth Narayanan 2024
Credits: Illustrations by Pratiksha Roy; maps by Kumar Ravichandran

The views and opinions expressed in this book are the authors' own and the facts are as reported by them, which have been verified to the extent possible, and the publishers are not in any way liable for the same.

All rights reserved.
No part of this publication may be reproduced, transmitted or stored in a retrieval system, in any form or by any means, electronic, mechanical, photocopying, recording or otherwise, without the prior permission of the publisher.

P-ISBN: 978-93-6156-117-7
E-ISBN: 978-93-6156-565-6

First impression 2024

10 9 8 7 6 5 4 3 2 1

The moral right of the authors have been asserted.

Printed at India

This book is sold subject to the condition that it shall not, by way of trade or otherwise, be lent, resold, hired out, or otherwise circulated, without the publisher's prior consent, in any form of binding or cover other than that in which it is published.

For Sangeeta
&
Street food vendors everywhere

Street food, I believe,
is the salvation of the human race.

—Anthony Bourdain

CONTENTS

Foreword	*xiii*
Preface	*xv*
Benne Dosa Paradise *Davangere*	2
Ghirmit and a Famous Pedha *Hubli–Dharwad*	6
From Gobi Manchurian and Mysore Pak to Thatte Idli *Mysore, Maddur & Bidadi*	11
The Malabar Street-Food Trail *Kozhikode, Thrissur, Ramassery*	17
Bun Parotta and Jigarthanda—the Blockbusters *Madurai*	25
Tiffin Rooms and Military Messes *Chennai*	35
Beyond Biryani: From Osmania Biscuit to Falooda *Hyderabad*	42
Odisha: The Land of Ghugni, Khaja, and Chakuli *Puri, Bhubaneshwar, Cuttack*	50
Steeped in History *Kolkata*	62

Tibetan Cuisine at Its Best 76
Darjeeling, Kalimpong, Shillong

More than Litti Chokha 84
Patna

Spirituality and Street Food 90
Varanasi

Streets Full of Surprises 102
Allahabad

Where Sharma Ji Ki Chai and Tunday Kebab Come Together 112
Lucknow

Sweets Fit for Royalty 122
Gwalior

Tea in the Winter, Rasmalai Dona in the Summer 129
Bhopal

Sarafa Bazaar and Chappan Dukan 135
Indore

A Hugely Popular Pakodewala 142
Nagpur

Perfect Misal and Parsi Baking 148
Pune

Fuelling a Massive Workforce 160
Mumbai

Where the Locals Go 168
Goa

Jalebi Fafda and Bun Maska, Chai: The Breakfast Icons 176
Ahmedabad

Locho: From Failed Attempt to a Signature Snack   187
  Surat

Kachoris Galore   195
  Udaipur

Doodh Bhandars: Where Milk is a Celebration   203
  Jodhpur

Patasi: Jaipur's Take on the Pani Puri   210
  Jaipur

Where Petha Rules   220
  Agra

Chhole Bhature to Mughlai   225
  Delhi

Puris and Maggi Points   236
  Dehradun–Mussoorie

Vegetarian Specials   241
  Haridwar–Rishikesh

An Abundance of Pedhas   247
  Mathura–Vrindavan

Kulcha Like No Place Else   255
  Amritsar

Begin the Day with a Girda   263
  Srinagar

Idli Vada Icons   268
  Bangalore

Acknowledgements   275

Glossary   277

FOREWORD

From the time National Association of Street Vendors of India (NASVI) was initiated in 1998, street vendors have been progressing towards a better future. But there has been no dearth of challenges that they face. A National Policy for Urban Street Vendors was drafted in 2004 and based on the learnings from its implementation, a Central Law was enacted in 2014; 30 lakh street vendors have been issued licenses under the law. Still, lack of urban planning and poor municipal governance create insurmountable roadblocks for street vendors.

The Food Safety and Standards Act was enacted in 2006. It was widely believed that its purpose was to drive out small food business operators like street-food vendors. We took the Act as a positive step and approached Food Safety and Standards Authority of India (FSSAI) for registration of food vendors under the Act. Registration began in many states in right earnest. It also generated interest in food vendors. We began organizing a National Street Food Festival in Delhi from 2009 and the crowds have swelled each subsequent year. Street-food vendors began participating in international festivals and in events organized by the Ministry of Tourism as well as other ministries.

We collaborated with FSSAI and began training food vendors across the country in hygiene and food safety. Street-food zones are being created and post Covid there has been a significant increase in street-food vending across the country and even in rural areas.

Street food has come a long way from the time we began working with food vendors. Now, multinational companies are entering this business and are opening more and more retail stores. All caterers now have a street-food repertoire. At our recent National Executive Committee meeting, we identified that preserving street food as the exclusive domain of food vendors was a formidable challenge. We have launched a campaign #streetfoodbyvendors and I am sure this book will go a long way in making people understand street-food vendors better.

We, from NASVI, congratulate Priya Bala and Jayanth Narayanan for taking the time and effort to write about a section of people whose livelihood contributes greatly to pleasing our taste buds, our culture and, most importantly, the availability of food for everyone.

Arbind Singh
National Coordinator, National Association of Street Vendors of India (NASVI)

PREFACE

The most outstanding aspect of Indian food is surely its staggering diversity. This abundance of variety spills over onto the streets and small shops of Indian cities and towns, becoming an immense cornucopia of inexpensive yet delicious food.

A long-nurtured desire to explore and savour this plenitude set us off on a journey, going where our tastebuds and tales of famed street-food vendors led us. Our two earlier books have been about restaurants, and the research was planned and structured.

But this time we decided, on a whim, to freewheel, careening from Davangere to Hyderabad, road-tripping in Odisha, and traipsing through the old quarters of Allahabad and Gwalior. We set forth, certain we would eat well wherever we went. What we hadn't anticipated were the deep insights we would gather about the crucial role street food plays in our urban culture. At the end of our journey, we had only the greatest respect and admiration for India's countless street-food vendors who feed the poor and the toiling.

In recent times, street food has risen from its shabby turf to acquire an element of cool. Proof is the popularity of tours that take visitors through the street-food hubs of a city, the explosion of blogs and videos on the topic, and the number of people who've come to enjoy the idea of slumming it and tucking into kachori or kebabs from modest little shops, while standing on the footpath, balancing foil plates in their hands.

Yet, in its essential purpose, street food was and still is the sustenance of those who cannot afford better. Hole-in-the-wall eateries, roadside food stalls and carts first came into being to serve migrant workers who had no access to home food and those who could not afford to eat in proper restaurants. Think of Mumbai's mill workers who found nourishment in plates of pav bhaji and the manual labourers of Madurai for whom a pile of salna-soaked parotta is hunger-quelling happiness.

Indian street fare, representing a culinary style completely different from that practised in homes and in restaurants, has evolved to encompass a repertoire of truly delicious foods that please and satisfy people across the country, from various social and economic strata.

It is an impossible task to contain the abundance that is Indian street food in a single-book, and we make no claim that this is an exhaustive compilation. It is merely our attempt to give you a glimpse into the vibrant street-food cultures we encountered in cities and towns during our uncharted travels. And in the process perhaps inspire you to undertake similar explorations. We were wonderstruck by the culinary imagination that can turn a few humble ingredients into such delightful foods, and their freshness and affordability. No two cities have the same street-food culture and that made our explorations unendingly exciting with surprisingly new dishes popping up at every turn.

There is a perception, especially among those who haven't really delved into the deep hearts of old cities and their underbellies, that street food is 'dirty'. In our experience, the settings may have been grimy, the dishcloths tattered, but the food was almost always made fresh in full view of customers. We are not being facetious when we say a hot-from-the-karhai samosa eaten off the street is nowhere as damaging as processed food that comes in pretty packaging. Having said that, there is scope to improve hygiene standards; street vendors can, for instance, have better access to water supply. The conundrum is that when our civic authorities set out to sanitize street food, they also take away long traditions and the very charm of it. We saw that in some of the modern hawker markets that have been set up.

Behind this culinary culture, which feeds cities and plays a key role in their street economy, are the people who sustain it: the cooks, the sellers of food, and the owners of these modest businesses, some of whom are carrying on a century-old tradition. This book also narrates their stories and focuses on their spirit of enterprise. These entrepreneurs, rarely highly educated, conduct their businesses in a way management institutes would probably wish to analyse. We were impressed by their commitment to quality, their focus on a single product or small range of products, their admirable customer relations and ability to evoke loyalty without any marketing or advertising.

Despite their utility in every urban landscape, street vendors, especially those selling food, are often at the mercy of city authorities. They are harassed for bribes and evicted, even though there is now a law that gives them rights. Still, they go on, displaying remarkable pride and joy in the simple task of making and serving the perfect papdi chaat or puri aloo.

We had completed over half of the travel and research for this book when the pandemic struck. The crisis that upturned lives and livelihoods meant we had to sit back and wait until travel became possible again. During those times we fretted about the plight of those who made their living selling food on the streets. Would they survive? It is a mark of their resilience and agility that they returned to add vibrancy to our street culture, warmly embraced by loyal customers.

While some street-food vendors have found recognition thanks to social media, many remain unsung and nameless. This book is a celebration of these humble food vendors and their modest enterprises. So, come take a street-food tour of India, along the way meeting the people who make Srinagar's best kebabs and getting to know the feisty woman who lent her name to Chachi ki Dukan in Varanasi.

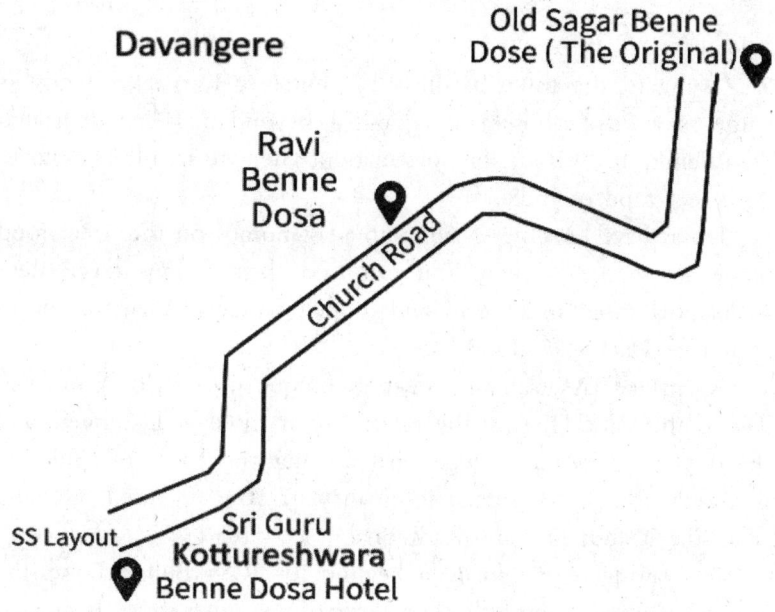

BENNE DOSA PARADISE

Davangere

Davangere, the town in the very centre of Karnataka, lends its name to a dosa whose fame goes far beyond it. Being dedicated dosa fiends, this was our first destination when we set off to discover the street food of India.

Dosas have become as ubiquitous as momos on the street-food scene across the country. You can find them being served next to kachori shops in Varanasi and topped with pav bhaji masala in Mumbai's *khau galli*s (food lanes).

Karnataka lays claim to a set of unique dosa styles, known as *dose* in the state. There is the *benne* (butter) dose of Davangere and the dose with its raised edges that the highway town of Mulbagal is known for. In Mysore, it is the Mylari dose, favoured by those who like it authentic and traditional.

In Davangere we made a beeline for Ravi Benne Dose, the iconic yet unassuming little shop located on a quiet street. It seemed some dose heaven had opened its doors to us as we ate the dose cooked to a golden crispness, while perched on plastic stools on the pavement. When we got a chance to meet the shop's owner, Ravi, he asked for a benne dose for himself as he settled down to chat.

The dose here is served with an *aloo palya*—mashed potato mixed with onions, cooked with salt and no other spice—and a coconut chutney. He mixed the potato into the coconut chutney and dipped bits of crisp dose into it. Nearing the end of the dose, he pointed to the edges, saying, 'It's dry. It shouldn't be like this. It's where you

place the benne—the butter. It has to go on the little mounds that form when you swirl the dose, not the ridges. Then, the butter pours down and keeps the edges crisp, yet moist.'

In need of knee surgery, Ravi hadn't been able to man the dose griddle in recent times. And he was clearly not completely satisfied with the dose-making skills of his staff. It's Ravi's attention to the smallest detail that has made this small shop the Davangere institution that it is.

Its beginnings go back to 1928 when a woman named Chennamma left her village and came to Davangere to make a living. She began to sell dose made from ragi flour at the Savalagi drama theatre. It was a night business, running from 7 p.m. to beyond midnight to feed those who came to the touring talkies. 'The ragi was ground on a stone, sieved in a dhoti and then turned into a batter. It was hard work and the yield was very little,' Ravi told us. Later, her sons Shanthappa and Mahadevappa, Ravi's father, stepped in and began to make the rice dose that would become famous.

BENNE DOSA PARADISE

In 1944, Shanthappa went on to open his own dose hotel, Davangere's oldest, and Mahadevappa also opened his own dose stall near the now-defunct Vasantha theatre. In 1988, he moved to the present space on Church Road, by which time Ravi had been inducted into the business. 'I started off cleaning tables and washing the water tumblers,' he said. 'I was allowed to make dose only after years of doing this.'

Ravi has been a dose master since 1967 and says it takes several decades to become an expert. The expertise involves making the batter of rice, *mandakki* (flattened rice) and just a pinch of soda, tending the wood fire, maintaining the griddle made of cold-rolled magnetic steel at the perfect temperature, pouring out the dose, and slapping on blobs of white butter—some 30 grams goes into one dose—with a practised rhythm and flipping the dose over. If you wish to, you can have a fluffier, fat-free version, the *khali* dose.

Continuing on the dose trail, we went to Old Sagar Benne Dose Hotel, famous enough for its name to be copied multiple times in the town. The original is on IB Road and has existed since 1992. It's a modest 24-seater and serves coffee along with the two dose staples. Umesh Vijayakumar, who manages this establishment, said it was previously known simply as the Sagar Benne Dose Hotel and the 'Old' was added to differentiate it from the competition.

Sri Guru Kottureshwara Benne Dose Hotel on Medical College Road is another reputed benne dose maker of Davangere. It was started in the early '90s by the brothers Revanasiddaiah and Basaiah, who came from nearby Anajigere. They were suppliers of white butter to restaurants in Davangere and then decided to set up their own benne dose place. There are two adjacent shops and here, too, there are just two items on the menu, benne dose and khali dose. We watched with amazement as regulars ate their first order of two benne dose and followed up with a stack of khali dose, having their potato palya and chutney replenished. Narendra, who now manages the business, has expanded and set up a corner shop across the road. 'Before any competition comes up there,' he told us with a smile.

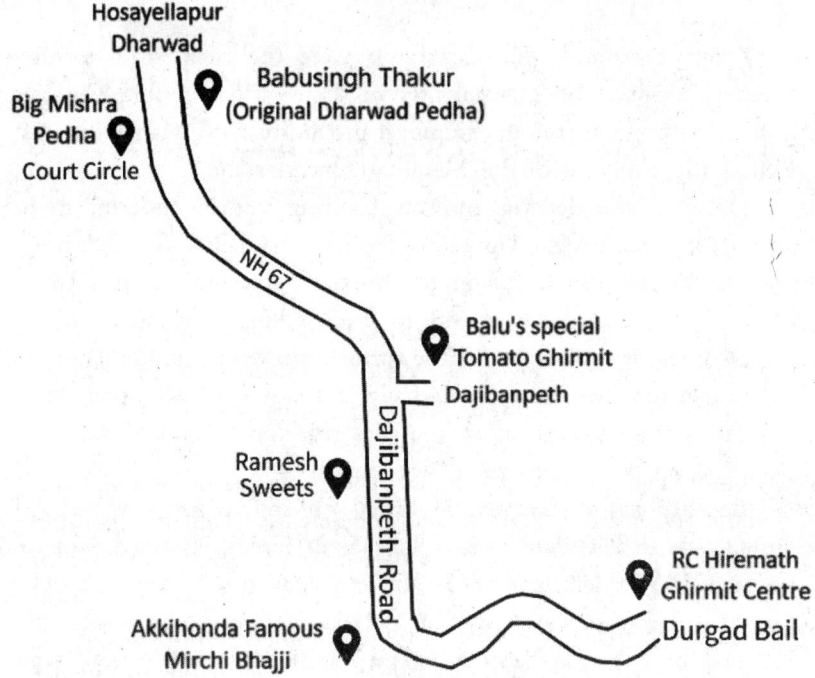

GHIRMIT AND A FAMOUS PEDHA

Hubli–Dharwad

After Davangere, our next stop were the twin cities in the northern extreme of Karnataka. Here, there's a perceptible Marathi influence, thanks to the geographical proximity with Maharashtra as well as the conquest of the Marathas centuries ago.

Hubli is crowded, its markets bursting with wonderful fresh produce. In quarters like Durgadbail, street-food stalls abound, dishing out *ghirmit* and mirchi bhajji to shoppers. You must dodge two-wheelers as you make your way to shops selling *papdi*-chutney.

Dharwad is quieter and more spruced up than Hubli, thanks to it being made over into a 'smart city'. It was the *pedha* that took us here, a unique confection that has received a GI tag and puts Dharwad on the sweet map of the country.

Bombay has its *bhelpuri*, Hubli its ghirmit. A savoury mix of puffed rice or *churmura* as it is known in Hubli, chopped tomato and masala powders, ghirmit is the city's favourite anytime snack. One that wins the popularity vote is Balu's cart, parked outside City Hospital, near the Dajibanpeth Laxmi Temple. Vishal, who now runs it, told us the cart has been in operation since the early 1980s. Even before he opens at 5 p.m., there are crowds milling around the cart. He has takeaway portions of dry churmura packed in foil bags. If you eat at the stall, he'll toss up a massive plate with puffed rice, lots of tomatoes, chickpea powder and masala that gives this ghirmit a distinct red tinge. At ₹40 a plate, it's an affordable, much-loved snack for the people of Hubli.

In the evenings, Durgadbail Circle is bustling with shoppers. That's also when the food carts start buzzing. Many though have begun to deal in generic fast food, like *gobi* Manchurian and Maggi noodles. One of the few serving an excellent ghirmit is the RC Hiremath stall, that's been here since the mid-1980s. Owner Prabhaiah says the secret to his ghirmit, unique to North Karnataka, is the special masala and, of course, the art of tossing it.

Passing by vendors of trinkets and cheap clothes and women selling piles of local vegetables, sacks full of millets and flattened rice, we reached a corner of Akkihond market. You only have to ask about the mirchi bhajji place and you'll be directed to a smoke-blackened hole in the wall that serves up this Hubli favourite. The shop has been operational since the early 1950s, said Sangaiah Hiremath, who makes the bhajjis here from 5 p.m. to 10 p.m. every day. The Hubli mirchi bhajji is special, made from a local variety of chilli, slender and pale green, with just enough heat to lend it a pleasant bite. The chilli is split and filled with a spice mix. It's then dipped in a chickpea flour batter and deep-fried to become pillowy, yellow bhajjis with a crunchy, hot centre. It is incredibly good and Sangaiah said it's because they grind their own chickpea flour, rather than using commercial ones that are almost always adulterated.

Established in the early 1990s, Shri Shakti Hotel in Janta Bazar, Dajiban Peth Road, rolls out a mirchi bhajji operation starting at 3 p.m. every day. Here you can have your mirchi bhajji in a bun, a take on Mumbai's vada pav. The owner, Ratnakar Gowda, also serves up *bonda* and samosa in a bun.

The most unassuming dish could become an amazing discovery, as we found during our travels. Right up there on this list is the papdi chutney of Hubli. Ramesh Sweets, a corner shop which has been there since 1990 in crowded Kamripeth, is known for it. Ramesh says his regular customers take away bags of the papdi and chutney, which keeps very well for three to four days. The papdi is made of chickpea flour and is light and crisp. The chutney, green with mint, also has ginger, garlic, green chillies and tamarind, giving it a

wonderful tartness. You dip bits of papdi into this wondrous chutney and savour the taste and the texture.

Babusingh Thakur Pedha laid the foundations of a sweet that would bring fame to Dharwad. In the 1870s, escaping a raging plague, Ram Ratan Singh Thakur left Unnao in Uttar Pradesh and arrived in Dharwad. A livelihood had to be earned and he turned to making pedhas with buffalo milk and sugar. The quantities were small and he would carry his wares to places where crowds gathered. After him, the family continued the business, slowly growing it. His grandson, Babusingh Thakur, worked to popularize the sweet and set up a shop in Line Bazaar. Old residents of Dharwad still refer to this confection as Line Bazaar pedha.

While the next generations chose to expand, setting up a chain of stores across the city and outside, the original shop is still functional and the family lives behind it. Umesh Singh Thakur, of the sixth generation who is now running the business, invited us in for lemonade and sweets. He told us the pedha enjoys the reputation it does because of the family's hands-on involvement in its making.

'We are all in the kitchen. Even after we've opened several stores, we only go to them on Dasara and Diwali. Every other day we are up at 4 a.m., when the making of the pedha begins by stirring the milk and sugar over wood fires.'

It takes hours of patient cooking for the milk to solidify and the sweet to caramelize. 'It cannot be rushed. And all the flavour comes from the quality of the milk and the technique. There's no colour, essence or other additives,' Umesh said. The ratio of milk to sugar, the cooking time and method are all closely held family secrets. 'You have to know how to manage the heat—that's what gives the pedha its structure—and the exact moment to take it off the fire.' Once cooked, the caramelized mass is 'cut', another special technique, and then hand-shaped. Finally, the pedhas are coated with powdered sugar and packed in boxes that are an ode to nostalgia.

Mysore

- Old original Hotel Vinayaka Mylari — Nazarbad Main Road / Vasanth Mahal Road
- Hotel Hanumanthu since 1930 — Akbar Rd cross
- Guru Sweet Mart — K R Circle
- Usman Dry Gobi — Devraj Urs RD / Krishna vilas Rd
- Univ. of Mysore
- Kukarhalli Lake — Mangalore Mysore HW
- Deepu Gadi

FROM GOBI MANCHURIAN AND MYSORE PAK TO THATTE IDLI

Mysore, Maddur & Bidadi

*M*ysore charms easily. Arriving here from Bangalore, we couldn't help thinking how much better Mysore does on the liveability scale. You immediately notice the change of pace, a slower, more laidback one, a refreshing change from the frantic movement of the big city. The homes are set amid gardens. In the old quarters of the city, you can go through the leisurely luxurious process of choosing and buying ittar. Or eat in restaurants that are nearly a century old. Plus, Mysore has all the tourist brochure attractions—from its opulent palace to yoga schools, the magnificent Dasara parade, its sandalwood and silk sarees, plus the Mysore *pak*.

Reaching Mysore as dusk fell one early winter day, we headed to the nearest snack shop that had achieved fame on Youtube. Karnataka's cities have a particular fondness for gobi, mostly made into 'Manchurian'. It is cauliflower dipped in batter, often a vivid red, deep-fried and then tossed in sauce.

Mysore's popular gobi spot makes a dry version. It's a shop in Devaraja Mohalla, begun in 1994 by Zain ul Abidin. Crowds wait patiently for up to 20 minutes for a plate of batter-fried gobi. The owners say it's the quality that brings customers to them. Usman uses fresh oil every day, up to 12 kg a day apparently. And it is not reused. The gobi, a moreish snack, is served with a thin green chutney and sliced onions.

Later, we went to a Mysore landmark, significant despite its inconspicuous facade and famous for its dose. The Old Original Hotel Vinayaka Mylari in Nazarabad is a tiny six-table eatery next to a stationery shop. Its reputation and success have spawned many imitations and a notice inside says 'No Branches'. There are just two items on the menu here: plain dose and masal dose. Commonplace as that sounds, you will be wowed when the dose arrives on a banana leaf. It's soft, airy, fluffy and topped with a pat of white butter. The chutney is excellent, too. The dose is cooked on wood fires. The batter is made to a recipe that has remained unchanged since the shop started in the 1930s. Usha Rani, who now manages the business, says it's a family secret. It was her mother-in-law's mother-in-law who began this dose shop. Usha Rani's son Sachin is also now involved. To eat in Mylari is to taste the perfect dose and laud the discipline and commitment it takes to run a two-dish eatery.

An entirely different dose experience awaited us at a cart known to regulars merely as Deepu Gadi. It stands in a lane near Kukkarahalli Lake and gets bustling from 7 a.m. in the morning. You buy a paper token—they come in different colours and codes, IV standing for idli-vada—and wait for your food, occasionally shouting out 'Deepu Anna, *ondu set masala dose*, extra butter.' Started around the year 2000 by Deepu, this cart sells masala dose that's smaller than in most places, crisp, golden and utterly delicious. Also on the menu are *thatte* idli, served steaming hot, masala vade and *uddin* vade, plus *bhaath*, the popular Karnataka breakfast of flavoured rice.

Locals recommended Hotel Hanumanthu for lunch. Like all successful eateries, it has spawned several imitations, prompting the owners to add 'Original' to the name. The *palav*, of rice and mutton, is the dish that has earned this place on Akbar Road in Mandi Mohalla its fame. The business was begun by Shriman Hanumanthu in the 1930s and is now run by Vishal Kiran Gowda of the third generation.

Hotel Hanumanthu starts serving palav from the early hours of the morning and it's not unusual for regulars to have a hearty portion for breakfast. When you take your seat, friendly waiters will

BAZAAR BITES

first spread a piece of newspaper on the table. The palav arrives in quick time on a leaf plate. It comes with a salad of cucumber and onion and a dark *sharva* (gravy). A half portion costs ₹200. The rice is small-grained and fragrant, the mutton is cooked to a lovely tenderness, and it's a truly satisfying meal. Several stars of the Kannada film industry are regulars here.

Before we left Mysore, we had to go shopping for the city's gift to the world of South Indian sweets. Mysore's best-known confection, the Mysore pak, is as famous as its fine silk sarees and its sandalwood.

Tracing the origins of food is never easy, tangled as it is in myth and hard-to-authenticate stories. However, it is easy to believe that the Mysore pak was born in the royal kitchens of the Mysore Palace. The story goes that the then ruler of Mysore, Krishnaraja Wadiyar IV, commissioned Kakasura Madappa to make a variety of sweets for a feast. Madappa came up with one made from gram flour, sugar and ghee. The king was pleased and called it Mysore pak.

The fifth generation of Madappa's family now runs Guru Sweets, a small shop at the corner of Devaraja Market. You must stop here to taste Mysore pak in the place of its birth. The shop sells two varieties: ordinary made with vanaspati and 'special' made with ghee. One bite of the special and you know why this is such a celebrated sweet.

If you drive from Bangalore to Mysore, there are two stops that must be made specifically for the food. One is in Bidadi, an otherwise nondescript industrial town some 40 km from the capital. There are a string of shops here specializing in one particular item, the thatte idli.

We stopped at the Sri Shiva Darshana Shashi Thatte Idly Hotel, SSD for short, lured by the signboard that announced it had been around since 1950. The eatery is now run by Shashi Kiran from the fourth generation and other members of the family that began this business. Originally, they dealt in the 'acrey' idli, which was a large idli cut into pieces, served doused with ghee and scattered with *podi*. SSD is one of the first places to serve the now famous thatte idli, which has put Bidadi on the food map of this region. Now there are more than 50 shops selling this idli. It's a tightly managed family business. The batter of *urad* dal and parboiled rice—it has to be aged rice—is made by the women of the family.

At the eatery, workers ladle the batter into trays and steam it. A seemingly endless stream of thatte idlis emerges. The idlis are served on yellow plastic plates and you can have yours anointed with ghee and scattered with spicy podi. It is accompanied by a chilli chutney made from a combination of Byadgi and Guntur chillies and a mild potato gravy they call Bombay sagu. We tucked into ours happily, enjoying the pillow-soft texture and the pleasing sourness of these perfectly fermented idlis. SSD sells up to 5,000 idlis in a day.

At our next stop, the owner politely declined to tell us how much he sold. That is an indication, too, of what a hotseller the vada at Maddur Tiffanys is. Current owner D.N. Chathura told us that the credit for making this vada can go to Ramachandra Budhiya and Madhavachar who sold food at the Maddur railway station. Budhiya's eatery was called Vegetarian Tiffin Room, VTR. On a particular day sometime in 1917, running short of time he converted his usual pakodas into a quick snack, flattening a mixture of semolina, rice flour, maida and onions into discs. What was it to be called? Maddur vada, he said. And this little town in Mandya district acquired a dish that would bring it food fame. Chathura's ancestor H.D. Hebbar then took over VTR and continued making the signature vade. It was passed down through the generations, but VTR at the railway station shut down in 2017, 100 years after the Maddur vade was born. We thought it sad that such a piece of food history should have been wiped away thus.

The family then set up Tiffanys, which now has three branches, including one in Mysore. These look like any highway restaurant in this part of the country and serve the staples. But Tiffanys stands apart with its vade, which is part of Karnataka's culinary legacy. It's now made in an industrial-scale operation, vast amounts of the flours and kilos of sliced onions kneaded together to be fried and sold by the thousands every day. They also have a 'special' version, studded with cashew and poppy seeds.

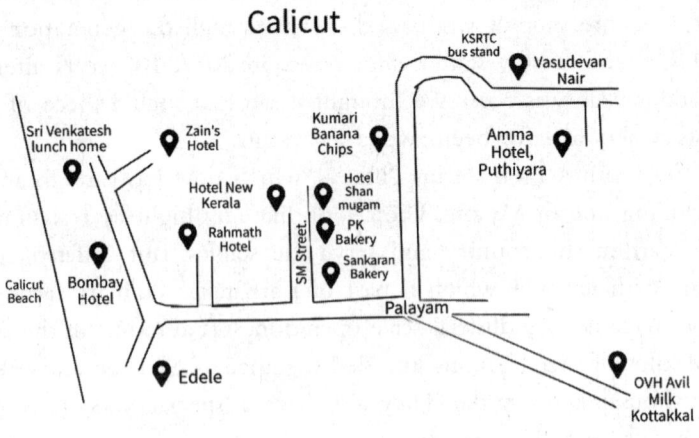

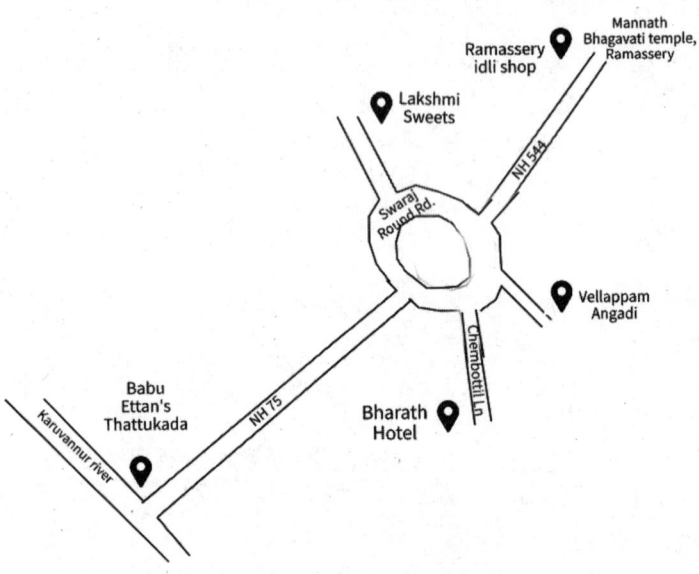

THE MALABAR STREET-FOOD TRAIL

Kozhikode, Thrissur, Ramassery

We arrived in Kozhikode (also known as Calicut) with the city basking in pleasant evening light. It has the charming air of old cities, with vintage buildings, amidst which pop up contemporary-style cafes and broast shops—ubiquitous sellers of fried chicken in these parts—cool or incongruous, depending on your aesthetic.

We headed first to SM Street (or Mittayi Theruvu, as it is known in Malayalam) and were told by a shopkeeper there that SM stands for Sweet Meat. The street is part of a sprawling market, a vast, pedestrian-only public square. It has always been a gathering place for the town and is the setting for the Kerala Sahitya Akademi award-winning work, *Oru Theruvinte Katha* ('The Story of a Street') by S.K. Pottekkatt.

At the entrance to SM Street is New Kerala Hotel, which has been standing here since 1930. The little eatery is known for its array of snacks displayed in a glass case.

The chicken cutlet and *ela ada* (rice flour packets stuffed with coconut and jaggery and steamed in a banana leaf) are popular items here and so is the *poricha ada*, a Malabar empanada, if you will, made with rice flour and stuffed with sweet coconut. We had one of these, with lemon tea, before walking further down SM Street.

Hotel Shanmugham, founded in the 1940s by P.M. Pachu, is the vegetarian version of Hotel New Kerala. It has lots of old-world charm and is famous for its dosa, vada, *aval* (flattened rice tossed with jaggery and coconut), *puttu*, and, of course, a range of local snacks like the *pazham pori* (batter-fried nendran banana).

As you amble further down the street, you'll probably have to brave shopkeepers of halwa stores, entreating you to buy their famous Kozhikoden halwa or dates.

We were headed to Sankaran Bakery, rated by locals as the best halwa maker in the town. This shop, begun by Sankaran Nair in the 1920s, is now in the hands of Rishil, of the third generation. There are over three dozen varieties of halwa in a glass cabinet, glistening in various colours, from black to neon green and orange. The halwas come in flavours of tender coconut, pineapple, the traditional banana, dates and a dark halwa made with rice flour. The others are made mainly from cornstarch, sugar and coconut oil, the mixture then enhanced with dried fruit, nuts, colour and flavourings.

Another popular store here is the 90-year-old PK Bakery, begun by Vishwanathan. It produces baked goods at the back of the store, making crunchy barley biscuits, raisin rusk and other goodies. Like most stores on SM Street, PK Bakery also sells a variety of Kozhikoden halwa.

After the sweet treats, it was time to check out some more of the unique snacks of the Malabar region. Bombay Hotel on Silk Street is in a quiet part of town, not far from the beach. It was begun in 1940 by Kunhahammed, a skilled cook who came from Thalassery to open an eatery in the flourishing town. His son, the soft-spoken Mohammed Najib, an advocate by training, now manages the restaurant that's a Kozhikode landmark. We went there late one evening and the place was abuzz with customers who come here for the *elanchi*, a turmeric-tinted pancake filled with coconut and sugar, the *unnakkaya*, a delicious banana fritter, the puffs, the *chemmeen* cake, a two-layered, soft, savoury cake filled with spiced prawns and more.

At lunch time the biryanis bring people here. Why Bombay Hotel, we asked Najib. 'It was a trend at the time to name hotels after places. So, we had Rangoon Hotel and Paris Hotel,' he smiled.

Rahmath Hotel in Mananchira is also famous for its Malabar snacks and is one of the few places where the names of the local

BAZAAR BITES

dishes are also written in English. The snacks—cutlets, pazham pori, egg box, beef *pathiri*—are served in a separate section. The biryani, especially the beef biryani, is the most ordered item here.

Kuttichira, at one end of Beach Road, is also well-known for its biryani. Zain's Hotel on Convent Cross Road is known for its Malabar dishes such as *muttamala* and *erachi pathiri*. So, off we went to stroll along the beach. It was pretty crowded even on a weekday evening and you had to admire a city for making this a public-friendly space with seats, shade and toilets.

Calicut's beach snacks are unique to this stretch. Close to the water is a string of vending carts all selling pickled vegetables. Large jars hold fat slices of raw mango, carrots, gooseberries, even pears floating in brine. You take your pick, squirt on a chilli masala that's kept there and enjoy the mouth-puckering mix. The pickle carts also sell ice *orathi*. A block of ice is shaved and the shavings scooped into a plastic glass. Syrup is added, plus a squeeze of fresh, local narangi orange. Some chopped cherries, soaked *sabja* seeds and, curiously, roasted chana dal tops it off.

We looked askance at this seemingly bizarre combination and were surprised at how lovely and cooling it was. Fringing the road by the beach are carts selling *arikadukka*, mussels fried in a rice batter to a golden crisp, quail eggs that can be had plain or with masala or tossed with boiled green peas.

THE MALABAR STREET-FOOD TRAIL

Just off the beach is Sri Venkatesh Lunch Home, with an eye-catching lilac façade, holding its own against the trendy cafes that have sprung up in the vicinity. Begun in 1969 by Vishwanatha Iyer, it's now run by his grandsons, Rajesh and Vishwanathan. We went there for breakfast. The place was spotlessly clean and the idli, vada and chutney were all excellent. Anyone who scoffs at *upma* should taste the one here.

If our breakfast was at this vegetarian landmark, our next stop was Edele, a meat lover's paradise near the Mishkal Mosque in Kuttichira. It's bang opposite a butcher's. Begun by Yahutty and now managed by his son Kunhalavi, Edele is known for its breakfast dishes such as *puttu* with beef curry. The shop opens as early as 5 a.m. and there are customers lining up. Fridays are special at Edele for that's when beef biryani is available. 'Only one day a week,' Kunhalavi told us. 'Other days, you can have *neichoru*, Kerala's ghee rice, with beef curry.'

One doesn't leave Kozhikode without a stash of chips. We went to Kumari Banana Chips at Paragon Junction. This is a tiny store and all the frying happens in a shed alongside. Two workers, sitting outside, patiently peel *nendran* bananas. The peeled vegetables are then put through a slicer to make thin chips. These are washed in water and a solution of salt and turmeric and fried in a vast karhai. Coconut husks feed the fire.

Paragon, famous for its biryani which lends its name to the junction, is next door and how could we not drop in there? So, we had pazham pori and tea before continuing on the chip hunt. The Vasudevan Nair shop opposite the KSRTC bus stand also has a reputation for its chips. These are still cut by hand and you can tell the difference.

Leaving Kozhikode, after truly loving its vibe, we went to Kottakkal, the town best known for its Ayurveda centre. Only slightly less associated with the place is *avil* milk. VH Avil milk on the main Kottakkal Road serves this unique Malabar drink. It has cold milk, soaked aval, or flattened rice, local bananas, with puffed rice and peanuts adding crunch. Like with the ice orathi, we were unsure

BAZAAR BITES

what to expect and were most pleasantly surprised. On a warm day, it was the perfect drink, cooling and nourishing.

The terrain was unremarkable, driving to Thrissur from Kottakkal. Our ennui was lifted by the discovery in Thirikannur of a cart selling freshly fried tapioca chips.

Thrissur, bustling and large, missed the charm of Kozhikode. But there are still quaint little lanes and small shops like Lakshmi Sweets in Palayam. Murali Swamy began the business in the 1980s and he's now assisted by his son, Akshay. In front of the store, a low table holds trays with vegetarian cutlets, bonda, vada, vegetable samosa, *unniappam* and *sukiyan*, fried balls of sweetened moong dal and coconut. Nearly every item is priced at under ₹10 and all of it is very good. The store inside has a range of savouries and sweets along with a popular curd vada.

There are other excellent vegetarian eating houses such as Bharat Hotel on Chembottil Lane. Established in 1964 by Balakrishna Menon, it has the gravitas and tradition of old eateries. Vijayakumar has taken over from his father and was keeping accounts in a ledger as we spoke to him. Bharat serves superb dosa, vada and exceptionally good coffee. If you want to have an unforgettable sambar vada, then here's the place.

Our main reason for going to Thrissur was to see the phenomenon of a street devoted to one food. That's Vellappamangadi, the *appam* street in the town. The road is wide and one side is lined with around ten stalls in front of houses, each making and selling appams. You can't really eat here as they don't serve any accompaniments. You can buy appams and take away or order in bulk for catering to a crowd.

We spoke to Katherine, one of the appam-making entrepreneurs. 'This business was started in the 1920s,' she said, then turning to a customer to ask for an advance as he placed an order for 100 appams the next day. Made with rice, coconut, yeast and a little local toddy to aid fermentation, the appams here are sweet and sour, with fluffy centres and crisp edges and priced at just ₹5 apiece.

THE MALABAR STREET-FOOD TRAIL

Wanting to check out a late-night *thattukada* (Kerala's street-food carts), we drove about 30 minutes out of Thrissur town to Babuvettan's cart parked under a bridge and alongside a river. Masala-fried liver, beef, *kappa*, quail eggs and a whole host of other non-vegetarian dishes are on the menu here. Customers eat at plastic tables scattered by the water's edge.

Our next stop became one of the high points of the Kerala sojourn. We had heard and read that the Ramassery idli comes from a small place near Palakkad. We were unprepared for how very rustic and beautiful it would be. You have to take a narrow, winding road that leads off the highway, past paddy fields and banana groves. There, opposite the Mannat Bhagavati temple is the Sree Saraswathy Tea Stall with the words 'The Ramassery Idly Shop' below that. It's a small eatery, with space for about 15 customers. At the back is the kitchen where all the magic happens.

'Go in and see if you are curious,' Rajamani who was at the counter told us. His sister-in-law Bhagyalakshmi is the owner of this eatery, known for its idli that has acquired fame far beyond the hamlet where it's made. The batter made of rice and urad dal was smeared on a cloth stretched over bamboo steaming plates. These were then stacked, three at a time, over a pot of boiling water and covered with an overturned vessel. The lady making the idlis then

BAZAAR BITES

moved to the next pan and then the next. She then removed the cooked idlis, peeling them off the cloth and placing them on a leaf. We watched for a few minutes, captivated by the meditative calm with which she worked.

The Ramassery idli looks like an uttappam but is soft and fluffy. It's served with excellent sambar, a red coconut chutney, a spicy chilli chutney and *chamanthi* podi, a dry chutney, with coconut oil. They leave the dishes holding these accompaniments on the table and you can keep drowning your idli in sambar if you wish. Three other shops here also serve this idli. 'They are all from the family,' Rajamani said, adding with a smile that the tradition is only about 300 years old. 'It's what we learned from our grandmothers, being passed on.' The members of this family are said to have moved here from Kanchipuram in Tamil Nadu when weaving was no longer allowing them even sustenance. We had seen this before, tribulations causing people to make and sell food and see the business achieve fame and success.

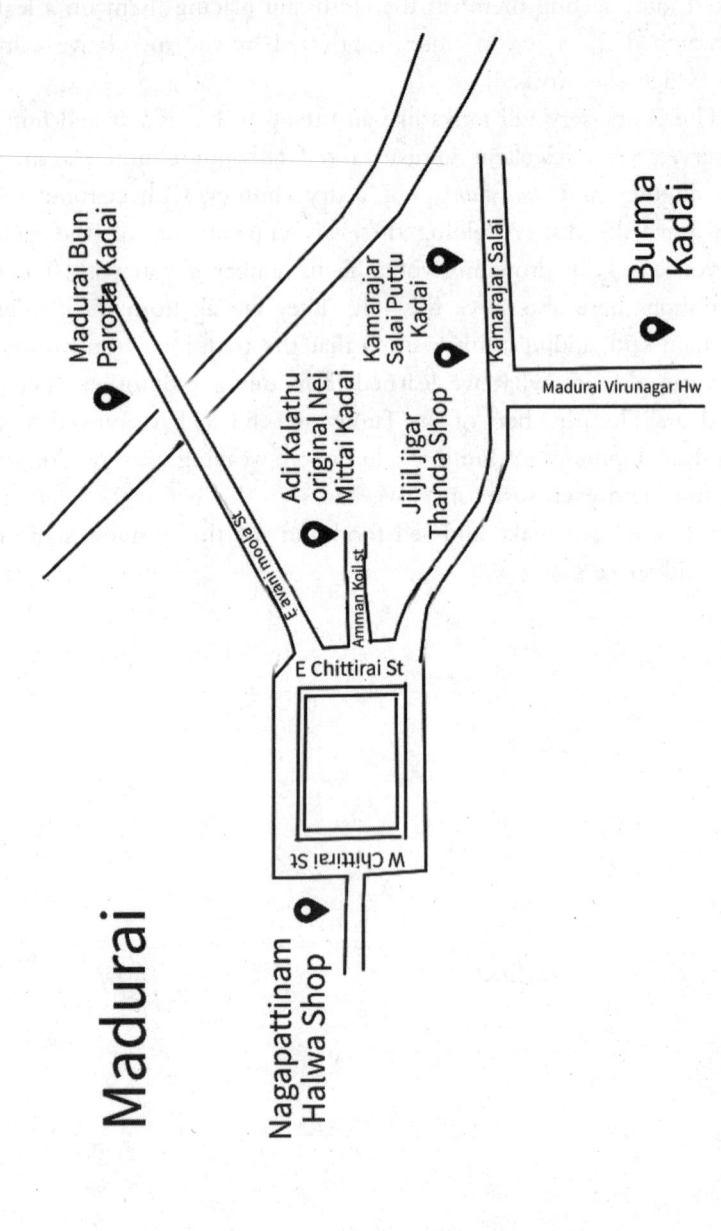

BUN PAROTTA AND JIGARTHANDA—THE BLOCKBUSTERS

Madurai

Continuing our travels in the South, we went to Madurai. You must invariably cross one of the bridges that span the Vaigai River to reach the beating heart of Madurai, the magnificent Meenakshi Sundareswarar Temple. Now, the river is for most part of the year a sand bed where clothes dry and donkeys graze amid the scrub. On the other side are all the bustle, colour, sounds and smells that make up the city of Madurai.

Celebrated in myth and legend, it is believed that nectar, or *madhuram*, from the locks of Lord Shiva fell upon the city. Sung about in Sangam literature and seat of the Pandya kings and later the Nayaks, Madurai is now crowded, dusty, noisy, a little careworn, like a once grand home allowed to go to seed.

Counterpoised with the faded facades and the scruffy streets is the verve of its people, loud, unapologetic and steeped in the culture of the place. It is a city where the fragrance of Madurai *malli*, the famed jasmine of the city—its essence makes its way to French perfume houses, fills the air as dusk falls around the temple.

Night brings a seedy charm to Madurai. Roadside vendors and 'high-class vegetarian hotels' serve up idlis, said to be as soft and white as the prized jasmine. At street corners, from vast vats of oil emerge an array of bhajji, bonda, *vadai*, the cheap, everyday snack for office-goers, workers, and families who step out to visit the temple or to shop in the colourful stores around the temple precincts.

Despite being a temple town, Madurai is also famous for its unabashed love of non-vegetarian food, particularly mutton in its many forms, including offal. The city gets its Thoonganagaram ('city that never sleeps') tag from, among other things, the *parotta-salna* shops that come to life at night. They serve *paya* and bone soup and *kola urundai*, minced meat balls. The *kari dosai* is Madurai's unique twist to the ubiquitous dosai, as it is called in Tamil Nadu. Into the wee hours, you can drink *paruthi paal* (cotton seed milk) from carts at busy corners.

Even if you are not devout, a visit to the temple is a must-do to take in the awe-evoking architecture with its perfect proportions and carved pillars. We sat by the tank, watching the sun go down and turn the towers into graceful silhouettes, and ate the temple *prasadam* of tamarind rice and pepper vadai.

Outside, right below the west *gopuram* tower, on West Chittirai Street is an iconic sweet shop. The blue-green paint is faded and the tiny shop is nondescript. Save for the crowd that gathers outside it every morning and evening, some people holding out their hands for a single portion of the shop's famous halwa, others taking it away by the kilo. The Nagapattinam Halwa Shop was established in 1901. Now run by the fourth generation, this shop was set up by K.S. Vishwanatha Iyer, who came from Kumbakonam. The original shop was opposite the Amman Sannidhi, the path to the temple's sanctum sanctorum. It moved to its present location in 1942 and not much seems to have changed since then. Certainly not the making of the halwa, which has its roots in Nagapattinam. This coastal town, some 280 km from Madurai, was an important trading port since the time of the medieval Cholas, whose influence extended across Southeast Asia. The halwa is not native to the sweet-making traditions of Madurai or, indeed, Tamil Nadu. Traditional sweets in this region are made from rice flour and jaggery. The old halwa makers of Madurai believe that this dense, rich sweet may have come from elsewhere and point to its similarity to *muscat* and *dodol* from the region.

On the other side of the temple, near the east gopuram, is another time-honoured halwa maker, Aadhikaalatthu Original Nei Mittai Kadai—the mouthful means 'ancient, original ghee sweet shop'. This one traces its history back to 120 years when an enterprising Muthusamy Chettiar set up his sweet business. He had no heirs and after his time the business passed on to Krishnamurthy and Sundaresan, also from the Chettiar community known for their business acumen. Those are remembered as the glory days in the annals of the Original Nei Mittai Kadai.

The Chittirai Festival, celebrating the celestial wedding of Goddess Meenakshi, is a highlight on the city's calendar. In the past, it would bring so many people into the city and they would all frequent the halwa shop. It's part of family lore now that the income from one festival would allow them to buy a house and the next year you could rake in enough to arrange the wedding of a daughter. Those were also the days when the affluent travellers from nearby Karaikudi would pay for the halwa in gold coins. The second and third generations of the family are now guardians of this halwa and its making.

As the family expanded, the original shop has spawned more outlets and there are now three around the temple; D. Balaganesh, one of the younger members, opened a sleek sweet shop format in Chokkikulam. Time has wrought these changes, but the method of making the halwa has not changed. It takes nearly a week for a batch to emerge. In a space above the shop, wheat is soaked for two days, then hand-ground on a stone, the milk-like liquid extracted and allowed to settle and ferment for a day. It's slow-cooked with sugar and ghee in massive iron pans over a wood fire; cardamom and nutmeg powder are added and it's allowed to cool for a day before being sold to customers in tiny single portions or packed up to be taken home or abroad by those longing for a sweet taste of home.

The Nagapattinam-style halwa is denser and chewier than its equally famous Tirunelveli counterpart, which has a slithery, soft texture. It has no added colour, chemicals or preservatives and comes with an assured shelf life of two months. The Aadhikaalatthu Original Nei Mittai Kadai is a reassuring sign that the hand-made food from a tiny shop can withstand cool trends and passing fads and continue to yield pleasure as it did 120 years ago. There are no plans to modernize or speed up operations at the older shops. 'You must seek peace in your work,' said Balaganesh's father, S. Dandapani, who operates one of the outlets with the air of a philosopher.

Madurai has three seasons: hot, hotter, hottest. How fitting then that its most loved drink should be called jigarthanda, that which 'cools the innards'. The origins of dishes are hard to pin down, especially in India where we have not been especially diligent about documenting food history. Jigarthanda is one such dish.

The famous jigarthanda version is the one that has gained currency and it is believed that Shaikh Meeran conjured up this creamy, sweet glass that Madurai cools down with. Meeran came from Aarampannai, an agricultural village near Srivilliputtur. Relatives from his village had constant contact with Rangoon in Burma. One of them was settled in Madurai and offered to take the young Meeran into the ice cream business he ran. These were hand-churned ice creams. Meeran mastered their making and learned to serve them on a *mandharai* (camel's foot) leaf with a twig from the palm tree as a spoon. Working with ice cream, Meeran began to experiment. Adding sherbets and syrups to it, mixing in fresh milk and cream. He worked on it for over 30 years, according to his son Shahul Hameed, who now runs the business along with his three brothers. Then he arrived at the caramel-hued concoction, part drink, part dessert, that Madurai calls its own.

In its present form, jigarthanda consists of reduced milk, thickened by cooking over a wood fire, *nannari* or sarsaparilla syrup—considered to be cooling, slithery strands of almond resin, a scoop of ice cream made from the same reduced milk and a topping of cream from the thickened milk. Shahul Hameed told us the use of almond resin may have sprung from his father's connections with the travellers from Burma and that the creativity with thickened milk could have been inspired by the influences that the Nayak rulers of Madurai brought in.

The first jigarthanda was sold from a cart over 40 years ago and at night Meeran found a kind shopkeeper who allowed him to park his vending vehicle there. But a crackdown on street vendors by the then commissioner compelled Meeran to get off the street and find a place for his jigarthanda. He took a space of 10 feet by 10 feet on East Marrat Street and a new chapter opened in the small food shops history of Madurai.

Scaling, joint ventures and franchises have made the famous signboard—Shahul Hameed came up with the name some years ago—a common sight in Madurai and in cities across the South.

Still, a glass of jil jil jigarthanda at this vintage spot on East Marrat Street is special.

※

In Madurai's distinct deep-south intonation, it frequently emerges as 'barotta'. The city eats several thousands of these disc-like breads made from maida, with salna, a spicy, fragrant gravy that is soaked up by the multi-layered parotta. The bun parotta is a sub-sect within the family. They are not buns, but simply parottas that are shaped, cooked and fluffed up with masterly dexterity to make them stand up brown and bun-like. Their crisp, golden exterior enfolds an intricate pile of layers that open up as you break into the parotta.

The temple town's most famous maker of this dish simply calls itself Madurai Bun Parotta Kadai; it's at the Aavin signal in KK Nagar. It is scarcely a *kadai* (shop), being merely a vast stainless steel-topped table where a massive quantity of dough is kneaded every afternoon to be cooked on a heavy iron griddle. Alongside is a small stall with basic seating for a handful of customers. Karuppannan and his wife Vijayam set up the business in 1991, starting off as a tea stall. He gives credit for the creation of bun parotta to Raman, their very first parotta master, the lynchpin of any parotta business. In any commercial kitchen that turns out parottas, the master has a revered position on account of his skill.

The offerings from this stall are not for those with queasy stomachs. For the bun parotta dough is kneaded out in the open, by a team of five men using their bare hands, while traffic fumes and dust from the street swirl around. But Madurai's bun parotta fans cannot be bothered. The stall sells 2,000 parottas a day. The preparation and cooking of the bun parotta makes for a daily spectacle. At around 2 p.m., 100 kilos of flour are emptied from sacks on to the worktable. Salt, sugar, dozens of eggs and litres of milk are poured in. Then a team of five men, including Duraipandi the parotta master, go to work, kneading the mixture to make a soft, silken, pliable dough.

BAZAAR BITES

It is rested for half an hour and shaped into small balls. The dough is rolled, shaped into coils and then tossed into flat discs about six inches across. The tossing technique is known as *veechu* and the quality of the parotta relies heavily on the veechu artistry of the master, says Karuppannan.

Around 5 p.m., the first batch of parottas hits the hot griddle that sits on a coal stove and oil is drizzled around each. When they are done, they are flecked with golden brown on both sides. One of the staff taps each parotta between his palms, teasing it to reveal its layers and take its bun-like shape. Hundreds of customers line up and the stall that opens at 6 p.m. goes on till midnight or later.

Like the halwa, the parotta could not have been native to Madurai. Maida or all-purpose flour wasn't a common ingredient in this rice belt and the layering technique was certainly learned from elsewhere. Today, though, it's one of Madurai's most eaten street foods. Buoyed by the popularity and success of his stall, Karuppannan opened Sivaranjani Hotel nearby in 2010, so the family crowd that might have found it difficult to eat at the crowded stall could enjoy a plate of bun parotta and salna, with a side dish of fried quail perhaps. Karuppannan and his wife manage this place and it's very much a family-run operation. We ordered a bun parotta meal here and tasted not just Madurai's favourite bread but also its hospitality.

An hour's drive away from Madurai is the now decrepit town of Virudhunagar. Parotta aficionados instantly associate it with *ennai parotta* or oil parottas. These are kneaded and shaped pretty much like the bun parotta, but their cooking technique is different and they are smaller, too. Small discs, the size of your palm, are first partially cooked at the edge of a vast tawa holding oil. They are then slipped into the oil to emerge brown and crisp, with biscuit-like crispness. There are scores of small outlets in the town serving these.

But if you want to eat in a slightly more comfortable setting, there's the Burma Kadai. This eatery is now a brand with four outlets, including one on the Virudhunagar-Madurai highway. Started by a family of refugees from Burma—hence the name—who set up a tiny shop in town, it is now a must-visit for foodies to this part of Tamil Nadu.

Madurai is a city of temples and festivals, all of them wrapped up in myths and fables. So, we'll tell you a little story about why *puttu* is so special to this southern town. Puttu is a tasty crumble of flour—rice, ragi and in these health-conscious times, also wheat—mixed with coconut and jaggery. Unlike most other Madurai street snacks, this is steamed and, therefore, considered a nourishing and healthy breakfast.

Around August every year, Puttuthoppu, situated near Arappalayam on the southern bank of the Vaigai, celebrates a festival known as the Puttu Thiruvizha, re-enacting one of the miracles or 'sacred games' said to have been performed by Lord Shiva.

Manickavasagar, a minister in the court of King Arimarthana Pandian, and a Shiva devotee, was dispatched to buy horses for the king. En route, overcome by devotion, he built a temple to his Lord at Thiruperunthurai with the money given to him by the king. Enraged, the king punished Manickavasagar and made him stand on the burning sands of the Vaigai bank. To save his devotee, Lord Shiva caused a flood in the river. The river breached the banks and the king ordered that one person from each household must come forth to build a bund to contain the river.

An old woman, Vanthi, made a living by selling puttu. She was too old for the work ordered by the king and prayed to Shiva. He appeared as a labourer. She had no means to pay him. 'No problem,' said Shiva. 'Give me all the puttu that crumbles, I will work for that.' The Lord was in a playful mood, and all of Vanthi's puttu failed to hold together. Shiva feasted on the fare and slept on the riverbank. The Pandya king who came to inspect the progress of the bund was irked to see the lazy worker and had him lashed. It is said that the pain was felt by all living creatures on the planet. Then Shiva revealed himself, blessed the king, the citizens and Madurai, making puttu part of the city's legend.

BAZAAR BITES

Possibly the city's best-known puttu seller sets up shop outside a large store on Kamarajar Saalai. It is known to locals as the Kamarajar Saalai Puttu Kadai. There is no shop. Just a father and son who bring their wares in large pots. Here, crowds wait as early as 6 a.m. when A. Antony and his son Jesus Regan arrive on their cycles, bearing two large drums holding three varieties of puttu: rice with jaggery, rice with sugar and ragi. It's only ₹5 for a *pottalam*, a small packet wrapped in newspaper. Customers crowd around as Antony gathers up a bit of the puttu, drizzles some sesame oil on the mound, places it on the square of paper, tops it with a little more jaggery and grated coconut, and wraps it all up to hand out. He works at amazing speed, wrapping dozens of packets within a few minutes. The fingers must pick up the puttu delicately, or the granules will clump together and spoil the texture. It is a rhythm he acquired from his father, Arockiasamy, who started the business 50 years ago. Now his son helps him with everything, from buying the ingredients to making the puttu, transporting it and selling it.

Work for the morning's puttu begins the day before. The rice is washed, soaked and powdered. Then it's kneaded into the granules that give puttu its unique texture, and that requires practice and a light hand. The flour is then steamed twice in copper vessels, mixed with jaggery and coconut and brought while the puttu is still hot. Until 10 years ago, the rice was hand-pounded; now it's powdered in a mill. They have loyal customers who come here every day for a packet of puttu. For some, it's a pre-breakfast snack. Others turn it into an inexpensive and nutritious breakfast.

'People from Madurai who live in other cities call me when they are coming home and arriving by morning bus to keep packets for them,' Regan says, happy at how his simple dish touches people. 'It's clean, fresh and good,' a customer who's been coming to the puttu kadai for decades tells us as we watch this street venture buzz so early in the day. By 9 a.m., the puttu is all sold out—there is rarely any waste—and father and son pack up and head home to prepare for the next day's sales.

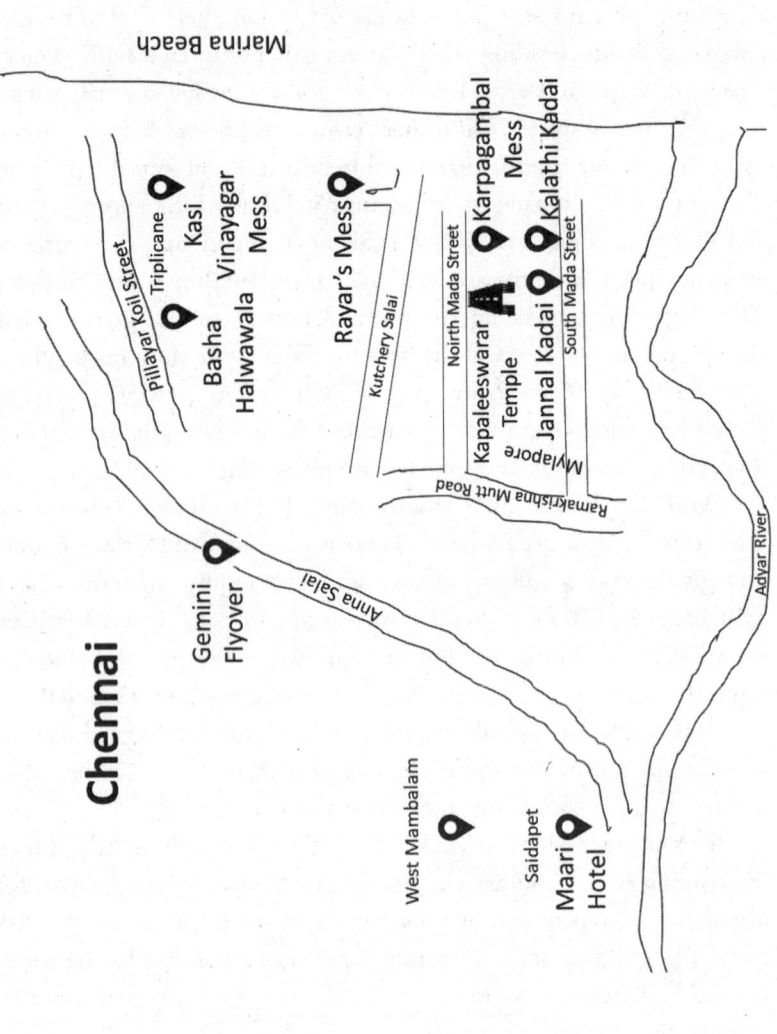

TIFFIN ROOMS AND MILITARY MESSES

Chennai

*S*prawled along the Coromandel Coast, Chennai is a vibrant metropolis, crowded and populous, with a strong sense of identity. It is distinctively South Indian and proudly Tamilian, yet expansive enough to encompass remarkable cultural diversity.

The Chennai vibe is equally varied. One of the earliest strongholds of the East India Company and the British Raj in India, it has colonial-era buildings that are landmarks, such as Madras Central railway station, Ripon Building, seat of the Chennai Corporation, and Fort St George that houses the legislative assembly. Juxtaposed with these neoclassical edifices are ancient temples, bazaars spilling over with sarees and jewellery, and massive markets for fish and vegetables.

Everywhere there's food. In the traditional quarters, old-world eateries serve fabulous tiffin and filter coffee. The wide swathe of sand that is Marina Beach is a favourite spot for Chennaiites to stroll, sit, watch the sun go down, and eat thenga-manga-pattani sundal and *murukku*. Roadside stalls serve biryani and *atho* of Burmese ancestry. Early settlers from Rajasthan and other parts of the North have brought chaat and milk sweets. The Deccani Muslims have their unique repertoire of confections. On the street-food trail in Chennai, then, you'll encounter everything from pani puri and podi dosai to bun-butter, vada curry and kebabs.

Chennai stirs to life early. Forewarned about crowds and queues, we arrived well in time in Mylapore, where the ancient Kapaleeswarar Kovil dominates the skyline. In the shadow of its gopuram is a place referred to as Jannal Kadai or 'window shop', and that's exactly what it is. A wooden window painted blue serves as the shop front. Behind the window a man seats cross-legged on a ledge handing out the food to customers, who jostle at street level. We spot another worker sitting on the floor inside frying vadai. Behind them, the everyday life of a Mylapore family carries on. All the food was fresh and delicious, the vadai being particularly so. This shop without a name or signboard has been serving its breakfast of idli, vadai and *pongal* to the neighbourhood for over 25 years. It was begun by two brothers and one of them, Sivaramakrishnan, succumbed to Covid-19, plunging Jannal Kadai fans into grief. His brother, Chandrasekaran, now looks after the operation. 'We'd like to meet the owner,' we told the rudraksha-wearing man at the counter. 'Kapali is the owner,' he said with equanimity. This unusual and hugely popular window shop is open from 7 a.m. to 10.30 a.m. and opens again at 5 p.m. to dish out hot and crisp bhajji and bonda with its signature tomato-coconut chutney.

The Mylai food trail leads next to Karpagambal Mess. The vegetarian mess in these conservative quarters is a uniquely Chennai phenomenon. In many places in the South, the mess almost always stands for 'military mess', a place serving predominantly non-vegetarian food. Here, though, it's a huge list of traditional, vegetarian tiffin items. Karpagambal Mess was started in 1953 by R. Soundararajan. After his passing, it is run by his son Prabhu Das. The place wears an old-world air, despite refurbishments and the addition of a tiny airconditioned space. The walls are lined with huge framed pictures of deities from the Hindu pantheon and devotional music plays loud. It's the ideal setting then to have breakfast after prayers at the Kapaleeswarar Temple. The crowd is regulars, plus NRIs—you can tell from the sneakers and the accents—who've come here to soak in some nostalgia. We had a Na Dosai, the *na* standing for *nallennai*, gingelly oil. It was perfect and so were the chutney and coffee, all served by a very surly waiter. The mess has no practice of presenting bills. Customers finish their tiffin, walk up to the cashier, tell him

what they ate, and pay. 'It's about trust and we've never thought of changing the system,' the restaurant staff told us.

Next stop in Mylapore was Rayar's Mess. On our travels we've seen a few food businesses in cramped spaces. Rayar's Mess surprises, located in an alley so narrow only one two-wheeler can move through it at a time. The eatery is even smaller, with seating at four tables cramped into a small hall. Customers must invariably wait outside, and they patiently do so.

Rayar's Mess—it was then called Rayar Café—was begun in 1930 by Srinivasa Rao. His grandsons P. Mohan and P. Kumar now run the place, assisted by K. Manoj from the fourth generation. Life begins as early as 4 a.m. at this mess. The idlis are poured out on cloth-lined moulds and the pongal is slowly cooked to its soft consistency. Everything is home-style, freshness and goodness being key. Manoj is hands-on at this modest but famous eatery, knowing the tastes and needs of all the regular customers. 'You need your coffee lukewarm, right?' he asks of one gentleman, who nods yes. Mohan remembers stories from his grandfather about the stalwarts of Tamil cinema, like Thiagaraja Bhagavathar and PU Chinnappa Thevar, being regular customers. Later, the likes of Nagesh and V.K. Ramaswamy would wrap up a night of shooting and arrive early to eat idli with podi and oil. Now, Simbu and Suriya drop in from time to time for their Rayar's Mess fix. 'Our customers are like guests in our home, we are here to serve them,' Manoj said. Despite their popularity and the constraints of space, they have no desire to expand. That is as it should be for this little gem in Mylapore.

The Mylapore street-food experience is incomplete without a stop at one end of East Mada Street. On the street corner stands a small shop with a fading board that says Kalathi Kadai, 'Kalathi Shop'. It was started as a newspaper mart in 1927 by Kalathi Mudaliar. At some point he began to sell the now-famous rose milk the shop is known for. Now sold in small plastic bottles at ₹20 apiece, the famous beverage is a crowd puller. It is the perfect sweet drink—made with milk and rose syrup—on hot Chennai afternoons. The third generation of the family now runs this shop that also stocks a few basic provisions.

Another star on Chennai's vegetarian mess map is Kameswari Unavagam in West Mambalam, which has been serving the area since 1988. It stands on a corner, with a kitchen that's open to the streets. Owner Krishnamoorthy, whose mother Thangammal started this food business named after their family deity, is at the cash counter from 7 a.m. The breakfast menu comprises soft idlis acquiring a sweet sourness from proper fermentation, pepper-studded pongal, and hot, crisp vadai with sambar laden with vegetables and chutney. The coffee is excellent. For lunch, the main offering is what is known in these parts as 'variety rice': *puliodharai*, pudina rice, *vatthal kuzhambu* rice, tomato rice and more. 'It's a tasty, satisfying meal and you can eat well for under ₹50. I come here two to three times a week,' a regular customer said, underlining again the role small food businesses play in our cities.

There are more messes to eat at for cheap, such as Kasi Vinayaga Mess on Akbar Sahib Street in Triplicane, which has been around for 50 years. Banana leaf meals are the signature here and you can get unlimited quantities of rice, sambar, rasam, buttermilk and vegetable dishes for lunch, plus chapatti and *idiappam* for dinner.

On the other side of Triplicane is Zam Bazaar, once the major retail market of the city. It comes alive at night with shops selling kebabs and biryani.

Find your way to Fakir Sahib Street and Basha Halwawala, which has been selling sweets here since 1915. Moinuddin Jalal told us his grandfather Basha Sahib started the business mainly to cater to the vendors and shoppers in the bazaar. 'It's lost much of its lustre now, but at the time it used to be the main market of Chennai. My grandfather started selling sweets in small quantities and the business grew.'

Basha Halwawala's most famous product is *dum ka roat*, a halwa with a fudge-like consistency. 'It's a sweet made in Deccani Muslim families,' Moinuddin said. The ingredients are simple: semolina, sugar and khoya. The secret lies in the technique, which involves a thick batter being slow-cooked, dum-style. This gives the sweet its signature brown crust. We tasted a portion and fell in love with it. It's being made in the same way for over a hundred years, according to Moinuddin. 'Even the wrapping must be the simple butter paper that we use. Try to do anything fancy and the sweet will spoil in a day,' he said. Basha Halwawala's other sweets, such as malida of Afghan origin, made with crumbled parathas, and a wonderful Mysore pak are all packed in old-fashioned cardboard boxes, indicating a style that stays true to tradition. You will also experience excellent service from the staff who take pride in this small but ancient shop.

Next, we went to Maari Hotel in Saidapet for breakfast. The place is credited with coming up with vada curry, a Chennai classic. The classic combination is vada curry with set dosai, soft, fluffy dosas tinged yellow. We absolutely loved the pairing. It's a spartan dining room, packed with locals tucking into their dosai, idli, poori or pongal. Kumaran, manning the counter, told us the shop was started by his father, Marimuthu Thevar, who came to Chennai from a small village in Thanjavur district to make a living. At first it was a small tea stall he had, serving bonda and vadai. At home, as was the practice in those frugal times, the leftover vadais were repurposed. Marimuthu Thevar took the same idea to his eatery, breaking up leftover vadais and allowing them to soak in a flavourful gravy. It was an instant hit and continues to have a fan following.

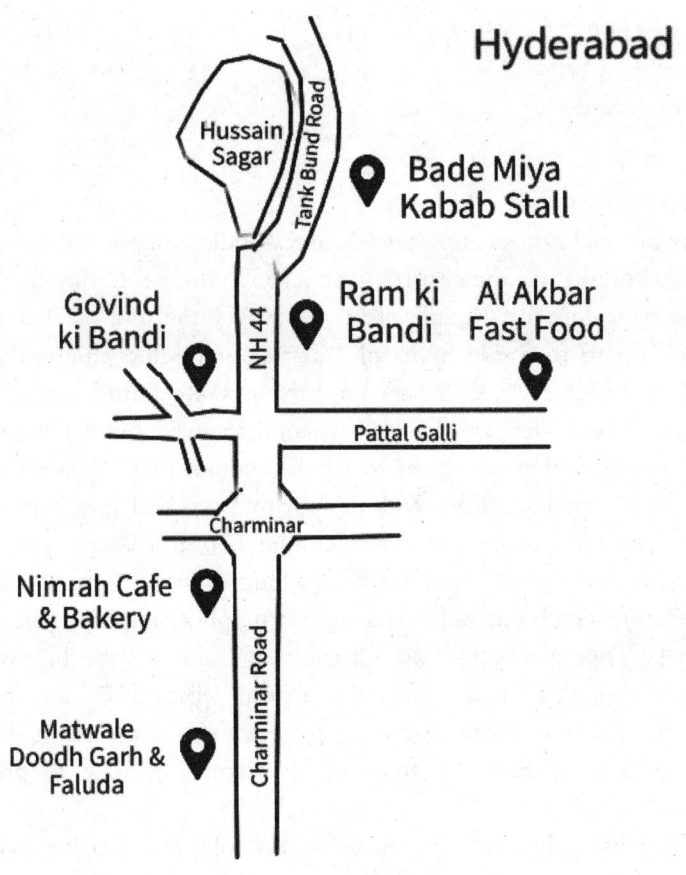

BEYOND BIRYANI: FROM OSMANIA BISCUIT TO FALOODA

Hyderabad

*H*yderabad is home to Google's largest India office and IKEA came to the country via the city. It's a modern city in every way and jousts with Bangalore for the title of IT capital. Yet, the soul of Hyderabad would seem to reside in its old quarters, far removed from glass-and-steel high-rises, tech parks and flyovers. We found that it's that colourful, crowded, infuriatingly chaotic sprawl around Charminar, the landmark that continues to be the symbol of Hyderabad.

The imposing edifice with its four minarets that give it its name stands sentinel while life whirls around beneath. Weave your way between the myriad street vendors, selling everything from artificial jewellery to embroidered *mojris*, and roving photographers, who want to take your pic against the Charminar. There are the brightly lit bangle shops of Lad Bazaar and the pearl sellers who carry on an ancient tradition. Hyderabad came to be known as the city of pearls, for its drilling centres where skilled artisans continue to prepare pearls for jewellery.

Craftsmanship is everywhere in this old part of the city. We stopped to watch the *warq* makers pound away at silver, turning it into gossamer thin sheets that will decorate sweets. Naan makers such as Munshi have been plying a craft for nearly 170 years, shaping the city's much-loved bread by hand.

Hyderabad's fondness for breads, indeed, food on the whole, goes back to its first Nizam, who chose the *kulcha* as the official emblem of the Asaf Jahi dynasty. According to legend, Asaf Jah visited the Sufi saint Hazrat Nizamuddin Aulia before setting off for the Deccan. Hazrat Nizamuddin invited him to share his simple meal, urging him to eat well. Asaf Jah finished seven kulchas and it is said that Hazrat Nizamuddin blessed him saying that seven generations of his family would rule the Deccan. A grateful Asaf Jah had the kulcha embroidered onto the royal flag. The Nizams did rule for seven generations and were connoisseurs of food.

The city continues to be known for its love of food—queuing up for paya and naan at 5 a.m. at Shah Ghouse, perfecting the art of biryani sold in upscale restaurants and holes in the wall, and adding southern spice to the middle eastern porridge of meat and lentils, turning it into Hyderabad's speciality, *haleem*.

We love the old quarters of any city and the area around the Charminar was endlessly fascinating. It is de rigueur to stop for chai and biscuit while here. The biscuits of Hyderabad are what *petha* is to Agra and *bhujia* to Bikaner, food that's synonymous with the city and taken away as edible souvenirs by visitors. While it now comes in fancy packing that you can buy in bakeries and stores across the city, the simple Osmania biscuit—sweet, buttery and crumbly—is part of the daily routine for many Hyderabadis. They stop any time of day to savour a biscuit or two dipped in the strong, thick, sweet Suleimani chai served in tiny white cups.

As dusk falls and the ancient façade of the Charminar is lit up, the crowds build up on the vast paved spaced around it. Many of them stop at Nimraah Café, famed for its biscuits and buns. The store is small and now there are steel tables outdoors where you can stand and have your biscuits and chai. Nimraah Café was begun in 1993 by Abood bin Aslam at this very spot, under the shadow of the Charminar. The café has now passed on to his son Ali bin Abood, who runs it with his brothers. It's still driven by the beliefs his father had and the practices he put in place, Ali told us.

Besides the biscuits, Nimraah Café is known for its malai bun, a large sweet bun served with butter. The plain bun costs ₹7, with

BEYOND BIRYANI: FROM OSMANIA BISCUIT TO FALOODA

butter and a cup of chai it comes to ₹19.

'We open at 4 a.m. and in two hours the buns are over,' Ali said. 'My father believed we should be a place where a person can satisfy his hunger without having to worry about the price.' The biscuits, too, are priced much lower than in other, newer places. They now have 33 varieties, including a delightful date roll coated with sesame seeds. The innovations have come in recent times, multigrain, chocolate chip and pista.

But the Osmania remains the star of the show. Ali told us the biscuit gets its name from Nizam Osman Ali Badshah, whose cook made him these melt-in-the-mouth baked morsels. Nimraah Café bakes its buns and all its biscuits on the premises. Many members of the loyal staff have been here for 25 years, as long as the café has been in existence. They get paid daily. 'It's a practice my father introduced,' Ali said. 'He wanted Hyderabadis to eat well and for his staff to be cared for. The first shift ends at 2 p.m., those on the shift get their wages in hand by 11.30 a.m. It's always been this way.' Along with sweetness, there's caring baked into Nimraah's biscuits, it would seem.

Walking further down from the Charminar, we went looking for another Hyderabad favourite, Chicken 65. Yes, it was invented at Buhari Hotel in Chennai and has travelled everywhere—a favourite in seedy bars and hip brewpubs alike. Hyderabad loves its Chicken 65. The best is a matter of debate, but most Hyderabadis will point you to Al Akbar Fast Food in the Charminar area. The glass-fronted counter dispenses mutton and chicken biryani, mutton and chicken handi and chicken tandoori. The Chicken 65 is the hot-seller, ₹75 for a half plate and double that for a full. It comes coated in the easily recognized red batter that packs a punch and is served with a thin green chutney. Syed Abdul Haji started Al Akbar 40 years ago, originally operating at Abids, moving to the present location in Charminar 15 years after that. 'We introduced Chicken 65 to Andhra,' he said, with the pride of the entrepreneur. 'And we continue to sell a lot of it.'

BAZAAR BITES

For our first breakfast in the city, we decided to eat dosas. Like most South Indian cities, Hyderabad consumes several thousand dosas every day, from grimy food carts, modern trucks, at chain stores that have made dosas the focus of their QSR operations.

Ask the Hyderabadis and each will have their favourite dosa eatery or vendor, who will custom-make the dish for regulars. There are dosa outlets in malls and in swank Banjara Hills. For off-the-street authenticity, it's got to be one of the *bandi*s or carts.

Ram ki Bandi in Mozamjahi Market is hugely popular, and so is Govind ki Bandi near Mecca Masjid in the Charminar area. It has been in the same spot for 40 years and was begun by Govind's father. The paan-chewing Govind, in his bright orange tee shirt, pours out 10 dosas on the long griddle with an easy rhythm, even as he engages in a steady stream of banter with his guests. Anyone who asks for less butter is told 'mazaa nahi ayega' and cajoled into having the loaded version. His father sold only idlis and dosas; Govind has expanded the repertoire with a special dosa, paneer dosa, cheese dosa and even a Szechwan version, and now serves up 25 types. But this is no run-of-the-mill 99 Varieties cart. The dosa batter is ground at home and includes urad dal, rice and rice powder, with no maida or soda. Perfectly fermented, it's poured out super thin and topped with *karam* podi and a big blob of Amul butter for the plain dosa. The special has runny upma spread over it, Govind crushes some tomato by hand over the dosa, tops it with karam podi and, of course, butter. Incongruous as the combination may sound to dosa purists, it all comes together in a crisp, buttery, spicy plate of deliciousness.

The Nizams brought the food from other exotic kitchens to Hyderabad, dishes from the culinary traditions of the Mughals and further afield. The falooda is said to have its origins in Persia. Enjoyed across the country, it's one of Hyderabad's most-loved foods, drink and dessert combined in a glass. At a walking distance from the buzz of Charminar, past stalls and carts selling socks, trinkets, cut fruit and piles of purple-red mulberries in winter is Matwale Doodh Ghar, the old city's preferred place for falooda and lassi. The unpretentious shop, begun by Moin Bhai, who originally hailed from Gulbarga, has been here since 1966. He named his son and his shop after the Matwale Shah Hussaini Dargah.

Mohammed Matwale, a soft-spoken, gracious Hyderabadi, was roped into the business as a young boy. 'Once I completed tenth standard, my father asked me to stop my education and begin work at the shop,' he said. He was an understudy in the shop for six years. After his father passed away in 1991, he took over the business. Matwale's signature items are the lassi and the falooda. The milk for these is sourced directly from buffalo farmers, not from a commercial dairy. The dahi for the lassi is set in-house. The malai and the ice cream for the falooda are also made at Matwale. This commitment to quality sees the crowds flock to the place throughout the year, with business peaking in summer.

'If I employ 12 people in the shop for the rest of the year, in summer I need 50 hands and often employ students who come here to work part time,' the owner told us. The Matwale falooda is simple and classic, with rose syrup, *sabza* seeds, milk, ice cream and malai, not too sweet and delightfully cooling. The lassi is lighter than, say, its Punjabi equivalent and comes with a hint of rosewater. This little store also sells kalakand, gulab jamun and rabri. When there's excess milk, we have to find a use for it, Matwale said. 'That's how we keep our demand steady with our suppliers and assure them of their income.' It's a small shop with a large-hearted owner. He absolutely refused payment for our faloodas. '*Aap Hyderabad ki mehmaan hai*,' he said.

Walking along Tank Bund on a balmy evening, we came upon another Hyderabad speciality. It is the food-loving Nizams who, again, can take credit for the *patthar ka gosht*. Between food historians and tellers of royal folklore, there emerges the story that Nizam Asaf Jahi VI once went on one of his frequent hunting expeditions and found the bawarchis had forgotten the skewers required for grilling meat. They came up with a solution and cooked the meat on a flat stone, heating it from below with foraged firewood. Seemingly, the Nizam so liked the dish that it was introduced in the royal kitchens. The dish with its royal origins is now the common man's meaty treat.

Some of the best patthar ka gosht is available at the Bade Miyan Kababs stall on Tank Bund Road. Trying to be a crowd-pleaser, this stall with street-side seating also serves pure veg chaat (the irony!) and Chinese food. But it's the kababs, especially the patthar ka gosht, that brings stylish Hyderabadis to eat here, unmindful of the grimy stall and the purely functional setting. The patthar ka gosht here is cooked by a cranky old man, who refuses to divulge what goes into it. He fans the flames heating the thick, time-worn granite slab and flips over the slivers of meat, basting them with ghee as they come off the fire. The meat, cooked in such rustic fashion, is spiced with a subtle elegance and has the melting tenderness of a far more sophisticated technique. Bade Miyan is now owned by Syed Shaji, the fourth generation of the family that began to serve up this delicacy. It was his great grandfather Haji Syed Ismail who started the business. He could well have learned the nuances from the bawarchis of the Nizam themselves.

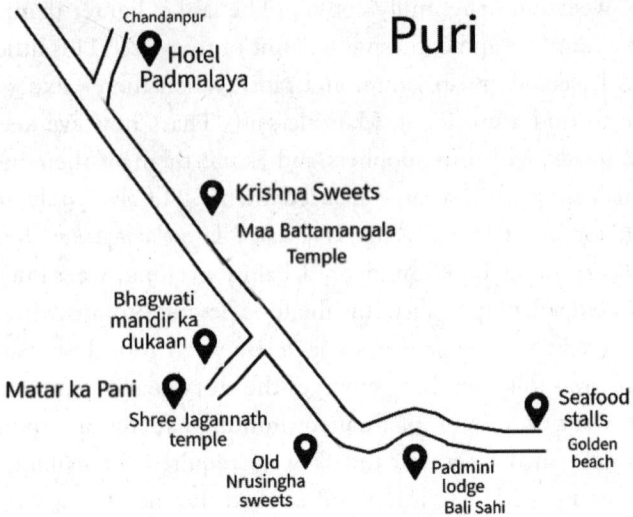

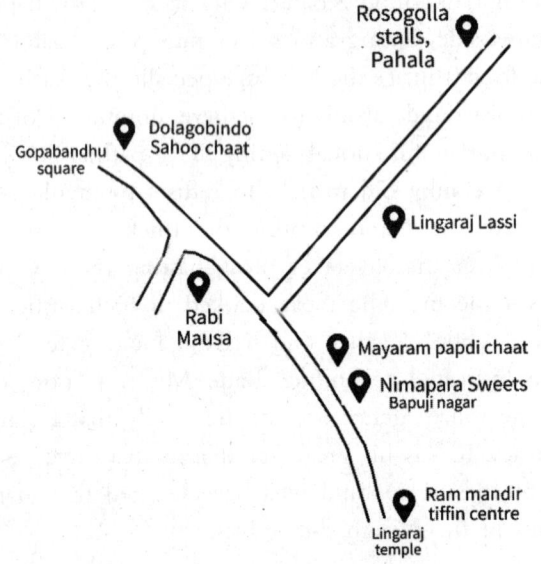

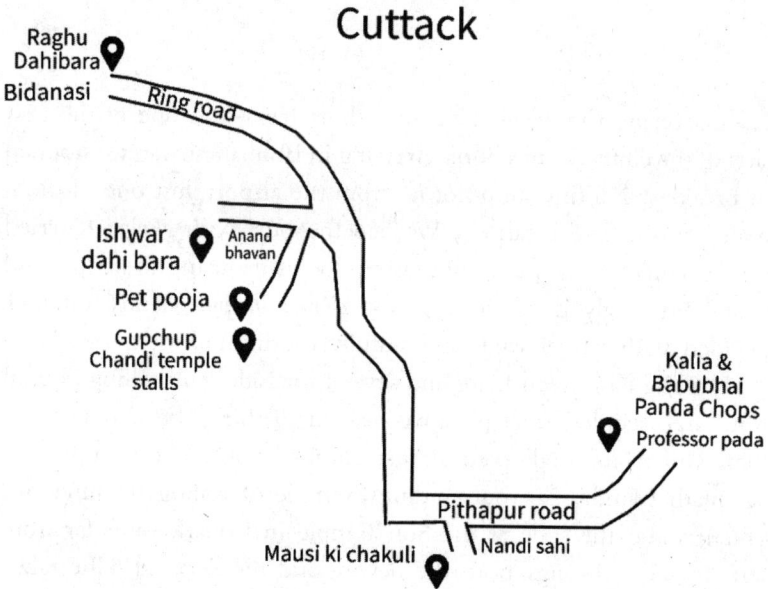

ODISHA: THE LAND OF GHUGNI, KHAJA, AND CHAKULI

Puri, Bhubaneshwar, Cuttack

Discovering Odisha—albeit on a short trip—was one of the best parts of travelling for this book. Arriving in Bhubaneshwar, we stopped for breakfast at a tiny shop not far from the airport, just one of those small joints where locals eat. We had the puri with *ghugni* (curried peas or chickpeas)—we would taste a lot of it during the trip—and it was amazingly good. So was the *chanar malpua*, darkly caramel, speckled with fennel seeds and sinfully toothsome.

Driving past green fields and several roadside stalls selling ghugni from large stainless-steel pots, we headed to Puri. The temple town holds you in its thrall even at first glimpse. There is the impressive Jagannath Mandir—an outstanding example of Kalinga architecture, which is also the style at the Sun Temple in Konark—not far from here. It draws throngs, both the devout and the devoted selfie-taker.

Our auto driver said, not without some disapproval, 'Who comes to pray and do puja? They turn their back on the Lord and click away.' To be fair, it is a picture-worthy backdrop.

The beach at Puri is another major attraction of the temple town. At night, it becomes a massive fairground; there are deck chairs for rent, stalls sell seafood from the Bay of Bengal, batter-coated and deep-fried, doing no justice to their freshness. At one end of the beach is Swarg Dwar, a burning ghat. Much like in Varanasi, death and the celebration of life and everything in-between coexist, without any seeming incongruity, in this sacred city.

The main street in Puri leading to the Jagannath temple comes alive at night with sellers of souvenirs, trinkets and food—from chowmein and dosa to *gupchup*—lining the streets. Narrow lanes leading off the temple squares are home to tiny, smoke-darkened shops dealing in milk, *chhena* and some wonderful dairy confections.

Around the temple precinct is where you'll also find *matar ka pani*; it's a soupy dish of white peas, served topped with masala, chopped onion and coriander and *sev*. Vendors sell it from cycles parked in the shadow of the temple with its white tower. *Khaja* is as ubiquitous in Puri as *vada pav* is in Mumbai. Shops displaying mounds of the crisp, gold-brown sweet glazed with sugar are a common sight. Traditionally, a large number of these shops that sold the sweet were clustered in Khaja Pati, a lane adjacent to the temple. The plan to create a security zone extending to a 75 m radius around the temple resulted in Khaja Pati being cleared in 2020. The sweet makers scattered and relocated, several of them moving to the street leading from the temple to Puri beach and Swarg Dwar.

Nrusingha Sahoo Sharma is credited with setting up the first khaja business in Puri in the year 1945. This sweet is made of a dough that's rolled and shaped to create many layers, then fried and dipped in sugar syrup. If you are eating it at a shop, it will be served sprinkled with a dark and fragrant spice powder. While the khaja was originally fried in ghee, most shops now use oil. It may have lost some of its original qualities, but the khaja still holds pride of place in Puri because it's part of the *chhappan bhog*, the celebrated feast dedicated to the temple's presiding deity. It is a tribute to the original Nrusingha sweet shop that there are dozens of others calling themselves 'Old Original Nrusingha Sweets'. In such a crowded landscape, it's difficult to trace and authenticate origins. After much searching, we learnt that the Old Nrusingha Sweets housed on the ground floor of Padmini Lodge in Bali Sahi belongs to the descendants of Nrusingha Sahoo Sharma. It's now run by brothers Harihar and Bhabati Sahoo Sharma. Besides the khaja, Nrusingha Sweets also sells excellent *malpua* and *chenna poda*,

ODISHA: THE LAND OF GHUGNI, KHAJA, AND CHAKULI

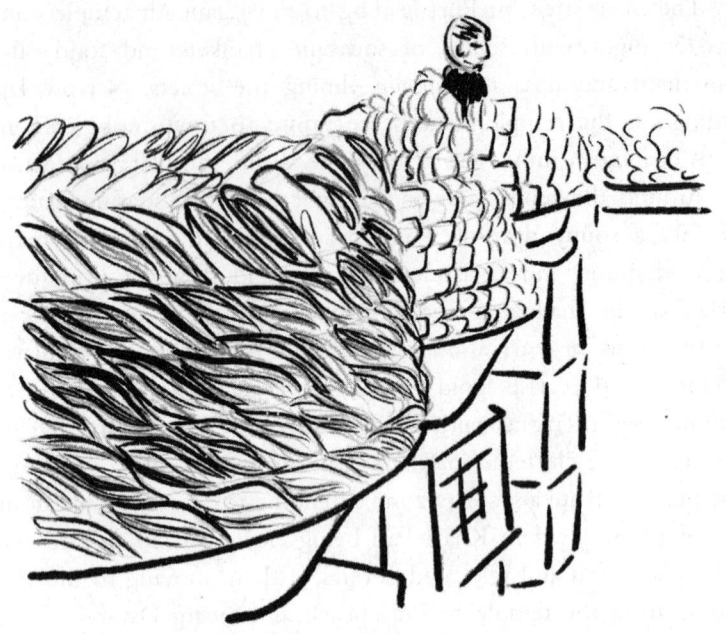

Odisha's signature sweet of chenna baked to acquire a caramel exterior.

We had heard of the malai puri maker of the town and he took some finding. The smoke-darkened shop is next to one of the smaller shrines that dot the area around the Jagannath temple and it has no name. 'It's just known as Bhagwati Mandir ka Dukan,' says Kaalia Behera, who runs the place started by his father Madhav Behera in the 1980s. Red-checked *gamcha* around his waist and shirtless, Kaalia moves between vessels, testing khoya, stirring rabdi and setting yoghurt. His speciality is the malai puri and it is a wondrous thing. Milk for this simmers away in a shallow cauldron. When you ask for the malai puri, Kaalia uses a long stick to deftly lift a thick layer of cream off its surface and places it, a glistening white disc, on a waiting plate made of dried sal leaves. The delicate layer of cream has to 'rest' a few minutes, before he weighs it and serves it sliced. A spoon of not too sweet rabdi takes this small plate of creamy richness to another level. Given the skill and technique this item demands, it's not surprising that it is so hard to find in Puri. It seems likely too that the making of malai puri is a dying art.

Driving back to Bhubaneshwar, we stopped at the Battamangala temple on the outskirts of Puri. Adjacent is a somewhat drab-looking eatery. It's called Krishna Sweets, but regulars refer to it as the Battamangala singhara place. Those passing on this highway or visiting the temple are compelled to stop here. The singhara—that's what the samosa is called in these parts, as also in West Bengal—is that good. It's small, stuffed with cubed rather than mashed potatoes, peas and carrots, and mildly spiced. These are fried in vanaspati and are a superb anytime snack. Of all the samosas across the country, we rate the Battamangala singhara one of the best. Jitendra Kumar Nayak, who's here managing the customers and cash, started this modest food shop in the early 2000s. In 20-plus years, he's built a reputation also for his puri-ghugni, *bada* made of urad dal, and sweets that include chhena poda and malpua. The tea is worth mentioning too. It's served in tiny cups with a dollop of fresh malai on top.

A short detour from the Bhubaneswar-Puri highway just after we left the temple town took us to Chandanpur. We stopped at the bright-red signboard announcing Hotel Padmalaya. It's a favourite breakfast spot for locals and now also tourists, thanks to social media and Youtube videos that feature the place. We met owner Kailas Chandra Senapathy and he spoke with a quiet contentment about his journey and the making of a landmark. He had been working as a panda, a temple cook, at the Basudev temple in Chandanpur for nearly 15 years. He considered the master cook who taught him his guru. 'In 1982, I told guruji I wanted to start a business,' he said. 'He gave me ₹1,001, a huge sum at the time, and his blessings.' He set up Hotel Padmalaya, with a large dining room and a kitchen at the back.

In the temple kitchen, he had been experimenting and one of the things he came up with was a dish that came to be known as *choora-kadamb*. Beaten rice is soaked and then crushed. To it is added

chhena and a little rabri, making it mildly sweet. The mixture is formed into a ball and served with *dalma*, the Odisha staple of dal cooked with seasonal vegetables. While Padmalaya now serves an array of sweets, such as malpua and chhena *jilli*, it is the choora-kadamb that is the star dish here. We ate this unusual combination off banana leaves. The detour from the highway was absolutely worth it.

Cuttack had an entirely different vibe and charm. This ancient city, the capital of Odisha before Bhubaneshwar, is now a significant commercial hub. Areas like Naya Sadak are colourful with shops selling the gorgeous handlooms Odisha is famous for. This is also where skilled artisans ply their trade in the filigree work that gives Cuttack its 'Silver City' sobriquet. There are sellers of *bara-ghugni* and gupchup dotting street corners.

There is also the Barabati Cricket Stadium, and the green expanse in front of it is a market for fish and local produce in the morning and a hub of street-food vendors by night. The Mahanadi which flows in an awe-inspiring wide sweep here gives Cuttack a beauty all its own.

In the early hours of the day, the streets of the otherwise buzzing Nandi Sahi are relatively quiet. But there's a bustle outside a narrow shop, while the shutters are still down in the adjoining ones. It has no name and has, for the longest time, been known as the place for 'Mausi ki Chakuli'. Annapoorna Devi, Mausi to all her customers, had been indisposed since the end of 2020 and handed over the reins to her daughter-in-law, Pramila Sahoo. The statuesque woman displays poise and grace as she tends to the steamer in which the *chakuli* is cooked. The chakuli is made of a fermented batter of urad dal and rice and is steamed not in a mould but on a cloth stretched over simmering water. It belongs to the family of Odisha foods known as *pithe*, which can include any number of steamed or fried items. It's served here with a spicy chutney of garlic and fresh chillies that's the perfect complement to the plain chakuli. Mausi began this single-product business in the 1960s to be self-reliant, and the freshness and goodness of this breakfast favourite soon earned her a place on Cuttack's street-food landscape. Considering the skill and assuredness with which Pramila made and served the chakuli, Mausi can rest assured that the legacy is in excellent hands.

If this particular chakuli required us to start the day early, without exception everyone we asked about Raghu's dahi bara aloo dum said, 'Go early, he sells out fast.' And sure enough, the crowds were beginning to gather by 4.30 p.m. in front of the shop in Bidanasi. It's an empty counter at this point. At 5 p.m., a cycle pulls up. It has a carrier attached and it's loaded with large steel containers holding the dahi bara and aloo dum which are made at home. When he was fitter, Raghunath Sasmal, now frail and in his 80s, would ride along with the containers. Now he comes occasionally to sit on a chair and watch the business he began in the 60s. His sons manage the clamour for what is unquestionably Cuttack's most famous dahi bara aloo dum. It's famous enough for News7, a TV channel, to include in its news capsule a segment on the plight of Raghu's business during the lockdown of 2020. This is stuff that Cuttack is concerned about. The shop is now managed by Raghu's two sons. What makes this street food stand out is its freshness. Regulars, who eat their fill here and take away several portions, vouch for its consistency. The bara is made of urad dal and is soaked not in yoghurt—though the name is dahi bara—but in a thin, seasoned buttermilk. It becomes soft and is infused with some tanginess. Four of these are placed on leaf plates and topped with the signature aloo dum, thin, red, spicy and piping hot.

Ishwar Dahi Bara on Biju Patnaik Chowk is also known for its dahi bara aloo dum. It's a more gussied-up version at this cart set up by Ishwar Behera in the 1960s. He used to carry his wares and trudge all the way to Barabati Stadium to sell them there. In 1999, the business moved to its present location where it's right outside Anand Bhavan. After Ishwar Behera's passing in 2021, his son Jagabandu took over. He's at the cart every evening, dishing out dahi bara aloo dum that has chutney, sev and chopped onions, making it more like chaat. Different from Raghu's version and still much-loved.

The narrow lane in Professor Pada is an unlikely place to find a food business that is famous enough to attract food-show TV crews. Tucked amidst the houses lining the street are the twin chop shops of Kalia and Babubhai Panda. Kalia, with a 100-watt smile, was cleaning his karhais and setting up for the evening when we met him. Though his shop is small and operates from the front of his residence, he's proud of the hygiene he's able to maintain in this cramped operation. 'My father started selling chops in the '70s and I took over from him,' he told us. The shop serves mutton, prawn and liver chops. These are made by the women of the house. Meat and prawn are spiced with masalas made in-house, wrapped in mashed potato, and crumb-fried to make one of Cuttack's favourite evening snacks. The adjacent shop is run by Kalia's cousin, Babubhai. They

co-exist, with no apparent disharmony.

The very name for pani puri in Odisha has a playful ring to it. A gupchup cart is somewhere to gather after class for college students, a pick-me-up for shoppers in crowded bazaars, and a must-stop spot for all lovers of street food. In Cuttack, the puri is much smaller than in other places. The filling is almost always a simply spiced mixture of boiled potato. The pani is clean, refreshing and spicy. Few vendors have a sweet version or flavoured variants as is common in, say, Indore. Some of the popular hubs for gupchup are Barabati Stadium, Dolamundai and Gowrishankar Park. We found an excellent vendor near the Chandi Temple.

The *piaji* is less common than, say, bara in Cuttack, but it has its fans. One place that's made these fried morsels famous is the cart opposite the Chandi Temple. A flex board announces that it's called

ODISHA: THE LAND OF GHUGNI, KHAJA, AND CHAKULI

Pet Pooja. The piaji is made of powdered chana dal and chopped onions, turned into a batter and fried. The exterior is crisp and the inside is soft and crumbly. The other speciality here is *gulgula*, which has a similar texture but is made of semolina and sugar. Odisha's love of combining sweet and savoury elements is evident here too; piaji and gulgula are served together and topped with a thin sabzi of aloo and *matar*. The shop functions from 7 a.m. to 2 p.m. and again from 4 p.m. to 8 p.m., drawing locals who wish to satisfy their 'pet', tummy, after pooja at the Chandi temple.

The capital of Odisha is an impressively smooth-running city. The old quarter, where Bhubaneshwar's many temples are, is crowded and chaotic. The modern city, designed by the German architect Otto Königsberger in 1946, has the ease of navigation usually associated with well-planned urbanscapes. The roads are wide and tree-lined; there's parking and pedestrian paths. Coming from Bangalore, these were a luxury while exploring the city.

Malls and gaudily illuminated jewellery stores light up the main thoroughfares at night. The lanes leading off these each becomes a mini street-food hub. Opposite Ramadevi Women's College, for instance, tandoori momo-walas and dum biryani sellers ply a brisk trade. *Jhalmuri* vendors patiently customize 'mixtures' for waiting customers. All the sweet shops are busy, chhena poda and *rasabali* being hot sellers.

To the casual observer, Bhubaneshwar looks like an easy city to live in, and the abundance of good, affordable food would seem to help.

We always look forward to our first breakfast in a new city. It becomes a prelude to what we can expect. Thus, we went to the Ram Mandir Tiffin Centre, a large stall abutting the temple. There's a throng of people outside and service is erratic. You have to try and catch the attention of the staff, place your order and wait, jostling other customers. But when our plates of puri and dalma arrived, we told ourselves it was worth the wait and the jostling. The dalma is the everyday dal of Odisha. It is made with lentils and a mix of vegetables such as potato, pumpkin, sweet potato, brinjal and whatever else is in season. Lightly seasoned, it's satisfying and nutritious.

This now bustling business was begun in a small cabin by Bhagwan Mahapatra. Later his sons Gopalbandhu and Surajkumar stepped in. We asked Surajkumar, when he could spare a moment in the midst of busy service, for the secret of his success. 'We do nothing extraordinary,' he said. 'Just use good ingredients and cook honest food.' Besides the puri-dalma, this tiffin centre, which opens early at 7 a.m., also serves dahi vada, samosa and Odisha's favourite sweet, chhena poda.

Nimapara Sweets in Bapuji Nagar is famous for its chhena poda as also other Odia sweets like chhena jilli and *arisa pitha*. Pithe are an important aspect of Odisha's culinary tradition and are an essential item at festivals such as Raja Parba. Pithe can be fried confections or griddle-cooked like pancakes. Wandering about the street-food hubs, we stumbled upon small shops selling an array of these, from arisa pitha to *chandrakanti* and *manda* pitha (steamed dumplings with a sweet filling).

The other sweet Odisha celebrates is, of course, the rosogolla, the subject of a long-running controversy between the state and neighbouring West Bengal on where this spongy, syrup-soaked sweet originated. In 2019, Odisha managed to secure a GI tag for its rosogolla. While you can eat excellent rosogolla all across Odisha, Pahala, a stop on the Bhubaneshwar-Cuttack highway, has now become a stretch of rosogolla shops. It's not unlike the surfeit of petha shops in Agra. The commercialization of a traditional sweet may seem excessive at times. Still, eating a warm rosogolla on the highway becomes a happy memory.

Evenings in Bhubaneshwar we spent hitting the chaat trail. Gopabandhu Square in Surya Nagar is a buzzing hub of street food with carts selling desi-style burgers, momos, lassi, traditional sweets and chaat.

One of the most popular chaat vendors is Dolagobindo Sahoo who sells his items from a battery-operated cart. 'Four batteries died and had to be replaced during the first lockdown,' he told us. But as soon as some form of normalcy was restored, his regulars came flocking back. Dolagobindo Sahoo, who began the shop in the year 2000, told us his chaats are so popular because he makes all the masalas and chutneys and keeps them fresh and zinging with flavour. Sahoo Chaats specializes in *papdi* chaat and *tikki* chaat, both served topped with a ghugni-like mix of spiced potatoes and white peas, sliced onions and perhaps some slivers of carrot and beetroot, a scattering of sev and chutneys that include a vivid orange one.

The chaat shop we really liked was Mayaram in Babuji Nagar. Pitambar Sahoo has been running this stall that is tucked into a line-up of food shops since the 1990s. The papdi chaat and the *vel muri*, Odisha's bhelpuri, are the hot-selling items here. According to local lore, it is Pitambar Sahoo who introduced papdi chaat here. His papdi chaat has papdi topped with potato masala, sev, peanuts and a sauce they say is homemade. Interestingly, this shop also adds a topping of crumbled dhokla to the chaat. We also loved the masala muri here, with its drizzle of mustard oil and coconut slivers.

Unit 6 Bhubaneshwar is a swank area. The smoke-darkened *bara* shop here is a bit of an incongruity. What's more, Rabindra Raut, or Rabi Mausa as he's known to his regulars, performs the amazing feat of picking of the crisp baras out of the hot oil with his bare hands. On account of that, he's also now a Youtube star and social media celebrity. The bara is good, but we ate better elsewhere. However, it's very nice to be here and chat with Rabi Mausa, who came to Bhubaneshwar from Konark and set up this shop in 1978. We asked him how he managed to work like that with boiling oil. 'My hands are just like yours, there's no magic,' he said, encouraging us to eat a gulab jamun, which, incidentally, is excellent here.

In between all the puri dalma, chaat and bara ghugni, we went to Lingaraj Lassi Sherbet which operates in what looks like a makeshift tent at a mela. Two surly men manned the shop one desultory afternoon. The lassi sherbet is a lassi with bells and whistles: rabri, khoya, grated coconut, cashew and chopped candied cherries to boot. It was pleasant for the first few sips, but then the richness overwhelmed.

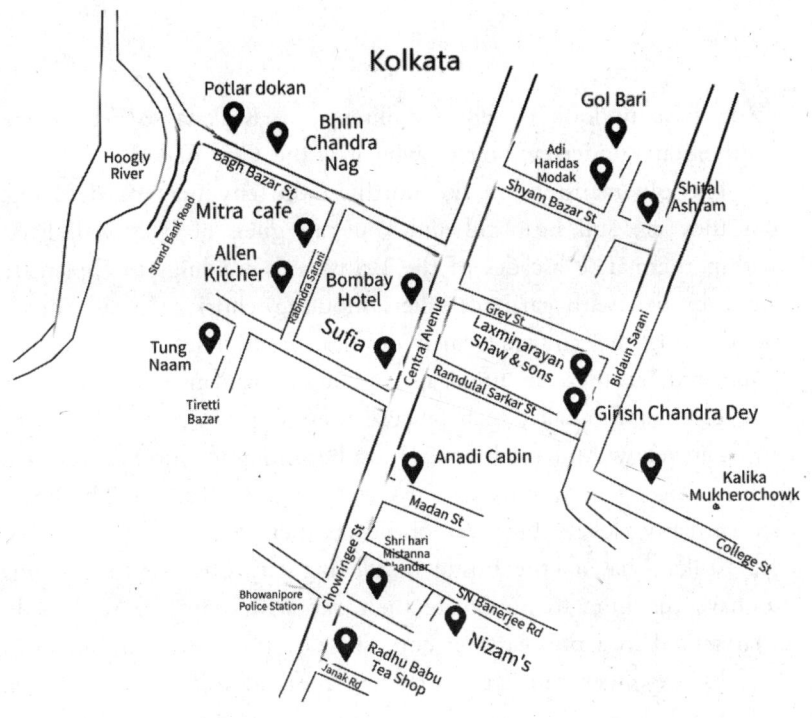

STEEPED IN HISTORY

Kolkata

*Y*ou have to look closely and intently at Kolkata to get even a rudimentary understanding of why it is the City of Joy.

The old mansions in the north of the city may be decaying, but they are still beautiful and you can guess at lives well lived within them. The arcades of the British-era buildings in Esplanade are crammed with garment sellers shouting 'chori ka maal'; there's no denying the vintage charm of these parts. The city is densely populated, but there are green spaces like the maidans where budding cricketers or footballers can practise their sport.

The yellow Ambassador taxis must be among the most ramshackle cabs in the country, but they are accessible and affordable. The buses are similarly rickety, but everyone takes them.

Kolkata has all the bustle of the big city, but everyone seems to have the time to punctuate their day with stops for well-made chai served in a tiny earthen cup. The poverty is evident, but even a rickshaw-puller can eat a satisfying meal of rice, dal and *maach*, fish, for ₹15.

From the crowds and the chaos emerge contemporary art, as it has for centuries. There's music, dance, theatre, literature. And there's *mishti*, available at big stores and tiny *parar dokan*, neighbourhood stalls, to sweeten the most difficult day. Kolkata, we have to say, entirely agreed with us.

On our first morning in the city, we decided on a breakfast of Kolkata-style *nihari*. The streets around Nakhoda Masjid were quiet on an early winter morning. But there was a bustle outside some eateries.

We stopped at Sufia on Zakaria Street, lying in the shadow of Kolkata's principal mosque with its Indo-Saracenic architecture. Customers sit on benches on the street and tuck into luchis and a light aloo sabzi. Inside the restaurant you can order an early morning special, the beef nihari, lighter than in other parts of the country and aromatic with a spice mixture, the recipe for which has been handed down over generations.

Further down the road, the 100-year-old Bombay Hotel, which began in the mid-1910s, is also famous for its nihari available from 6 a.m. 'Begun by Noor Mohammed, it was originally a tea shop known as Bombay Tea Stall,' Mohammed Faizan told us. Here, you can order a plate of deliciously slow-cooked nihari with roti or puris. The puris are also famously eaten with a brown halwa made from maida. We found it just the thing on a cool morning. 'It's an honour and a privilege to preserve a legacy that belongs to the people of Kolkata,' Faizan said.

If you are on the street-food trail of Kolkata, you will inevitably stop at Anadi Cabin in Esplanade. It was established in 1917 by Balaram Jana and has an unshakeable reputation for its Moghlai paratha. Food historians say its origins go back to the time of Mughal rule in East India and that a cook in the Mughal emperor Jehangir's court conjured up this dish. It became popular in the urban centres of the Mughal Subah like Dhaka and Kolkata. This crisp paratha, stuffed with egg, is undeniably delicious.

The 'cabin' is an essential part of the culinary landscape of the city. Now merely holes in the wall with fading paint and suffused with nostalgia, they go back to the early 1900s. They were originally intended to provide privacy for women and families when they ate out. The plywood partitions and curtains are all but gone now, but the food remains a draw in many of Kolkata's cabins. At Anadi, most people order a double duck egg paratha. The skilled paratha maker spreads out the dough thin, tosses in a mix of onion, chillies, coconut and peanuts, breaks the eggs atop and gives them a mix with his fingers. The dough is then folded over like an envelope and slapped onto a tawa with lots of Dalda (vegetable shortening). It's fried till golden and crisp and served sliced with a potato curry, some salad and tomato ketchup. 'Anyone who loves food and comes to Kolkata comes here for our Moghlai paratha,' said long-time manager Sudhanshu Dutta. His pride in his product is completely justified, we agreed, after our Moghlai paratha meal.

One lunch time, we walked towards Fairlie Place and BBD Bagh, bustling hubs for street food. There are several government offices in the vicinity and vendors serve their staff with freshly fried luchis and delicious potato curry, besides everything else from chai and toast to biryani, sandesh and lassi.

The luchi is Kolkata's puri, made of refined flour instead of wheat, fluffy and creamy white in colour. Paired with slightly sweetened *cholar* dal or an aloo sabzi, it's a satisfying anytime meal.

Eating that classic combination at one of Kolkata's oldest establishments, Haridas Modak at Shyam Bazaar, is a special experience. The shop is probably over 200 years old, certainly not less than 150, said the manager, an old-timer. Begun by Haridas Modak, it is now run by Mainak Modak of the fourth generation. Apparently, Ramakrishna Paramahansa ate the luchi dal here. The original menu of this tiny eatery comprised luchi, cholar dal and sweet *bundiya*. The luchi dal is still there, made at the back of the eatery in a smoke-darkened kitchen and served on banana leaves. Haridas Modak now also sells an array of sweets, and the *chhanar* pulao, the chhana being shaped to resemble long grain rice, is very good.

Shree Hari Mistanna Bhandar in Bhowanipore has also won the loyalty of customers for its luchi cholar dal, an affordable meal for many people. It's in a time-worn corner building opposite the Bhownipore police station. The *kochori*—with a spiced filling—with dal is also a popular order here.

Evenings were for a uniquely Kolkata pursuit. Say what you will about the calories present in deep-fried snacks, Kolkata's *tele bhaja*

trade is alive and well. For a vast number of locals, stopping at the neighbourhood tele bhaja seller is a daily ritual. They may buy *fulori*, lentil fritters, or *pyaaji*, onion bhajia, for breakfast and opt for *narkol* chop, coconut cutlets, or *aamer* chop with potato and raw mango as an evening snack. Battered and deep-fried snacks are what the tele bhaja shops specialize in.

One of the oldest is Laxmi Narayan Shaw & Sons on Bidhan Sarani in North Kolkata. Keshto Kumar Gupta now manages this shop, which is a relic from the past. The business was begun by his grandfather Khedu Shaw in 1918 and named after Keshto Kumar's father, Laxmi Narayan. Showing us old albums containing photos of the many celebrities who've frequented the shop, Keshto Kumar told us that in the pre-Independence era this modest tele bhaja shop was a place where freedom fighters gathered. Notes and information would be exchanged here. 'My grandfather was arrested a few times by the British for his role. When the activists gathered elsewhere in the area, tele bhaja, muri and *cha* would be sent from here,' he said.

Acting on the fringes of the freedom movement, Khedu Shaw became a devoted fan of Subhash Chandra Bose. 'He wasn't Netaji yet,' Gupta said. On the fiery leader's birthday in 1942, Khedu Shaw distributed free tele bhaja to the entire locality. It's a tradition that continues to this day. Intertwined as it was in the freedom struggle, Laxmi Narayan Shaw & Sons celebrated Independence by decking the shop with marigold garlands. 'It was like Diwali,' Gupta told us. This is not just a shop to get a taste of history and nostalgia. The tele bhaja is very good, too. It's fulori, pyaaji, *beguni*, *aloor* chop and dhoka, dal cakes that are steamed and then fried, from 8 a.m. to 12 noon, and a more elaborate list of fried goodies between 3.30 p.m. and 9 p.m. when paneer chop, narkol chop and *aam* chop are available.

Potlar Dokan on Bagbazaar street has no name. 'The taste is advertisement enough,' says a taciturn Dipendu Sen, who manages the shop, seated at floor level, while the bhajas are fried fresh alongside. The business was set up in 1928 by his grandfather Shashi Bhushan Sen, a cashier at Calcutta Tramways. He had a large family with

seven sons—one of them was called Potla—and began to sell tele bhaja to supplement his income. Besides the beguni, fulori and aloo chop available in the morning, Potlar Dokan is known for its dhoka. This, to many Bengalis, is a substitute for fish or meat on days when vegetarianism is prescribed. The process of soaking, grinding and frying dhoka is considered too tedious and many homes buy the readymade ones from Potlar Dokan and drop it into a gravy at home to make dhokar dalna.

Kalika Mukhorochok Tele Bhaja on College Street began life in 1965 selling only the traditional vegetarian items. Sukumar Dutta opened the shop on the auspicious occasion of Kali Pujo and hence the name. 'There was only beguni, aloo chop, etc., and those were available everywhere. Also, people were acquiring a taste for other things, so we decided to introduce fish, prawn and chicken as cutlets, chops and fries,' says Bablu Dutta, who inherited the business from his father. He sits at the cash till at this shop, which is a long roadside counter. College goers and book buyers who come to Kolkata's Boi Para are his clientele. The chops are delicious and inexpensive.

The Bengalis' love of crumbed and deep-fried foods is hard to beat. You can eat excellent versions of these almost anywhere you go in the city, from vegetable chops and egg chops at a roadside stall in BBD Bagh to the egg-battered dishes, known as *kabiraji*, in the cabins. The kabiraji belongs uniquely to Kolkata. It is believed that the dish came to be when desi cooks made 'cutlets' for their British masters. A possibly apocryphal explanation for the name is that it is a distortion of 'coverage', referring to the egg coating the meat, fish or prawn gets. What is certain though is that it takes skill and patience to make this. The main ingredient is marinated and crumb-fried. Beaten eggs are streamed into hot oil by practised fingers, the fried cutlet is placed on this chiffonade and enfolded in it. It's greasy, golden, crisp and very tasty.

Mitra Café near Sovabazaar Metro Station is reputed to make some of the best. This tiny space on Jatinder Mohan Avenue was set up in 1920 by Sushil Roy. His grandson Tapash Roy now runs the business, expanding it to five outlets across Kolkata. There are only four tables and often there are crowds milling on the pavement outside. The staff work at their own pace. You have to exercise patience if you want to eat at Mitra Café.

We went to Allen Kitchen near Sovabazaar Metro Station for their famous prawn cutlet. The place gets its name from a Scotsman who began the business in the 1880s. It was then taken over by Jeevan Krishna Saha. His great grandson Deepak Saha now manages the outlet. His mother is a welcoming presence here as well. Allen Kitchen is spanking clean and all the cooking happens at the front of the eatery. 'Besides the prawn cutlet, we're also famous for our fish cutlet and chicken batter cutlet,' Deepak said. The seafood and meats are marinated and either batter- or crumb-fried. 'Special' dishes are fried in ghee here, regular ones in refined oil.

A chai shop that's a local landmark, Radhu Babu's Tea Shop, on Janak Road, Kalighat, is both adda and eatery. Locals throng the place for chai and buttered toast, as well as the hugely popular fish fry and kabiraji. It was begun in 1933 by Radha Krishna Datta, who hailed from Purulia. His little shop was patronized by the likes of film stars Uttam Kumar and Raj Kapoor, all of whom knew it as Radhu Babu Chayer Dokan. It is now managed by his nephews Satyasundar and Somnath.

Snacking on chaat and jhalmuri are other much-loved evening rituals. The gupchup eaters, the fans of gol gappa and lovers of *patashe* may all be up in arms to hear us say this: Kolkata does have some of the best, if not *the* best, pani puri in the country. *Puchka* sellers dot the landscape, especially in the bazaars and bustling commercial quarters, near maidans and parks. The Kolkata puchka is a very large mouthful. The filling is almost always boiled potato mashed with an assortment of spice powders and condiments that the puchka makers blend in perfect proportion with practised ease and assurance. The pani is often spicy and some vendors will offer a sweet one as well. The result is a delightful burst of flavour in the mouth.

Vivekananda Park has long been a destination for puchka eating. When we went there, however, the place had lost much of its buzz and we surmised it was a fallout of the pandemic. But the vendors outside Vardaan Market—which is also a hub of cheela, dosa, bread toast and lassi sellers—do brisk business. The vendor near Basanti Devi College in Gariahat has been popular for decades. One of our best puchka experiences was at an unnamed stall at the entrance of Janak Road right next to Lake Market. Esplanade and the line-up of stalls outside Victoria Memorial are also places for brilliantly satisfying puchka.

Jhalmuri is Kolkata's very own bhelpuri. It may have been introduced here by migrants from Uttar Pradesh and Bihar, but it's become as essential a part of Kolkata as the yellow taxi or Victoria Memorial. Muri or puffed rice is the main ingredient; an array of add-ons, from boiled potato to chillies, soaked white peas, sprouted chana, slivers of coconut, peanuts, masala powder and a pungent drizzle of mustard oil make it the much-loved and affordable snack that it is. Like puchka, it's available across the city, in shopping districts, outside Metro stations, and pretty much anywhere with floating crowds.

What's more, the jhalmuri is excellent everywhere, whether you eat one with bits of singhara crumbs in it near Ram Mandir, at Girish Park, outside Rabindra Sadan metro station, from the decades-old cart near Basanti Devi College, or from the numerous vendors who set up their portable stands at Esplanade. In the residential quarters of North Kolkata, you can have jhalmuri with 'exotic' additions like aam *ada* (mango ginger) or *amra* (hog plum). Customers can pick their combinations and the vendor will toss and give you a taste before he wraps it up in a newspaper bag.

The culinary history of Kolkata has a chapter dedicated to the roll that is now a pan-Indian favourite. It is believed it was created by Hasan Reza, who came to the city from Lucknow and began selling kebabs near Esplanade. Members of the British Patrol who went on their rounds on horseback wanted kebabs-to-go and Reza came up with the idea of wrapping them up in a paratha. From a street stall, Nizam's, named after Reza's son Shaikh Nizamuddin, grew to be a full-fledged restaurant and is now a New Market landmark. Close to a century later, this is still a good place to order the perfectly made roll.

How can you be in Kolkata and not wander down Park Street? Kusum Rolls is the most famous street-food joint on Park Street serving delicious kathi rolls. Established in 1971, the place—there are two counters, one on the main street and one in an adjacent bylane—sure makes some delicious rolls. Staff roll out and fry parathas, add your choice of filling, from egg to chicken, mutton and veg— you can have doubles of any of these—top it with sauce and sliced onions, and voila! Wrapped up in butter paper is a roll that ticks all the boxes and stands for complete satiation.

Gourmet friends in Kolkata pointed us also towards Gol Bari. Few modest eateries are as famous for one particular dish as is Gol Bari at Five Point Crossing, in one of Kolkata's heritage quarters. Its original name was New Punjabi Restaurant. Being located as it is in a building with a semi-circular façade, it came to be known as Gol Bari and the name has become attached to its hugely popular

STEEPED IN HISTORY

mutton dish as well. The 100-year-old eatery was set up by Ratan Arora, Punjabis who settled here and is now run by his son Kishan Arora. 'No Beef' says a sign at the entrance. In any case, it's the mutton dish, dark, rich, robust and unashamedly oily that customers come here for. It is eaten with rotis. The tiny eatery has changed little over the years and is likely to be the same for some decades to come.

There's no dearth of excellent mutton dishes served by small shops in Kolkata. We went to Delhi Darbar on Acharya Jagadish Chandra Bose Road in the Beniapukur area. It was established in the 1960s and is most famous for its mutton tikka. This deep-fried kebab is made of minced mutton, subtly spiced with a hint of the edible ittar you'll taste in several meat dishes in the city. It's usually eaten rolled up in a flaky, slightly sweet paratha with sliced onions for crunch. Delhi Darbar is also known for its mutton *chaamp* (chop) in a rich gravy.

We spent another morning walking through Tiretti Bazaar, getting glimpses into a past and the lives of a people who once thrived here. A sugar factory established by an early settler in the eighteenth century and the creation of tea gardens in Darjeeling and Assam by the British brought the Chinese to Kolkata. They put down roots in and around Tiretti Bazaar, the earliest China town in the city, and later in Tangra. During the week, this broad street is lined with sellers of poultry, fish and seasonal vegetables. Early on Sunday mornings it transforms into a street-food market, with makeshift stalls selling dumplings and pork bao. Over the years, many Chinese have left the area and the city and the number of stalls has dwindled; the pandemic had its role too. Still, you can get a satisfying meal of dim sum or momos and soup if you get here early.

Tung Naam is a small restaurant in the area serving Cantonese and Hakka cuisine. It was begun in 2001 by Michael and his wife, third-generation Chinese in Kolkata. Michael is a self-taught cook and had worked in the US and Hong Kong before returning to look after the family property.

'We were in the paper business earlier. When the older generation passed away and the young people all left the city, this place was abandoned. I came back to keep it in the family,' he says. From a spotlessly clean kitchen emerge some of the best wontons you will taste. And the chilli pork is spectacular, too.

Between eating meal after delicious meal, we would stop for sweets in shops across the city. Few other cultures accord sweets the place of prominence Bengal does. Sweets are both an everyday ritual and a symbol of celebration and festivity in Kolkata. Sandesh, crafted from chhana and sugar or jaggery and made by skilled craftsmen, is possibly the most favoured of these.

One of the oldest sweet makers of Kolkata is Bhim Chandra Nag in Bow Bazaar (with one branch on Vivekananda Road). With its unpretentious façade, clean interiors and single-glass showcase for its delicious wares, the shop does not seem to have undergone any drastic changes since it was set up by Paran Chandra Nag in 1826. It is now managed by Pradip Nag of the fifth generation. He traced for us all the members of the family who have been involved in the business, pointing to black-and-white photos that hang on one wall.

'We are specialists in the making of sandesh,' he said. This sandesh has a loyal clientele now as it did nearly 200 years ago. Ramakrishna Paramahansa is said to have had a fondness for Bhim Nag's sandesh. For the inauguration of the Kali temple in Dakshineshwar, its founder Rani Rashmoni, who appointed Ramakrishna Paramhansa the priest of the temple, is said to have ordered 2.5 maunds (a maund is just under 40 kilos) of sandesh. 'They were taken by boat down the Hooghly,' Pradip Nag told us. If you go to this heritage store, look for the wall clock dating back to 1858. It was a gift to the shop by Thomas Cooke of Cooke & Kelvey, renowned for their time pieces. None of Bhim Chandra Nag's staff could read Roman numerals. So, the letters were inscribed in Bengali. 'It's the only one of its kind,' according to Pradip Nag. It's working perfectly well in a shop where time seems to stand still.

STEEPED IN HISTORY

Across town on Ramdulal Street in North Kolkata is Girish Chandra Dey & Nakur Nandy, another venerable sandesh maker so well-loved that they were commissioned by then Chief Minister Mamata Banerjee to make the celebratory sandesh cake to mark Kolkata Knight Riders' 2012 IPL victory. The shop with its vintage air is set in a heritage quarter, not far from the ancestral home of Swami Vivekananda. While Mahesh Dey began selling sweets from a cart, his son Girish Chandra Dey set up this shop in 1844. Later, his son-in-law, Nakur Chandra Nandy, joined the business and lent his name to it. It is now in the hands of the fifth generation. Brothers Pritid and Prajesh Nandy, like most young people who have inherited glorious food legacies, are conscious of their responsibility and committed to keeping tradition alive.

'We only make sandesh. The milk comes from the doodh bazaar every day and everything is done by hand, from the cooking of the chhana to the shaping in traditional moulds,' Pritid said when we chatted with him after a sweet-buying spree here. The result is sandesh that tastes of milk and cream and has the most exquisite texture. Now, they also make sandesh in flavours like strawberry and mango. Customers line up outside a green-painted grill to buy these; from exotic names to intricate shapes, degrees of softness and flavour, sandesh is a world unto itself. In the aftermath of Covid-19, a sign outside the shop says 'No mask, no sandesh'. Everyone heeds it.

You cannot speak of sweets in Kolkata and not dwell on the rosogolla. Chittaranjan Mistanna Bhandar in Shyam Bazaar is a shop set up in the early 1900s by Hiralal Ghosh. He was a devoted follower of Chittaranjan Das, a nationalist and freedom fighter, and named the shop after him, according to fourth-generation owner Sumit Ghosh. Chittaranjan originally served the traditional breakfast dishes of *radhaballabi* and singhara, introducing rosogolla in the 1970s. The rosogollas here are small and white and often available warm.

Other recommended places for rosogolla are Park Sweets near Park Circus and Bhim Chandra Nag. The truth is, you can get great mishti nearly everywhere in Kolkata. We've just brought you the smallest, sweet glimpse into an entire world of chhana confections, which take top-quality ingredients and great craftsmanship to perfection.

Kolkata runs on chai. On the busiest roads and in the quietest residential areas there will be a little shop selling tea. It's almost always of excellent quality, just strong and just sweet enough. In Fairlie Place, a tiny clay kulhad of cha costs a mere ₹3. The practice in these parts is to usually have a 'biskoot' or some toast with tea.

One of the quaintest tea shops we found was Sital Ashram in Shyam Bazaar. Over 100 years old, it was being run by the 86-year-old Kedar Modak who beckoned passers-by to come in. The shop serves tea in white ceramic cups, along with toast with butter and/or jam. You can order an omelette if you want a light meal. 'It was begun by my father Madanmohan Modak and originally sold sherbets; hence the name Shital Ashram,' Kedar Modak said. In the '50s, the shop began to sell tea and toast, and has been a popular adda for locals ever since.

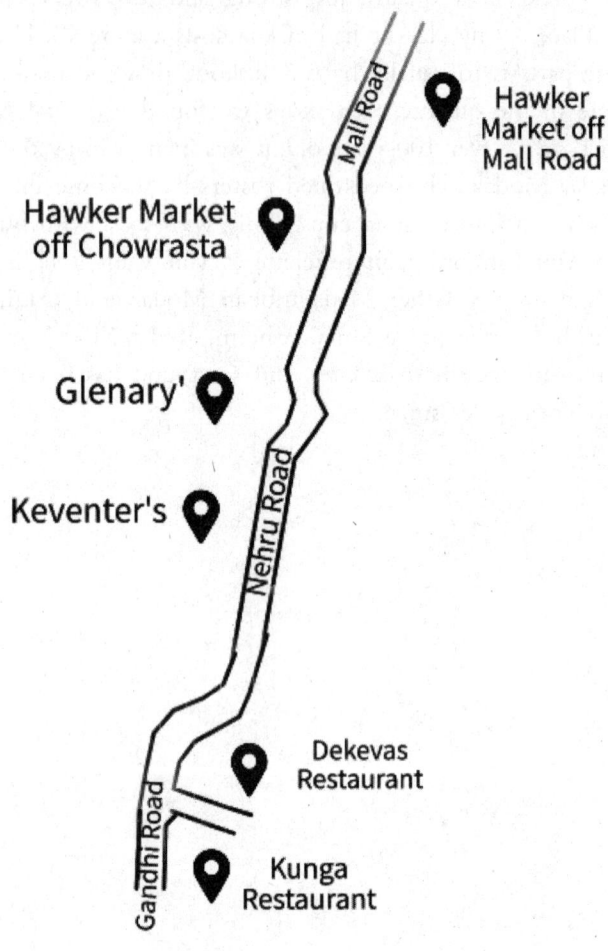

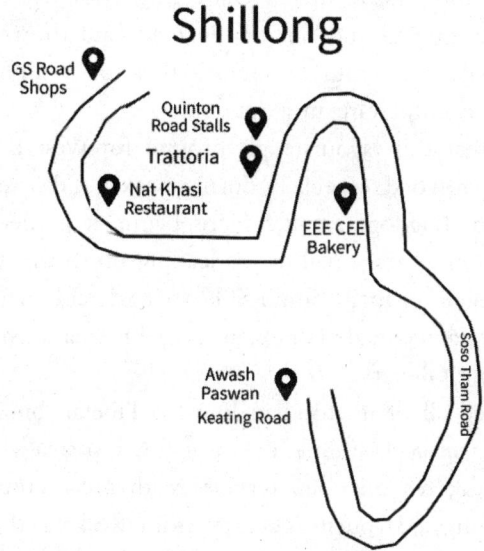

TIBETAN CUISINE AT ITS BEST

Darjeeling, Kalimpong, Shillong

If you'd always imagined Darjeeling as the fetching backdrop—it was for the vintage Bollywood song 'Mere sapno ki rani' or the more recent 'Kasto mazza' from *Parineeta*, you might do a double take when you see it for the first time.

Don't get us wrong. The town has all that it takes to be a sought-after mountain getaway. The narrow, sloping streets are quaint and perfect for ambling, the Chowrasta is a welcoming public square where bands play frequently, the mountain views have everyone pulling out their phones for photos, there's Darjeeling Himalayan Railway, the rail tracks weaving in and out of the road, and the tea is splendid, whether masala chai from a vendor's flask or a sophisticated first flush served in chinaware in a café.

It's just that this favourite playground for West Bengal can get infuriatingly crowded, especially during peak holiday season. On the drive up from Bagdogra, traffic snarls begin at gorgeous Kurseong and continue in all the small towns leading up to the 'Queen of the Hills'. Parking is virtually impossible to find and there are queues outside every eatery made famous on social media, such as Keventer's and the iconic Glenary's.

We braved all of it, stood in line for Tibetan bread and *thukpa gyathuk*, ate *shapaley*—veggie or meat-filled pastries—for the first time and drank tea on open terraces with great Himalayan views. With this being a favourite getaway from Kolkata, there are many vendors selling the city's popular snacks here. The hawker market

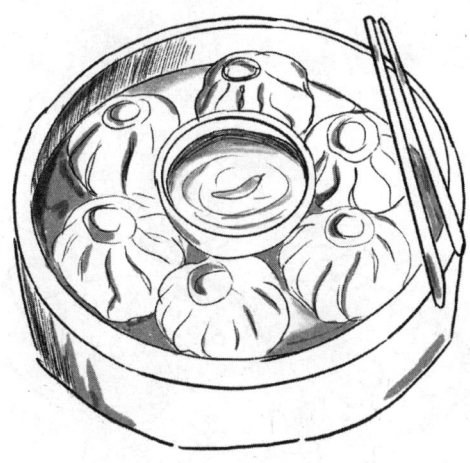

leading off Chowrasta, where every stall sells fashionable winterwear, is a good place to get a packet of jhalmuri, spiced to your liking. There are puchka sellers as well. Holes in the wall also sell singhara and luchis with aloo sabzi.

In the evening, Mall Road begins to buzz with vendors setting up their stalls. The entire line-up sells similar products: chowmein, tossed on a huge tawa with lots of soy sauce and a generous pinch of ajinomoto, chicken momos, *taipo* (super-sized momos), and shapaley. Chicken koftas, tinged orange and spicy, were also a hot seller.

Having been turned away the previous evening as the queue was long and the place was closing, we headed to Kunga for breakfast the next day. At 10 a.m., the family that runs the place was still seated around a table peeling garlic. The space is tiny with seating for no more than 15 people. The kitchen is even tinier. Yet, from here emerges some of the best Tibetan food you will eat in Darjeeling. We ate Tibetan bread, leavened with soda and deep-fried to have a crisp crust and soft, pillowy insides. Then momos, which the menu says, will take 20 minutes. It's worth the wait. These dumplings are shaped and steamed only after you place your order and they are superbly soft and light; the fillings are delicious, and so is the fiery chutney that accompanies every plate of momos. Chimme Bhutia,

TIBETAN CUISINE AT ITS BEST

who was taking orders and serving the food, told us Kunga had been a family business for years. With their roots in Tibet, they specialize in the cuisine of the region, making thukpa *bathuk* with hand-rolled noodles and *thentuk* with hand-pulled noodles, made in-house.

Next door is Dekewas, which has also achieved popularity thanks to making it to social media. It rides the wave of Korean cool with dishes such as *gimbap*, plays BTS, and also serves Chinese and Tibetan dishes.

Then, on to Kalimpong, after a drive through spectacular scenery that changes every few kilometers and skirting the Teesta flowing in a deep ravine. The town that was once an important trading hub with Tibet is now a crowded town with traffic that's nearly as crazy as in Darjeeling. The eateries in Kalimpong are small and nondescript. Many have succumbed to catering to tourists' tastes and demands, and authentic regional foods have to be hunted down.

We had our first taste of this at a cart calling itself Kalimpong Street Food Taste at 10th Mile. The aloo thukpa, a potato gravy served over noodles, is one of the items here.

The *haat*, a market sprawl where you can buy clothes, spices, fresh produce, *churpi* (the local hard cheese), a profusion of greens such as fiddlehead ferns, and mushrooms, seemed to us the culinary heart of this mountain town.

Within the market are half a dozen vendors making and serving momos and shapaley. Interestingly, they are all vegetarian, the filling being mainly cabbage and coriander. We watched with awe an entire family engaged in deftly shaping, steaming and serving momos to customers and other vendors in the market.

A unique product to look for in this market is *phumbi*, a sort of firm, translucent 'tofu' made of fermented moong bean paste. The yellow cubes have a neutral flavour and are served tossed in a chilli-garlic sauce. 'This is the way to eat it, but young people nowadays top phumbi with whatever they please,' shuddered one vendor.

Another moong bean product to buy in the Kalimpong haat is *phing*, a fine glass noodle. Dolly, a vendor with a smiling weatherbeaten face, has a stall at the entrance and sells phing, along with other noodles, churpi and a milk candy that is unique to the region. She gave us recipe ideas for using phing and we felt again the connectedness between people that is so much a part of local markets such as this one.

Outside the market on Damber Chowk, momo and shapaley vendors set up stall every evening. Ritu Rai's cart has been here since the early 2000s. Her products are all beef and she also sells home-cured beef sausage, sliced and tossed with condiments. Other vendors specialize in chicken. Everywhere the momos are excellent. On the approach to the Deolo Hill viewpoint, we stopped at a little shop for vegetable momos and chai. Chopped mustard greens had been added to the filling and the dumplings were, as in most places in Kalimpong, steamed fresh and utterly delicious.

One finds momos everywhere now. Perhaps it is the mountain air or the smiles that accompany the serving of the momos—in Kalimpong they seem to taste better than anywhere else.

TIBETAN CUISINE AT ITS BEST

It's a scenic drive along smooth roads from Guwahati to Shillong. The vast Umiam Lake presents a gorgeous spectacle as you enter the capital of Meghalaya. Beset by traffic snarls, Shillong is a small hill town with narrow roads.

The street-food hub of Shillong is Police Bazaar and the crowded road connecting it to Lal Bazaar. The main circle of Police Bazaar has seven roads leading to it from different directions.

One of them is Quinton Road alongside the MarBa Hub shopping mall. In the evenings, Quinton Road is lined with food carts, a cluster of them selling chow—which is how they refer to chowmein here—plus papdi and aloo chaat. Other carts serve up rolls, aloo parathas and momos. The aloo paratha is served with channa curry. The rolls were delicious. You can order a spiced boiled egg alongside.

The must-try foods on Shillong streets are the flame-grilled smoked pork, chicken and fish. The meat on skewers is finished over a flame and served with a cabbage and onion salad and spicy red chili sauce. The pork skewers are the most popular, tender meat acquiring a glazed, crisp surface.

Most of these stalls are run by the local Khasi people. Adjoining the flame-grilled meat stalls are carts selling *jadoh*, rice cooked in pork fat, sometimes blood, and topped with aloo curry, *doh khlieh*—a salad of pork, usually brain, onions and green chillies, and *tungrymbai*, the fermented soybean condiment unique to Meghalaya.

Trattoria, despite its name, is a small eatery serving local Khasi food and snacks. Started by Lasarabah Suting, the place sells pork dishes, besides fermented fish and a local chicken curry. The platters come with jadoh and your choice of toppings: *dohjen*, a minced pork curry, doh khlieh, *dohnud*, a dish of pork liver, and more. There's tungrymbai and a salad of radish. If you do not want to eat pork, you can order a platter with *jakhaw khasi*, sticky rice from the hills, with doh *syiar kylia*, homestyle chicken curry, or *dohkha* kylia, fish curry and *tungtap* made with fermented fish. We were delighted to see a tourist town serving such authentic and utterly delicious local food.

BAZAAR BITES

There are momo stalls aplenty, selling both the small mouthfuls and large momos that are like baos. A hugely popular cart that sees the well-heeled stop by is on narrow Keating Road, just before Hotel Sapphire. This blue momo cart run since the late '90s by Awash Paswan who hails from Bihar serves only vegetarian momos that are wrapped in leaves and steamed.

The most popular bakery in Shillong appeared to be the Eee Cee Bakery on Jail Road, which has been around since the 1960s. Besides puffs and savoury buns, the top-seller here is the cream roll filled with fresh cream.

GS Road is lined with shops selling everything from clothing to handicrafts. The best time to explore this area is in the mornings before the shops open. Outside the shuttered shops, vendors sell Khasi breakfast fare along with vegetables and fruits. You will need to

TIBETAN CUISINE AT ITS BEST

explore the small alleys in this area to find these places. If you take the trouble, you could tuck into a serving of *pu maloi*, small steamed rice cakes made with glutinous rice and stuffed with coconut or sugar. We also discovered *pukhlein*, oil cakes of rice flour and jaggery fried in mustard oil, which lent them an unusual flavour. Then there's *puswa*, made of red rice flour and baked in an open fire. We dipped these into tea and ate, taking our cue from the locals.

The Iewduh area is home to several jadoh stalls throughout the day. Nat Khasi restaurant and the very old Durka Pybrot Jaintia Jadoh stall are landmarks here. The Nat Khasi restaurant serves jadoh or plain steamed rice topped with your choice of pork or chicken. We had what most locals were ordering at the shop for breakfast, the jadoh topped with mixed pork curry and boiled egg. The person at the counter told us that everyone who came here ordered the jadoh, except those who didn't eat pork.

The Durka Pybrot Jaintia Jadoh stall is over 100 years old and is currently run by the fifth generation of the family. The restaurant is named after the daughter of the woman, Ka Durka Pybrot, who set it up in the 1900s. Here we had a platter of plain steamed rice topped with *dai nei iong*, dal cooked with sesame seeds, tungtap and doh *sniang*, boiled pork. The simple dish served in a small portion in a leaf plate was a fulfilling breakfast dish.

The Iewduh area is also home to big momo vendors who set up shop later in the day. The big momo is cut into half, slathered with red chutney and topped with sliced onion. The big momos here are mostly vegetarian, but if you are lucky, you may find a pork momo vendor too.

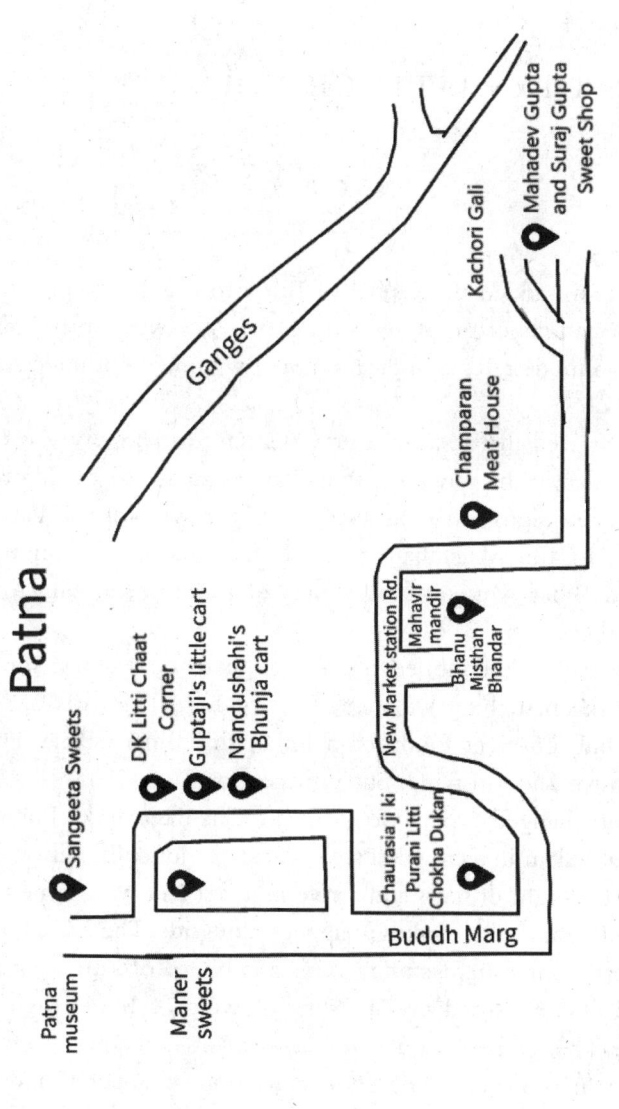

MORE THAN LITTI CHOKHA

Patna

When we added the capital of Bihar to our list of places to go, our expectations of the street-food experience were, to be frank, no more than modest. It's an indication of how limited our understanding of it was.

We arrived in Patna on a grey winter day. The city was chaotic and crowded in the way most Indian cities are. To the casual observer, there are few signs revealing its glorious past when it was Pataliputra and seat of the Magadha empire. But it has an arrestingly well-designed Bihar Museum and scores of buzzing shopping quarters and markets.

Litti chokha, mentioned often enough to be a cliche for Bihari food, is the first thing we wanted to eat here. The carts of Maurya Lok, a hub of street food, sell a lot of this Bihari staple. They are inexpensive and satisfying, but unexceptional.

That changed when we went to Chaurasia ji ki Purani Litti Chokha Dukan in a crowded area near Patna Junction railway station. You take a flight of stairs and arrive in a vast hall with some benches scattered about. The cooking happens alongside. The littis, little balls of wheat flour dough stuffed with a mixture of sattu, dal powder and spices, are roasted over brightly glowing coals and then dipped in ghee. The kitchen counter displays tins of 'desi' ghee as proof that they use nothing else. The chokha, a mash of potatoes and brinjal, simmers away in a vast pot outside. You crush the litti or tear it up and scoop up some of the chokha with it. And it simply hits the spot. Owner Ajay Kumar Chaurasia is effusive and proud of what he does.

This modest shop was begun by his father Govind Prasad Chaurasia in 1956. 'There's both sadness and joy in how this business came about,' he told us. 'My father was a seller of *kachri*, fried snacks, and we were a large family. Often, we ate just kachri. My mother had asked my father to make some litti chokha alongside and bring it home so we could eat a bit better. Customers who saw the litti my father made wanted some. They ate it and loved it and the word spread. Having started with litti made with half a kilo of atta, we have grown to this size, thanks to blessings from above and the love and trust of our customers.'

Nearly all of Chaurasia's customers are regulars. And he feels responsible not just for feeding them tasty food, but also for their well-being. 'A lot of our customers come here several times a week. They have four littis at ₹12 each, having as many refills of chokha as they want,' Ajay Kumar said. The spices used in the *sattu* filling of the litti and the chokha change according to the season. 'Now it's winter and you will taste warming spices like ajwain and pepper in the food. Come summer and it's jeera, to keep the stomach cool. In the rainy season, we add spices that will provide immunity against colds and coughs.' As we descended the narrow stairs after our litti chokha here, we experienced again the joy of eating an excellent meal and meeting a man who did just one thing and did it with such commitment and concern for his customer.

This Purani Litti Chokha Dukan is in the crowded New Market area. It was here next morning that we ate a satisfying thali of puri-aloo and jalebi, all for ₹20. You can eat similarly well all across the city; you'll just have to share a bench with auto drivers and vegetable vendors for whom this is daily sustenance. Wander into the narrow lanes of New Market and more food awaits: affordable thali places, shops selling sweets like *tilgud* and *anarsa*.

Another morning well spent was in old Patna City. In early winter, Sabzi Chowk bustled with the vibrancy of seasonal vegetables.

There were bunches of green garlic and hara chana, pink potatoes, the earth still clinging to them, and gorgeous striped brinjals, which, no doubt, make their way into many a chokha.

We were looking for the famous dum aloo kachori place here. It seemed to have shifted address, but we did manage to eat a scrumptious plate of baby potatoes simmered in a tangy gravy and tiny kachoris fried in mustard oil. Near the Marwari School in this area there's another excellent puri-aloo seller, and you should top off the meal with a jalebi.

Also near Sabzi Chowk is the Mahadev Gupta and Suraj Gupta sweet shop on Kachori Galli (but no kachoris are sold here anymore). Started in the 1940s, this small but clean shop, with paper clippings about its fame plastered on the walls, is best known for its *khurchan*. This sweet, made by slowly reducing milk in karhais till it becomes a sheet of creamy richness, requires patience and skill. We ate some and bought some, and had a fabulous chai at a little stall frequented by the sabzi sellers.

When evening falls, Maurya Lok is the place to be for chaat lovers. Street vendors serve up bhelpuri, dahi puri, papdi chaat and other ubiquitous chaat items. And yes, the tandoori momo is here in Patna too. Slightly more gussied-up than street carts, food trucks serve rolls and Chinese food.

The DK Litti Chaat Corner grabbed our attention with its photos of having represented India at a street-food festival in Singapore. We stopped here for an aloo tikki chaat.

Next, it was Guptaji's little cart for one of Patna's most popular puchkas and aloo cut. The latter is a tangy aloo chaat and the puchka is pronouncedly Kolkata-style. This isn't surprising because Guptaji came here from Kolkata, bringing his puchka-making skills with him.

Wandering around Maurya Lok, we stopped to take in the array of ingredients—rice, chana, wheat flakes, peanuts and an assortment of condiments—stacked on Nandushahi's Bhunja cart. He puts rice into salt being heated in a karhai and it fluffs up and pops as you watch. The *bhunja*, ₹10 for a paper bag full, is customized with

sprouts, nuts, other crispy bits and chutney. It would be perfect with a drink, we thought. But Bihar is a prohibition state and we had to settle for eating the bhunja without the rum.

Another street-food hub is Boring Road and share autos take you here. One stretch of the street is lined with carts selling 'burgers', tandoori momos and chicken litti. We were tempted to try the latter, but decided to let the taste of Chaurasia's classic linger.

There are quite a few small eateries in Patna all calling themselves Champaran Meat House. They aren't part of a chain and all claim to be the oldest or the original. Mutton or chicken is cooked in sealed earthen pots over coal—the dish is called *ahuni*—and is the speciality at these eateries.

We decided to taste it at the Champaran Meat House in Kankarbagh. The hype seems to have overtaken all else, and this wasn't our best meal in Patna.

Unique to Patna and living up to the hype was the bunia sev at Bhanu Mishthan Bhandar adjacent to the Mahavir Mandir. It looks like a makeshift tent, but it has been around several decades. The third generation now runs the place and say it was their family that constructed the Hanuman temple here. The bunia—boondi in other parts—was the best, with every orange globule soft and syrup-filled. It's eaten here with savoury sev and frequently with a dollop of dahi; the yoghurt here is very good, as is the tea.

On the quest for Patna's sweet confections, we went to Maner Sweets at the corner of the Maurya Lok complex. The owners told us it was in the town of Maner that the *motichoor* ladoo originated. This is the shop that brought the meltingly soft and sweet Maner ka ladoo to Patna. The sugar syrup-soaked besan globules are tiny pearls—hence moti—and the ladoos are a rich delight.

Sangeeta Sweets, occupying a line of sweet shops opposite Patna Museum, is a 40-year-old shop famous for its Silao-style khaja that now has a GI tag. Begun in the mid-70s by Basant Kumar, it is now run by his son Mukesh Kumar, who multi-tasks, keeping an eye on the sweet-making process via CCTV cameras and maintaining excellent customer relations. Sangeeta's top-selling item is the khaja, thin, flaky layers of pastry deep-fried and sugar-coated. These are absolutely delicious and, in our opinion, far superior to the khaja of Puri. Another sweet to try here is *lai*, originating in Gaya and made from an amaranth-like seed known locally as *ram dhana* or *kobhi dhana*. And if it's winter, there are sesame sweets in many shapes to choose from. We bought some for gifts and left with the happiest memories of Patna.

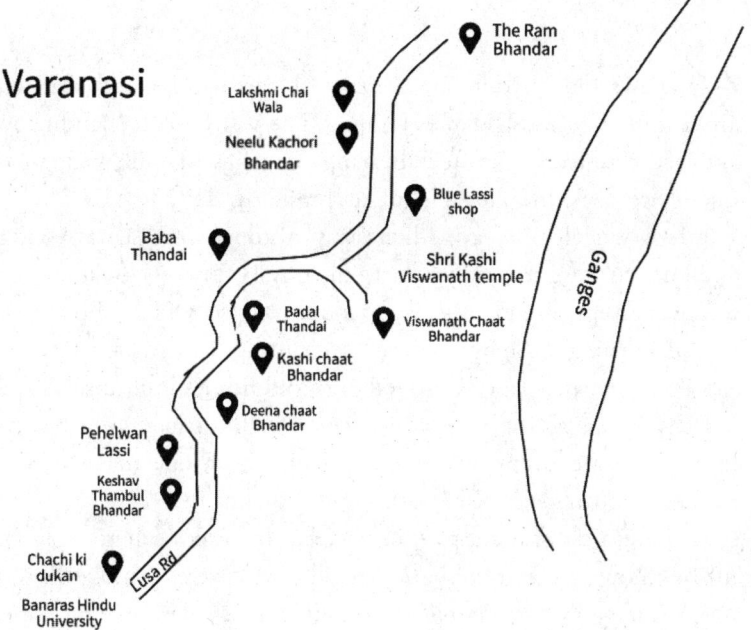

SPIRITUALITY AND STREET FOOD

Varanasi

Varanasi's old quarters are a maze of narrow alleys among which are scattered a thousand-plus temples. The Vishwanath Mandir towers above the rest and devotees bearing offerings of milk wait in long queues to seek the blessings of its presiding deity.

Two-wheelers weave their way through the lanes, dodging ambling cows and vendors carrying trays of sweets on their heads to their shops. Frequently, a garlanded corpse will be borne along to the burning ghat by pallbearers chanting 'Ram naam satya hai'.

These narrow lanes are lined with old homes built upwards, now faded versions of the vibrant edifices they must have been. At street level, there are shops selling *rudraksha* beads, fridge magnets, Ganga *jal*, and food and chai for locals and pilgrims.

There are chaat shops tucked away in places where only those in the know can find them, *chaiwala*s brewing tea in smoke-darkened shops, Varanasi's famous *mithai*s winking in shades of white, cream, yellow and green from glass counters, and kachoriwalas who open shop early in the day.

Outside the bewilderingly complex web of alleys is the Chowk area. Here, bike riders weave about as if high on bhaang, rickshaw pullers struggle for road space, and there's the relentless press of people. At every turn, there's more food: chaat, fruit, toast and tea, thandai and sweets. When the noise and the clamour become overwhelming, you can vend your way to the ghats and feel the calming embrace of the river.

Varanasi begins its day with a sumptuous serving of kachori-sabzi, often adding a jalebi or two to go with it. The kachori in this part of the country isn't the palm-sized crusty-flaky disc chockfull of aloo-pyaaz or dal. Here, they take the form of hing kachoris, tiny, crisp rounds filled with a little moong dal or aloo and a pronounced amount of asafoetida. The manner of their serving is what adds a tasty twist. The kachori is broken and placed in a *dona*, leaf cup, and topped with a chana masala, made of black chickpeas and a punchy spice mix. The other kachori here is a puri, stuffed with a paste of ground urad dal and spices known elsewhere as *bedmi* or *bedai*. When it's rolled out and deep-fried, the filling becomes a thin smear, giving the puri a little taste twist. These kachoris are served with aloo sabzi, making for an utterly enjoyable breakfast.

Kachoris are everywhere in the city, available in small eateries and from roadside carts. Varanasi even has a Kachori Galli. In its heyday in the 1970s and '80s, the stretch connecting Vishwanath Mandir Chowk and Manikarnika Ghat housed several vendors serving the old part of the city. Today, it's a pale shadow of its former self, with just two specialist kachori vendors.

Neelu Kachori Bhandar, a tiny shop in Kachori Galli, serves hing kachori and chana masala, topping off each katori with a mound of grated radish. Around 120 years old, the shop is currently run by Ravi Gupta, from the third generation of the family that started the business. From Gowri Shankar, who started this eatery over a century ago, it passed to Ravi's father, Neelu Kumar Gupta, who lent his name to the shop. The lone shop in what was once a street bristling with kachori sellers, is a sad reminder of old, traditional food businesses that are struggling to survive.

The other kachori vendor in the heart of old Varanasi operates just off Kachori Galli. It's a nameless shop set up by Ratan Gupta 45 years ago. Ratan makes the puri-like kachori and serves it with an aloo-sabzi, made without onion and garlic and yet packed with flavour and a distinct tang. Ratan Gupta also makes an exceptional jalebi and a *jaleba*, larger, softer, juicier, which even the toothless can relish, he says. For the last 20 years, it's the two Gupta shops that have been keeping the name of Kachori Galli relevant.

Several of the kachori vendors have moved to other parts of the city; like Sanjay Gaur, who sets up a temporary stall every morning on the main road connecting Godowlia junction and the Chowk. Sanjay's family used to run a shop in Kachori Galli and moved here in the late '90s for better prospects. He has a small table on the footpath. On it, the chana simmers over a coal fire. A big tin holds the tiny hing kachoris. Sanjay puts four of these in a small *kulhad*, breaks them and swirls chana on top. He makes the kachoris at home and brings a few tins every morning. He stays open 'Till Stocks Last', and that isn't long at this stall that's a favourite with locals, including cops employed for duty at the Vishwanath temple.

Another kachori shop, Shri Gowrishankar Kachori, with a 70-year history in Kachori Galli, moved to the main Chowk area about 15 years ago. Started by Gowri Shankar Prasad and currently run by Bharat Lal Prasad, this shop sells hing kachori and *khoye ki jilebi*. Similarly, Ashok and his son Shivam, who run a kachori shop in the narrow lanes leading to Meer Ghat, have moved here from Kachori Galli.

One place which serves both types of kachori is The Ram Bhandar, located in the inner gullies leading to the Kaal Bhairav temple from the Vishwanath temple. The owner insists on the 'The'; this shop is an offshoot of the original Ram Bhandar which was started in 1888. Ram Bhandar started off as and still remains a mithai shop. Started by Shri Raghu Nath Prasad, the shop gained popularity for its milk-based sweets. His son, Bihari Lal Gupta, continued the business, which is now helmed by the third and fourth generations of the family, Radhe Shyam Gupta and his son Arun Gupta. One of the family members, Rajendra Kumar Gupta, broke away from the main mithai business and started The Ram Bhandar, a few blocks away from the mithai shop, in 1992. The Ram Bhandar sells *gol* kachoris, the small hing kachoris served with brown chana, and the *badi* kachori, stuffed puris, with aloo sabzi.

Fresh jalebis also draw locals and tourists to the place. While this kachori shop does not boast a long history like many others, the Ram Bhandar brand name works in its favour.

Over the years, the lane in which Ram Bhandar is located became known for its mithai bhandars with several shops selling high-quality milk sweets. Notable among them is Shree Satyanarayan Mishthan Bhandaar, which now has four shops with the same name in the area, thanks to different members of a family branching out with their own outlets. One of the outlets of this mishthan bhandar begun by Mala Prasad Gupta, who was a halwai, 120 years ago is now run by Madan Kumar Gupta, of the fourth generation. The family split in 1938 made way for the four outlets, all specializing in a similar range of mithai. The *parwal ki mithai*—pointed gourds stuffed with *mawa* and fragrant spices and immersed in sugar syrup—and petha, different from the Agra one, are specialities, Madan Kumar said. 'You can buy sweets anywhere, but the products of Varanasi are unique. It's the jal-vaayu (water and air) of the place,' he told us.

A Varanasi breakfast isn't complete without a serving of jalebi. It's also a preferred pick-me-up through the day. In the vicinity of the Banaras Hindu University in the Lanka area is a small shop, known to locals as Chachi ki Dukaan. Located at the edge of land belonging to the Sankat Mochan Temple Trust, the shop begins to stir to life as early as 3.30 a.m., and the first kachori-sabzi and jalebi are ready by 5 a.m. It has no name or signboard, but everyone in the area knows the shop that has been at this spot since the 1960s with a history going back to the early 1900s.

Varanasi resident Vishwanath Sardar had a dairy business and sold milk, yoghurt and malai in the 1900s. His aunt, Bageshwari Devi, supported him by making milk sweets, which they sold as itinerant vendors. Vishwanath set up a modest shop in the space allotted by the Sankat Mochan Trust in the 1960s. It was the entry of his wife, Channi Devi, that would give the business its iconic status. Channi Devi started making jalebis and kachoris, and buoyed by the success of these, she added on *launglata* and samosas to the menu; they continue to be among the most-loved and best-selling items here. BHU students began to frequent the shop and started calling Channi Devi Chachi.

Chachi was a feisty woman. She would fling *pyaar ki gaalis*—affection garbed in abuse —at customers who were unable to pay. They would touch her feet and she would bless them. Over time, the belief built up in this part of Varanasi that a gaali from Chachi was a blessing. Customers lined up to eat her delightful jalebis and kachoris and to be blessed or taken to task for wasting food or making a nuisance of themselves. There are many stories of students eating kachori-jalebi at Chachi's shop and getting her blessings before heading to write their entrance exams. Not just students, politicians from Varanasi and film crews shooting here are all Chachi customers. The quality of food, coupled with the shopkeeper-cook's unique connection with her customers, made Chachi ki Dukaan an intrinsic part of life at BHU. Channi Devi—and few knew her real name—became everyone's Chachi.

By the late 1970s, Chachi's sons began to help with the business. Two decades later, the streets of Varanasi were busy and the traffic became crazy. There was a real concern that bike riders might veer into the big vats where sweets were made at this roadside shop. So, in the 1990s, the family set up a small *karkhana*, factory, a couple of minutes' walk from the shop. That's where all the sweets are now made. Tough entrepreneur that she was, Channi Devi worked till she passed away at the age of 89 in 2012. She used to come to the shop every day on her own in a rickshaw. The rickshaw-pullers considered it good luck if she was their first customer and lined up outside their home in Assi Ghat to ferry her to her shop.

The kachoris and jalebis are still made fresh in the shop, but everything else is toted from the factory, fresh trays of samosas and launglata arriving to replenish stocks. Everything made in a day is sold on the same day. You do not get fresher than this. All the sweets and savouries are still handmade. 'It cannot be any other way,' Chachi's son, Ramji Yadav said. A BHU employee, he managed the shop before and after work hours, assisted by his brothers. The next generation of the family, including Ramji's son Vinay Kumar, is also involved in the business now. While Chachi is missed—her photo is up on a wall in the shop—her dedicated sons and grandsons are working to preserve her legacy.

We chatted with the dignified Ramji Yadav on a mellow winter evening, as he sat in the courtyard outside his kitchens with some of his friends from the neighbourhood. It was a pleasant moment, but tinged with melancholy as he told us he was uncertain about the future of this iconic food shop. He didn't know if the younger generations would want to sit amidst karhais and vats of sugar syrup. Also, they didn't own either the shop or the place where the food was made. We can only hope that Chachi ki Dukan goes on forever.

Chaat, that all-encompassing word that stands for the spicy, sweet, tangy delights of the street, is the pride of Varanasi. Locals will stubbornly maintain that no city makes chaat like here. That can be argued, but there's no doubt the city has an amazing and delicious variety, claiming invention rights for *tamatar* chaat and tossing up *choora matar* with flattened rice and the tender, sweet peas of winter. Then, there's the *palak patte ki chaat*, aloo chaat, gol gappa and dahi *bhalla*.

'It's Deena Chaat Bhandar that gave Varanasi its reputation for great chaat,' says Atul Kumar Kesari, who runs the legendary shop on Luxa Road. It has come down from his grandfather who entered the food business, selling gol gappa from a khomcha near Chitra Cinema nearly 80 years ago. Later, he set up a small shop in Chowk, where it still exists and is run by Atul Kumar's uncle. The Luxa one came later and there have been attempts to modernize it; there's now fried rice and chowmein on the menu here. Still, it's the chaat you should go here for. The tamatar chaat is the star of the show and there's speculation that it contains, among other ingredients, the sugar syrup from gulab jamuns. Deena's chaat is so popular, the chaat makers and their paraphernalia have travelled as far as the US and Singapore to cater at weddings. The Ambanis fly them down for their functions as well.

Another venerable chaat shop in crowded Varanasi is Kashi Chaat Bhandar, also begun by the Kesaris. It was opened 70 years ago by Deenanath's brother, Kashinath. His son Rakesh Kumar Kesari is the current owner. 'It was our grandmother who began the business, selling chaat items from a basket,' he told us. Kashi is close to the main ghats and stopping by here for a serving of bhalla papdi or samosa chaat is the thing to do after taking in the grand spectacle of the Ganga *aarti* at Dashaswamedh Ghat. There's almost always a rush for a place to sit in this tiny store. That's the fame that Kashi Chaat Bhandar's tamatar chaat, made with a secret blend of garam masala, enjoys.

Less known, but making spectacularly good chaat, is the Vishwanath Chaat Bhandar tucked into Vishwanath Gali on the lane leading to Dashaswamedh Ghat. While it sells papdi chaat and dahi bhalla, among other things, the gol gappa is the hot seller here. Pilgrims and locals line up, holding out their *dona*s for the crisp puris filled with aloo and dipped into the spicy pani. Customers can ask for different spice levels and a mixture of sweet-and-hot if they so prefer. The gol gappa man can serve over half a dozen customers at a time, moving to a rhythm that looks as if it's choreographed.

Lassi, the sweet, cold, frothy yoghurt drink, is as popular in Uttar Pradesh as it is in Punjab. In Varanasi, there are scores of lassi shops in the busy bazaar areas of Godowlia, Chowk, Luxa and Lanka. Ask anyone for the best lassi and they'll point you to Blue Lassi in Kachori Galli, not far from Manikarnika Ghat. Begun by Ram Das Yadav 80 years ago, it was then a nameless shop serving plain lassi. It was a young South Korean customer visiting sometime in the early '90s who christened it Blue Lassi Shop because of the colour of the walls here. The name stuck and it's now a Varanasi landmark.

This is even more applause-worthy since Ramdas's son, Pannalal, who took over the shop from his father juggled its running with his career in films. Trivia fans may like to know that he worked in Satyajit Ray's *Joi Baba Felunath*. Pannalal's son and grandson Vijay Kumar and Chanchal Yadav now run the lassi bar that enjoys huge popularity, especially with foreign tourists. Passport photos of hundreds of them are stuck on one wall. The present owners went all out innovating and there are now 120 different lassis to choose from: chocolate, berries, seasonal fruit and various other flavours. They buy milk from the bazaar and set the yoghurt themselves. Customers must wait up to 10 to 15 minutes for their lassi, for each one is made fresh before being topped off with a squirt of saffron syrup and rose water. 'Premixing would kill the freshness and the flavour,' Vijay Kumar Yadav says, going back to the stainless-steel jug in which he churns the lassi.

The other big name in lassi here is Pehelwan. Arrive at Ravidass Gate in Lanka and you could be confused. For there are three shops in a row, all calling themselves Pehelwan Lassi. While Manoj and Vijay Yadav who run one of these claimed to be the original, this is clearly the result of a split in a joint family that once did business together. In a rare case of women's entrepreneurship, this dairy venture was begun by Vijay Yadav's grandmother Sahodra Devi in the 1940s, supported by her husband Heeru Sardar. Vijay's father, a well-built man who wrestled for fun, gave the business its present name. While each of the Pehelwans now boasts of making the best lassi, there isn't much differentiating their offerings. The lassi, served in kulhads, is thick and sweet, topped off with rabri, a drizzle of saffron syrup and pistachio slivers. Part drink, part dessert, it's rich and refreshing. In winter, this row of shops, like many lassiwalas here, put out *malaiyo*, the whipped milk sweet that is as delicious as it is fleeting.

You may be surprised to hear us mention bread in the city of the hing kachori. But yes, Varanasi also has a taste for toast and chai. It's evident at Laxmi Chaiwala, a 60-year-old institution in the city. It's tucked into a lane off the Chowk area, an unusual arrangement with the shop occupying both sides of the lane. Started by Laxmi Prasad Chaurasia in the same spot, it is now run by his son, the coolers-sporting Sitala Prasad Yadav, who oversees the making and serving of toast and tea and chats with the regulars.

After the banter, they occupy the rickety benches in the two-part tea shop and eat crisp toast and perfectly made tea served in kulhads. It's an all-male gathering at this place, which opens at 5 a.m. and shuts only past midnight. The bread from a local bakery is toasted over coal, six slices at a time, in an iron contraption that looks like a fish grill. The coal lends it an appealing smokiness. You can have your toast with lashings of Amul butter or homemade white butter. You can have it sprinkled with sugar, pepper or chaat masala. The bread can also be buttered first and toasted, an item known as the Caesarian here. Ganesh, who has been working here for 40 years,

BAZAAR BITES

said the coal cooking makes all the difference, both to the toast and the tea. The quality of both these offerings here is so special that Laxmi Chaiwala is a local icon, not just another tea shop. That is why hundreds come here every day.

Varanasi is counted among the best places to celebrate Holi, the festival of colours and abandon. *Thandai* is the traditional drink of the festivities and the city has a reputation for this concoction of milk, nuts and spices, and, on request, bhaang. Jayanth decided to be adventurous and asked for bhaang in his thandai. Going by his mood soon after, we'd say it's the thandai that makes Holi revelry in Varanasi so special.

Negotiate your way through two-wheelers that threaten to run over your foot and arrive at Badal Thandai, which sits on a corner of Sonapura Road in Godowlia. It's a tiny cubicle of a shop and has been here for 70 years. Narendra Kumar Kesari has now taken over from his father, Babu Prasad, who started the business. Badal Thandai's reputation rests on the quality of the ingredients—milk, almonds, pistachio, aniseed, pepper, saffron—and the technique of grinding these together, according to Narendra Kumar.

Those who wish to explore and experience the high of bhaang—sale and consumption of the cannabis leaves are legal in Varanasi—can ask for it to be mixed into their thandai. A lurid green spoonful will be stirred in and you can go tripping (at your own risk).

The 50-year-old Baba Thandai, enroute to Dal Mandi, is another preferred spot for thandai. It's called Baba because that's a name for Shiva, who presides over this holy city, explains Ganesh Sarin, present owner. A large portrait of Shiva, who is said to have consumed bhaang to quell the toxic effects of the poison he consumed after the *samudra manthan*—the churning of the oceans to obtain nectar—adorns one wall. And, yes, you can have a bhaang thandai here too.

Paan is ubiquitous in the city. The anointing, folding and serving of the betel leaf is so elevated an art in Varanasi, it made its way into a hit number in the Bollywood film *Don*. Vast quantities are chewed, by rickshaw pullers and the elite alike; it's a mouth freshener

SPIRITUALITY AND STREET FOOD

and digestive, offered to guests as a symbol of hospitality and part of various rituals.

There are paan shops at every turn and Keshav Tambul, which sits under the spreading branches of a bo tree in Lanka, is among the most favoured. It's run by Rajendra Prasad and Narendra Kumar Chaurasia, the third and fourth generations of the family that entered this business. The paan leaf is to be treated as gently as you would a woman, says Narendra Kumar, with no apparent intention of being lyrical. 'We store it in a cool, closed room before folding and serving,' he says. Perhaps because of this process, the Benarasi paan is a paler shade than what you get elsewhere. Carefully selected ingredients go into the many varieties of paan here. The supari is from Assam and some of the spice mixes that flavour the paan are ground in-house. The *gulkand* paan with its hints of rose petal is hugely popular and the *navratan* paan with its heady aroma and flavour is also special. This old shop also doubles as an 'adda' for locals. They gather to talk about politics and the events of the day, while ordering or chewing their favourite paan, a uniquely Varanasi tradition. We stood here awhile, letting the feeling of being in this most ancient of cities soak in.

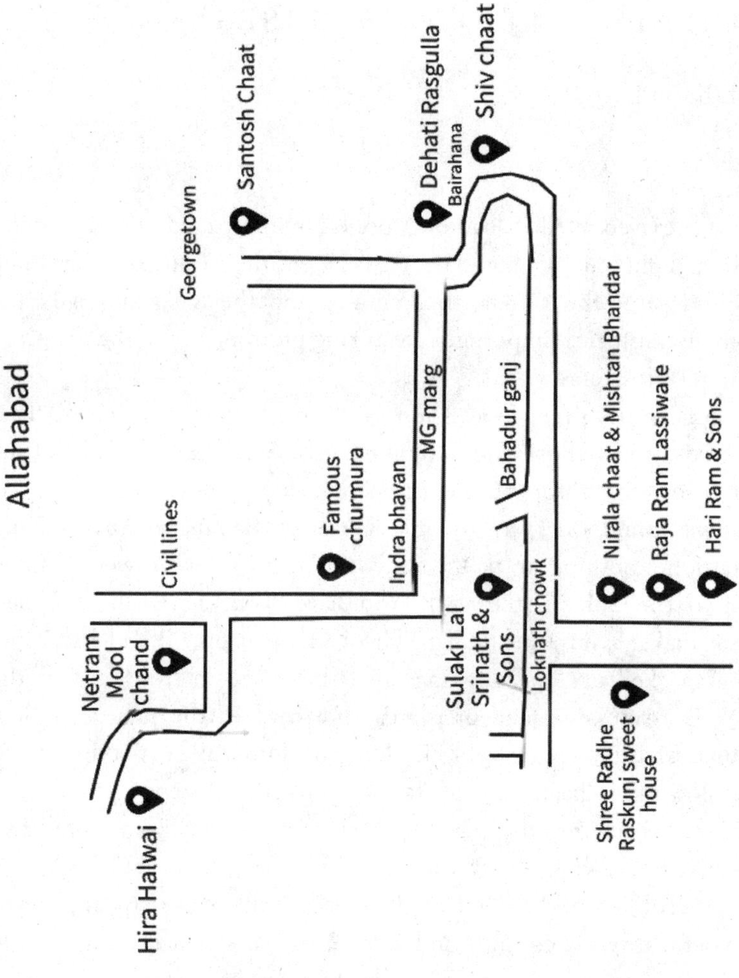

Allahabad

- Hira Halwai
- Netram Moolchand
- Civil lines
- Famous churmura
- Indra bhavan
- Santosh Chaat
- Georgetown
- MG marg
- Dehati Rasgulla
- Bairahana
- Shiv chaat
- Bahadur ganj
- Sulaki Lal Srinath & Sons
- Loknath chowk
- Nirala chaat & Mishtan Bhandar
- Raja Ram Lassiwale
- Hari Ram & Sons
- Shree Radhe Raskunj sweet house

STREETS FULL OF SURPRISES

STREETS FULL OF SURPRISES

Allahabad

We arrived in Allahabad on a bone-chillingly cold winter evening with a light rain falling. The city lies at the confluence of three major rivers—the Ganga, the Yamuna, and the Saraswati—and has immense historical importance, featuring prominently in the country's history across eras.

Allahabad's street food is just as diverse as its history. From chaat and lassi to kachori and much more, we had a wonderful time exploring this historical and fascinating city.

We found our way to Shiv Chaat at Bairahana. The weather had done nothing to keep away the regulars who were milling around the hole in the wall. 'You have come to Allahabad's best chaat maker,' said a gentleman who had eaten his fill and had more chaat packed up. The cooking and service are in front, and at the back is a smoke-stained prep area and store. In the prep area, Shiv Kumar Yadav, wearing a black checked cloth bandana style, 'builds' the aloo tikki chaat. One of the assistants fries dozens of tikkis in a vast tawa, smashing them in the final stages to get them extra crisp. Shiv Kumar Yadav then breaks up tikkis into a leaf katori. On top goes a ladle of cooked and mildly spiced white matar (peas), a swirl of yoghurt, sweet chutney and a spicy one, and a scattering of aloo *laccha* (potato straws) that lift up the aloo tikki chaat.

Yadav, who started the shop in 1978 and now runs it with the help of his son, works mostly in silence with the calm of someone who understands the rhythm of the kitchen, no matter how humble.

But he looks up to say, 'You ate it wrong. It's not to be all mixed up. You have to taste the layers together without disturbing them.' A lesson learned. Shiv Chaat is also famous—and we do not use the word lightly here—for its dahi bhalla, all sorts of gorgeous textures of spongy bhallas, cool, creamy yoghurt and sweet-sour-spicy flavours, and its sharp, piquant pani puri. The chaat traditions of Allahabad turned out to be an unexpectedly delightful surprise.

In Georgetown, there's an equally popular chaat vendor, Santosh. He begins preparations at 6 a.m. in order to open his shop at 2 p.m. He operates from a makeshift shack, with *phulki*s being served from a small counter in front, while he mans the tawa on which is cooked the tamatar chaat that is his speciality. It's the spice mix that makes this dish a standout and Santosh says all the spices and condiments are homemade. Another signature at this modest shop is the karela papdi chaat. The 'karela' is a layered papdi, peppered with ajwain, which is shaped to look as if it's woven. This is broken, topped with matar and chutneys to make the chaat. Santosh's father began this business 20 years ago, naming it after his son, who now runs it with all the commitment to quality we noticed to be common among street-food makers.

By day, we got a clearer look at the city distinguished by being one of the four holy sites of the Maha Kumbh Mela celebrated once every 12 years. This is when pilgrims throng the place and dip in the sacred waters of the Triveni Sangam, alongside tourists and photographers on a quest to capture exotic India.

Allahabad, rechristened to its earlier name Prayagraj, got an impressive makeover for the 2019 Maha Kumbh; arterial roads were widened and attractive street art came up on traffic islands. Clusters of buildings were painted red and black in the northern part of the city that's divided by the railway line.

South of it is 'City' or the Chowk area. While Civil Lines, developed by the British, is all wide streets and gracious buildings, Chowk, particularly Loknath, the vibrant ancient heart of Allahabad, is an infuriatingly chaotic maze of narrow lanes and bazaars.

Wandering through this part of the city was one of our best Allahabad experiences. Shops here sell rhizomes of turmeric, their pungent aroma wafting into the street, bags full of papad and *vadi*, stacks of bags made from old newspaper and leaf katoris, the last meant for the food shops in the area. There are scores—lassiwalas, *makhan* malai vendors in winter, namkeen makers—who have been in business for a century, and chaat specialists who pride themselves on having served prime ministers, writers and artistes.

In Loknath, with its abundance of street food, Nirala Chaat & Mishthan Bhandar enjoys a fine reputation on account of its age and quality. The paan-chewing Jagannath Kesarwani is the fifth-generation owner of the business, keeping an eye on the boys tossing up chaat. On the mithai counter are stocked specialities such as the winter offering of *sonth* ke ladoo, made with dried ginger, and *tarbooz*, a finely crafted sweet, which when cut open resembles a slice of watermelon. 'It was chaat we began with and sweets were introduced sometime in the '70s,' Jagannath Kesarwani told us. He's not particularly concerned about the scores of new chaat and sweet shops that call themselves Nirala. Perhaps a 100-year-old legacy entitles you to such equanimity.

Lift your eyes from the narrow lanes of Loknath and you'll see buildings with delicate trellises and ornate trim, harking back to more glorious times. The area may have a timeworn, even shabby façade now, but those who come here to shop and to eat don't seem to mind a bit.

Follow your nose and arrive at Hari Ram & Sons, a shop that would slip with ease into a period film. There's a set of brass scales on the counter and it must have some antique value. 'It's decades old,' says Shri Ram Purwaha, third-generation member of the business. His grandfather came from Agra and sold samosas on the street. In 1890, Shri Ram's father Hari Ram set up shop in the present address, to sell 'unique delicious salted food products' as one signboard says. An ageing Shri Ram now runs the store with the help of his nephew, Arvind. But he has lost none of his passion for the business.

The savoury snacks are all hand-made and fried at the back of the store. 'The masala, and they are a secret, is what makes our namkeen special,' Shri Ram tells us. The spices are measured and mixed by him or Arvind and handed over to the staff to make *mathri*s, *namak para* and the famed masala samosa. Hari Ram has mastered the seemingly impossible technique of using spiced potatoes to make a dry filling for the mini masala samosas. They keep for weeks and are taken away by Allahabadis who live away from the city. Hari Ram is a legend because it values substance over style. The savoury snacks, including the samosas, have an appealing handmade quality to them—some are imperfect in shape, but all taste superb. They are packed in simple paper boxes and tied up with string to be taken away.

What's a trip to the crowded bazaar without a stop for some lassi! Loknath has many lassiwalas plying their wares—a simple collection of dahi, lassi, rabri, and in winter, malai makhan, also known as *nimish* and *malaiyo*.

Raja Ram Lassiwale is among them. It's 125 years old. That's not surprising, says Sushil Kumar, who runs the place. 'Here in the gallis of Loknath you'll find lots of food shops that have been around for a century.' It was his grandfather, Laxmi Narayan, who began the business. His father, Raja Ram, then built it further and it became a Loknath landmark. 'Indira Gandhi used to come for a lassi after offering prayers at the nearby Bhola Mandir,' Sushil Kumar recalls. His lassi is the classic, just yoghurt, sugar, a dollop of rabri and a squirt of saffron syrup on top. The milk for the yoghurt, which he sets himself, comes from cows and buffaloes in the nearby villages. Sushil Kumar makes every kulhad of lassi fresh, whipping the yoghurt with a wooden churner.

During winter, the malai makhan vendors also put out their wares in this area. Made by boiling sweetened milk and whipping it to a froth at dawn while the dew still lies on the ground, this is a seasonal delight which makes the cold months even better.

If the cold winter of Allahabad is sweetened by the availability of malai makhan, fruit cream makes the perfect cooler for the searing summer. Shri Radhe Raskunj Sweet House in Loknath was one of the first in the area to introduce this refreshing medley of seasonal fruit and cream. Founded by Siddhi Ram Purwar, Shri Radhe is today popular for its fruit cream, besides an array of milk-based sweets. Some are traditional, such as the *sohan* halwa, which is excellent here, while others are innovations. The makhan *anda*, introduced 50 years ago, is a result of simple ingredients and sophisticated sweet-making techniques. White butter and milk solids are coloured and shaped to look like a boiled egg, with a golden yolk. Here, too, we experienced the warm hospitality of small food vendors who want you to taste and enjoy their wares.

Kachori-sabzi must be, without a doubt, the most eaten breakfast in the cities and towns of UP. The kachori here is a puri but stuffed with a thin smear of dal and spices. Hot off the karahi—the best shops use desi ghee for frying—accompanied by an aloo sabzi, almost always cooked without onions and garlic, *boondi* raita and a sweet chutney, it's loved by locals and visitors alike. One of Allahabad's oldest establishments to indulge in this breakfast—here available all day—is Sulaki Lal Srinath & Sons in Bahadurganj, a little away from the press of people and the chaos of Loknath. The business is 120 years old, begun by Buddhulalji who came from Banda. Handed down over the generations, it has grown from the humble venture it was, selling ladoo and jalebi. Present owner Alok Gupta is conscious of the legacy he has inherited. 'All my education has been here,' he tells us.

Besides the kachori-sabzi and masala samosa, another Allahabad speciality, Sulaki also has a rich array of sweets, being patronized particularly for the *balushahi*, the sonth ladoo known as *sethaura* ladoo in these parts, and the sohan halwa.

Netram Moolchand in Civil Lines also competes for the title of the city's top kachori-sabzi maker. The shop is best known, though, for the ingenuity of combining sweet, warm jalebis with slightly tart, cool yoghurt. In Allahabad, it is an oft-eaten combination, particularly at breakfast time. In the world of food, claims to invention of dishes

are made and contested, but in no way hamper their enjoyment. The shop in Katra stakes a claim for being the first to introduce this delicious combination in these parts.

Begun in 1855, Netram is now run by the four Agarwal brothers. They pay tribute to their enterprising forefathers with sepia-hued photographs adorned with garlands on the wall of their tiny eatery. Netram was originally a seller of sweets and is even now known for its motichoor ladoo and sohan halwa that's made in winter. It was only 70 years ago that they began to serve kachori-sabzi, said Mukesh Agarwal. Opening by 7 a.m., Netram sells a huge volume of this breakfast order alongside its speciality of dahi-jalebi.

It's a deceptively simple thing—a fairly common sweet and some unsweetened yoghurt served in disposable katoris. The making of it here makes all the difference; a batter of the perfect consistency is fried in ghee in swirls and soaked in saffron-hued syrup. It's hot and

STREETS FULL OF SURPRISES

crisp, oozing syrup with every bite. Combining beautifully with the cold, creamy yoghurt, it makes for the sort of indulgence 'foodies' describe as #foodporn. Netram's offerings, both sweet and savoury, have earned it a legion of fans, some famous, like Indira Gandhi who enjoyed dishes from here when she visited Swaraj Bhavan, and Lal Bahadur Shastri. No wonder it's such a landmark in Civil Lines. 'Yes, the *chauraha*, intersection, is named after Netram,' says Mukesh Agarwal with justified pride.

The samosa is ubiquitous across India and is present everywhere in Allahabad as well. As with many street foods, it's the quality of the ingredients and the skill in the making that set one humble samosa apart from another. The samosa chhole is a popular combination in Allahabad and Sainik Sweets in upmarket Rajapur has quite a reputation for its version.

There is also a samosa that stands apart because it's so good it needs no accompaniment, not even chutney. The samosa at Hira Halwai stands apart because of its taste, rendering the need for any accompaniment unnecessary. It's an unpretentious stall nestling under a canopy of trees on Maharshi Dayanand Marg in Civil Lines. It is a legacy from Hiralal, who sold puris and jalebis from a cart in the area since 1938.

In 1954, he managed to put up a small wooden shack and business was growing, with samosa and sweets on the short menu. The nascent business was threatened when, in 1967, the civic authorities evicted Hiralal from the premises. He may have been a humble vendor of sweets and namkeen, but he wasn't giving up without a fight. Hiralal went to court and the judgement was in his favour. The court stayed his eviction and ordered the authorities to give him an alternative space. That is how this little legendary shop moved to its present address. Now, Hiralal's sons, Ashok and Ramesh Kesarwani, run the place. The long-haired Ashok sits cross-legged at the counter, while his brother oversees the kitchen, ensuring items arrive hot and fresh as each batch is sold out. The samosa, crisp with a spicy potato filling, is a hot seller here and so are the *gujiya*s, pastry crescents filled with

BAZAAR BITES

khoya and dried fruit. There are regulars—lawyers, students, office-goers from the area—who come here just for the gulab jamun or the dahi-jalebi. Hira Halwai also stocks dal moth, fried chana and masala samosa, which have a dry filling of moong dal and hing. It's also somewhere you can get a *dona* of paneer sprinkled with chaat masala. 'It's all made in-house,' says Ashok, who's here from 7 a.m. to 10 p.m. every day. It's a long day and there's a steady stream of customers. The sons of Hiralal aren't complaining.

The street-food repertoire of a place isn't complete without a 'time pass' snack. Allahabad's is *churmura*, the crunchy, spicy mix of puffed rice, spice and crunchy bits. It's available at various street corners and you must applaud a vendor who's become famous selling this simple snack.

Famous Churmura near Indira Bhavan in Civil Lines is a tiny stand. It was begun in this very spot 50 years ago by Beni Madhav. His son Ajay Yadav now sits there, tossing up various combinations of puffed rice, peanuts, sev, chopped onions and coriander and masala powders. In winter Ajay adds sweet, fresh peas to his mise en place. He custom-makes the churmura for his customers, many of who are regulars, his fingers skimming over the ingredient containers with practised ease. The fact that the inconspicuous-looking Famous Churmura is a known landmark in a city is proof not just of the vendor's skill, but also of the locals' capacity to embrace and celebrate food, no matter how simple.

Our final stop in Allahabad was for its famed sweet. It's called a rasgulla here, but is, in reality, a gulab jamun. Allahabad locals display a particular fondness for these gold-brown balls, bobbing in sugar syrup, and every area has its shops selling gulab jamuns alongside other sweets and savoury snacks.

Dehati in Bairahana is different. Here is a single-product specialist who makes only gulab jamun. The business, started by Ramsevak Yadav, is 20 years old and now his sons Ajay and Mahadev Yadav are in charge. The quality of the khoya and the restrained use of maida are keys to their product quality, according to Ajay. The Dehati

STREETS FULL OF SURPRISES

rasgulla is large and soft, the texture a touch grainy and with a smoky whiff, thanks to the coal fire on which it's cooked. The shop opens at 3 p.m. every day and the crowds gather to eat their fill of the gulab jamuns served in small white ceramic saucers. For those who wish to take away, the syrup-soaked sweets are packed in earthen pots. Dehati demonstrates what much bigger brands fail to do: focus on a single product and deliver it better than anyone else.

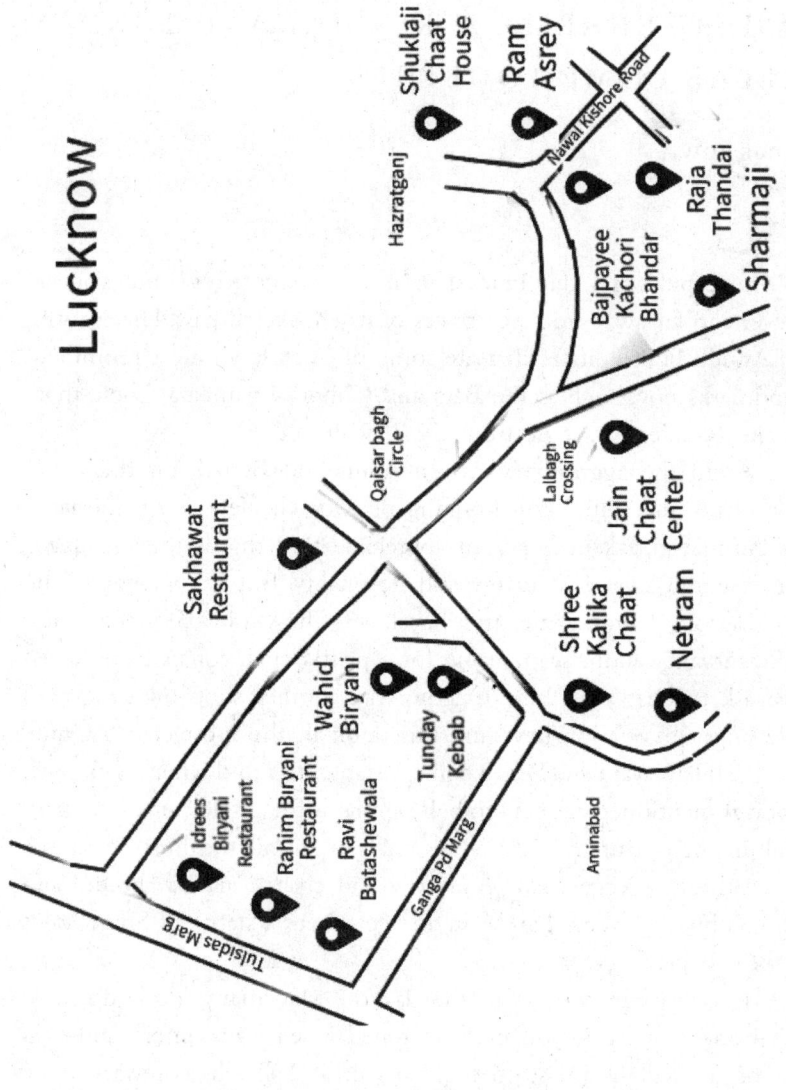

WHERE SHARMA JI KI CHAI AND TUNDAY KEBAB COME TOGETHER

Lucknow

The capital of Uttar Pradesh is now a modern city, but you are never too far away from the traces of its checkered past. The Nawabs of Awadh built edifices that are some of Lucknow's most prominent landmarks now, such as the Bara and Chhota Imambara. Then, there is the Residency, a relic from the British Raj.

Amid the aggressively driven Audis and Benzes on the roads, the chaos and infuriating honking of two-wheelers down the lanes of Aminabad, it's not easy to appreciate that this is the birthplace of *adab* and *tehzeeb*, courtesy and hospitality. But it's evident in the singing of a Mirasi artiste in a haveli off Chowk, in the graciousness of a biryani vendor scampering for a plastic chair for us to sit when we ask to chat with him. Or, the way another shop owner evokes blessings for our journeys and this book in the most chaste Urdu.

While biryani and kebab come instantly to mind when Lucknow's food is mentioned, it's easy to believe that is the predominant culinary culture here. But the city is an amalgam of all the histories it has lived through. Vegetarian *bhojanalay*s and chaat *bhandar*s abound and there's bhaang-laced thandai in a shop where a statue of Shiva holds centre stage.

On this trip, we began the day the way many locals do, with chai and samosa. If you ever imagined a seller of samosa and chai to be a small business, go to Sharmaji at Lalbagh. Forewarned by locals, we went as early as 7.30 a.m. Already there was a crowd milling at the counters that separate customers who stand on the street and the brisk pick-up service inside. Owner Manav Sharma sits on an elevated spot, smiling at regulars and managing orders and cash. He has much to smile about. The business begun by his grandfather Omprakash Sharma, in 1949, has won Lucknow's heart and loyalty. Locals who've been away for a while are known to stop here for a chai and samosa on the way back home from the airport or railway station.

The shop that occupies a corner building in Lalbagh overlooks a small park. Morning walkers pick up their chai and samosa and move to occupy park benches and enjoy a daily ritual. Tourists who've heard this is a must-do in Lucknow join them. The samosa here is uniquely shaped, more ball than triangular. The masala is dark and spicy. The tea is made from a special blend they have custom-made, Sharma says. The milk for it comes in 20-litre cans from a goshala in Sultanpur. Besides the legendary chai—you can also ask for it in an earthen kulhad which costs more—and samosa, Sharmaji also serves bun maska. Some customers squish a samosa between the bun.

The staff at this always busy shop work like a well-oiled machine. The milk for the tea is constantly stirred by one man as it boils on a stove on the curb. Two others mash mounds of potatoes for the samosas. These are then moved into the shop, where cooks and tea makers 'finish' the products. The serving staff remember every order and move with astounding speed. 'We took care of our staff during the lockdowns of 2020 and '21,' Manav tells us. 'It's difficult to find skilled *karigar*s and we have to keep them.' Sharmaji is a lesson that a single store and a minuscule menu can be a remarkable success. You just have to make the sort of food that evokes love and loyalty in customers.

Later, we went looking for Lucknowi kachori, a puri by another name. There is also a variant known here as *khasta*, closer to what we recognize as a kachori. There's no real need to grapple with the names though; both are equally satisfying and among the most common breakfast choices for locals.

Some may say the hype has overtaken the quality, but Bajpayee Kachori Bhandar on Naval Kishore Road is the frontrunner when it comes to kachori in Lucknow. It was started in 1975 by Balkishan Bajpayee. He owned a flour mill and thought up a food business that would use the atta he milled. So, the Bajpayee kachori is made from atta, not maida as is more common. It is served with a spicy *chhole* that includes potatoes. Initially, this kachori vendor was a modest shop in Hazratganj, doing brisk business until 2019, when it felt the full impact of celebrity endorsement. Kartik Aaryan, who was shooting in Lucknow, dropped in to eat a kachori, which made it to social media and the small kachori bhandar became a tourist attraction and a must-do. This explains the long queues any time of day outside this shop. Go early in the morning so you don't have to wait too long for your fill of kachori and sabzi.

Another excellent spot for a breakfast or evening snack of kachori is Netram in Aminabad. This is a neat, old-fashioned sweet and savouries shop and there's some seating indoors. Outside, skilled workers turn out piles of kachoris served with a delectable sabzi. Netram is a respected name originally from Allahabad. 'When the state capital moved from Prayag to Lucknow, many government staff who had been eating at Netram in Allahabad wanted the same food and taste here,' said Anup Agarwal, whose grandfather began the business in 1854. He inherited the shop from his father, Ajay Agarwal, and now Anup's two sons are also hands-on here. 'It takes the constant and focused attention of the owners to maintain quality,' according to Anup Agarwal. 'We use the best ingredients, such as desi ghee,' he said, pointing to the pile of tins. 'And yet, the malai or the khoya can sometimes fall short of perfect if a close eye is not kept on every step.' Which is why Netram in Lucknow has no intention of ever branching out or giving out franchises. 'You don't need a dozen outlets, you need one which draws people because of the goodness of its food,' he said.

At the risk of sparking a minor controversy, we might venture to say Uttar Pradesh holds a position of predominance when it comes to the vast world of chaat. We had some of the best chaat in Varanasi and Allahabad. Lucknow will not be left behind. The aloo tikki chaat is possibly the most popular chaat in the city. Matar, a spiced mass of cooked white peas, sitting alongside the aloo tikkis as they fry on wide tavas, is also ubiquitous.

One of the most patronized chaat vendors is Shuklaji Chaat House on Shahnajaf Road in Hazratganj. A paan-chewing Dinesh Shankar Shukla sits atop the counter, serving *batashe*, Lucknow's pani puri. The batashe filling here, as it is everywhere in Lucknow, is made of boiled and mashed white peas, ever so mildly spiced. The pani, in contrast, is spicy with a sharp, clean flavour. He works with the assured rhythm of someone who has been doing this for a very long time. The chaat business was started by his father, Mangala Prasad Shukla. 'The lockdown hit us hard,' Shukla said, 'but who was spared?' It is a tribute to the resilience of these small businesses that they managed to bounce back after the lockdowns of 2020 and 2021.

Another place for excellent batashe is Jain Chaat Corner near Lalbagh. The tidy shop, where you pay inside and eat standing on the street, is 25 years old. Started by Santosh Kumar Jain and now managed by his son, Sandeep Kumar Jain, its batashe is a big seller. The aloo tikki is also popular. Crisp aloo tikkis are pressed down, placed in a leaf cup, topped with yoghurt, sweet chutney and a sprinkling of masala. It's a palate-pleasing combination of textures and tangy flavours.

Weave your way through Aminabad's maddening press of people and cycle rickshaws, past shops selling cheap chikan kurtas and arrive at Shree Kalika Chaat. A feisty Babita Gupta runs the place she inherited from her grandfather and father. The little shop was begun in 1880 by Kalika Prasad. 'My grandfather was my teacher,' Babita tells us, in-between taking orders and collecting cash from customers. 'The *sont* papdi is a speciality of ours and you are unlikely to find it anywhere else.' It's a seasoned papdi, topped with cubed potato and a sharp spice powder on top. 'Eat it in one mouthful,' Babita instructs. The matar is also a Kalika speciality. Fans of this dish buy it and take it far. It keeps and travels well.

Ravi in Chowk, who sells his wares from a cart, is a batashewala, of renown. Pani in a dozen flavours—pudina, hing and more—is his crowd-puller.

Perhaps on account of the epic status Tunday kebabs have achieved, *galawati* kebabs are ubiquitous in Lucknow, from sit-down restaurants to street carts, which will smear one on a roomali roti and turn it into a roll. The galawati is made from a mixture of raw meat, spiced with an astounding number of ingredients. It is so soft and gooey, it is slapped rather than shaped onto the tawa. The kebabs are cooked over coal fires as they have been for a century and more.

The history of Tunday kebab makes for captivating foodlore. Murad Ali, who lost his arm in a kite-flying accident—hence the name Tunday—is credited with creating this deliciously soft and nutritious kebab in consultation with a hakim, in order to please an ageing nawab who had lost his teeth. Tunday had no sons and his nephew Rais Ahmed inherited the business, passing it to his son Mohammed Usman.

The Tunday Kebab outlet in Aminabad is now a full-fledged restaurant even if the famous kebab and the equally reputed biryani are made street-side. The origins of the Tunday kebab, however, lie in Chowk, which most Lucknow residents say is the true and old heart of the city. Weave your way past ittar shops and makers of traditional breads, and find yourself at this venerable landmark dating back to the early 1900s. At Chowk, four pieces of bade ka kebab (beef kebab) cost a mere ₹20 and with a roomali roti, ₹7, it makes a fulfilling meal even for those who can't afford more.

'God has given me so much, I don't wish to burden my customers,' Mohammed Usman told us when we interviewed him for *Secret Sauce*. He believes fulfilling a purpose is more important than making money. At the newer Aminabad outlet, mutton galawati is available and costs ₹60 for four pieces. Tunday has also taken to selling the uncooked kebab mixture, which they call 'batter' by the kilo for those who want to shape and fry their kebabs at home. The bade ka kebab paste costs ₹450 a kilo. Awadh culinary experts say the galawati's surging popularity—social media and food blogs have had a role to play—has seen other kebabs from the cuisine, such as the *shami*, lose currency. There are, however, a few restaurants like Sakhawat in Kaiserbagh that continue to make shami and *pasanda* kebab.

Lucknow's Chowk is a little less crowded and chaotic in the early part of the day. This is when you should go to taste one of this city's most celebrated foods, nihari. In the Awadhi tradition there are specific breads to be eaten with dishes. *Kulcha*, which is nothing like the bread that goes by the same name in Amritsar and Delhi, is considered the perfect and only accompaniment to nihari, the slow-cooked stew with mutton on the bone flavoured richly, but subtly. It doesn't have the in-your-face punch of, say, the Delhi-style nihari. Whether you are able to appreciate the nuances of the nihari or not, you'll definitely be impressed by the kulcha, known in these parts as the *ghilafi* kulcha, which accompanies it.

At once crisp, flaky and soft, the best version of the kulcha is available at Raheem's at Akbari Gate in Chowk. There is some confusion here as to whether Raheem's or Rahim's is the original and we chose to go to the former. Zubair Ahmed, wearing a pastel-pink chikan-embroidered kurta, sat at the counter at this tiny basement eatery with just a few seats. If you are a family or a large group, staff will direct you to a larger dining space in the narrow lane adjacent to the shop where all the food is cooked. Bread makers squat on a raised platform, kneading, shaping and cooking kulcha and *sheermal* glazed with saffron colour. Zubair Ahmed told us the shop was over 100 years old and was begun by his grandfather who cooked for erstwhile royalty. The family has been in Lucknow for centuries. 'I'm told my grandmothers threw stones at British soldiers as their part in the Freedom movement,' Zubair Ahmed reminisces.

He believes there is value in staying in the same place and doing the same thing to achieve perfection. 'You cannot standardize these recipes or methods. The sourness of the yoghurt varies one day and the moisture level in the kebab mixture varies, depending on the meat

IDREES BIRIYANI

and even the weather. You have to be sensitive to these and make the small adjustments.' That level of commitment to quality and the skill to achieve it is what makes food vendors like Raheem's go on.

We tasted biryanis everywhere. Lucknow can justifiably lay claim to making the very best. Culinary excellence achieved over centuries in royal kitchens has flowed onto the street too. So, you can eat beautiful biryanis—subtle, aromatic and delicately flavoured—at very affordable prices in eateries that provide only the most basic amenities.

Enter Chowk and find an outstanding biryani at a most innocuous-looking eatery, one that looks like a lean-to. Abu Bakar was outside, discussing a catering order with a customer. It is his father, Mohammed Idrees, who started the business in the late 1960s. 'Walid Sahab [his late father] mastered the art of making Awadhi biryani. There is *hunar* and *ilm*, skill and knowledge, to the making of great biryani. He shared these with the cooks he employed as the business grew. He wanted each of them, armed with the knowledge, to go out and begin enterprises of their own.'

We do not know how many people went on to set up their own biryani businesses, but the culinary tradition he nurtured certainly seems to continue at Idrees Biryani Restaurant. The biryanis are cooked over coal fires in *deg*s, each holding about four kilos of biryani. Mutton on the bone is simmered with spices—sieved for refinement—and milk to make the *yakhni* in which the rice is 'finished'. The copper *degchi*s are covered with a cloth as the meat and rice dum cook to become the Idrees biryani.

'It takes anything between three and four hours to make the biryani,' Abu Bakar tells us. 'After that it has to "rest" for about half an hour to emerge at its best.' Besides the signature biryani, Idrees also serves korma, sheermal and mutton stew. The seating space at this eatery is basic and cramped. That does not stop Lucknow's elite from coming here and taking away their biryani. Box upon box of biryani is scooped out of the deg and served. '*Hum mehnat daalte hain, mazaa Allah dete hain,*' Abu Bakar says, the contentment in what he does obvious.

Across the city, in Aminabad, right next to the famous Tunday Kebab is Wahid Biryani, another popular place for Awadhi biryani in Lucknow. It began in 1955 by Wahid Ali. Now 89, he still comes to the shop for an hour every evening. The business is managed by his son Abid Ali Qureshi and the third generation has stepped in as well. 'My father tells us, he sold biryani at one anna a portion,' Abid Ali Qureshi relates. Wahid Ali first sold his biryanis in Chowk and then moved to Aminabad. 'The price then became one rupee and regulars were outraged, but only briefly.' His other memory is of Dilip Kumar, the Bollywood star, coming to eat at Wahid. 'I was in school then and it was a major event,' Abid Ali Qureshi smiles. We found the biryani here to be slightly greasier and denser as compared to the light elegance of Idrees. The eatery has also expanded its menu to include dishes like chicken fry and Mughlai kebab paratha.

Covid restrictions hit Raja Thandai hard. It was not possible to serve iced drinks and their only product, thandai, suffered. Still, Ashish Tripathi had not lost his equanimity. He had time to chat with his regulars who stopped by on a hot October afternoon. This thandai business was begun by his grandfather Ramadhar Tiwari and brother Shivadhar Tiwari. Ashish Tripathi's father then took over and the business passed to him. A small paper cup of thandai costs ₹50. 'Everything that goes into it is natural,' Ashish Tripathi tells us. The speciality is the bhaang thandai. 'Bhaang is a great thing,' he adds. 'It has no bad side-effects at all. Bhagwan himself used it,' he says, pointing to a large Shiva statue that occupies pride of place in his small, tidy shop.

There is no dearth of sweet shops in Lucknow. They make an array of confections. We noticed that the jalebi and *imarti* rule the sweet stakes here.

Ram Asrey in Hazratganj, right opposite Bajpayee Kachori Bhandar, is an old and respected sweet shop, established in 1805. The business has been at its present location since the early '80s. Pankaj Behari continues the family tradition and manages a thriving business. Ram Asrey is so popular, staff scarcely bother with customer relations. You simply have to wait for your order of jalebi. In the evenings, it's imarti, made with a batter of urad dal, instead of maida. The malai *gilori* is another signature sweet here.

Motilal, established in 1983 and run by M.D. and L.K. Ahuja, also has a well-deserved reputation for its morning jalebis. We are also partial to the jalebi and imarti at Netram, both made in desi ghee, sinful, and sensationally good.

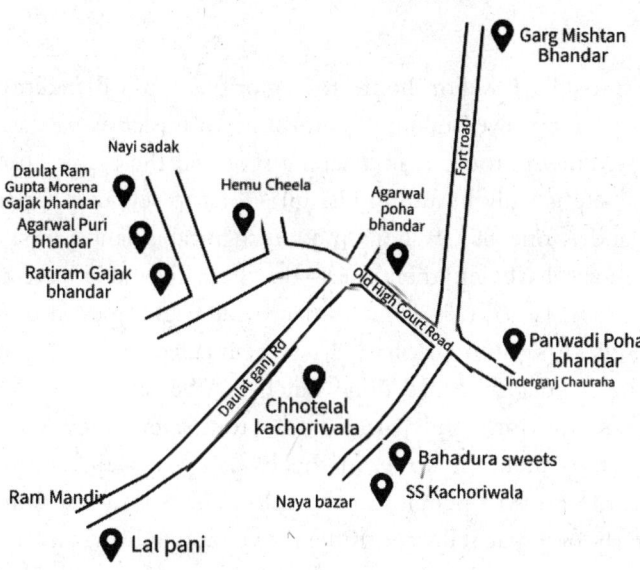

SWEETS FIT FOR ROYALTY

Gwalior

It's easy to like Gwalior, home to a glorious musical tradition and a string of impressive buildings connecting to the city's past as a princely state. Tansen's tomb is in a serene spot and the architecture of this burial site is truly beautiful. The qila (fort) towers over a part of the city and is one of Gwalior's most recognizable landmarks.

The Scindias have left their mark on the city and a part of the family palace, Jai Vilas, is a museum providing glimpses into an opulent lifestyle. Our auto rickshaw driver bemoaned the passing of Madhav Rao Scindia, who had done much for the city.

Away from the forts and palaces, it's a tourist-brochure whirl of colour, not to mention noise, in the bazaars. At Maharajwada, for instance, the press of people can be daunting, as they go about their festive shopping at stalls and itinerant vendors who crowd the roads and pavements under the shadow of heritage buildings. Here is also where you can find carts selling Gwalior's unique karela chaat, not made of bitter gourd but a light and flaky papdi, shaped like the vegetable, and topped with yoghurt, chutney and spices. And then stop for kulfi on a stick from Ishwar's cart.

All across Madhya Pradesh, poha, seasoned flattened rice, is a breakfast staple. Street vendors across Gwalior start heating up their poha as early as 7 a.m. Gwalior has more than a few shops that call themselves Agarwal Poha Bhandar or Centre. We went to the one on Phalka Bazaar Road in Lashkar. It's a small, narrow shop. The poha is made at a counter at the entrance. It is as minimalist as the setting, eschewing peanuts or tomato, just beaten rice, topped with sev, chopped onions, a sprinkle of masala and a squeeze of lime juice. It was begun by Piyush Agarwal in the early '90s. TV personality Vinod Dua seems to have been a fan and the signboard include an inset of him with the owner.

A more recent poha vendor who has gained an impressive following is Panwadi Poha Bhandar at Inderganj Chauraha. It was started in 2012 by Sonu Chaurasia, who has the ebullience and confidence of the self-made entrepreneur. He started off selling namkeen and then decided to do poha, his way. The cart at this busy circle holds a massive tray of soaked and mildly spiced poha. It's served on a leaf and Chaurasia is proud of this 'innovation' as most pohawalas use foil plates. The leaves are lined up, poha is spooned onto them, it's topped with sev, fried peanuts and chopped onions, masala is showered atop this mound, and a squirt of lime juice finishes the dish. Chaurasia's younger brother, who now manages the cart, plates up a dozen pohas at quick speed while helpers serve it to customers. There's a reason this poha is so popular. We found it softer and with a subtle richness which most pohas in Gwalior did not have. The success of the cart has led to the Chaurasias opening a full-fledged restaurant a stone's throw away.

In this part of the country, the kachori is a breakfast staple as well. A shop that calls itself SS Kachoriwala has to be a specialist. It's in Naya Bazaar and crowds mill in front of it, waiting to be handed their leaf cup of kachori, samosa or bedai. The accompaniments to these fried delights are aloo sabzi cooked in mustard oil, a relish of mango pickle and jaggery, and a coriander chutney. Brothers Hitesh and Hirdesh Bhargav now run this iconic eatery begun by their grandfather, Ramcharan Lal Sharma, in the late 1950s.

'It's said in our family that he began business with one anna selling samosas,' Hitesh said, inviting us behind the counter as he continued to serve the throng of customers. His father Ram Swarup Sharma then took over. He wasn't particularly keen that his sons run the shop. But then in 1996, he had a paralytic stroke and the very future of SS Kachoriwala was at stake. 'We couldn't allow it to collapse or to let thousands of our customers down, so my brother and I stepped in,' Hitesh said. The shop is open from 8 a.m. to 1 p.m. and reopens again at 4 p.m. to go on till 8 p.m. The offerings vary slightly between morning and evening, and they change according to the seasons too. Imarti is available in summer and gulab jamun and gajar ka halwa are available only during winter. *Mawa* sweets aren't at their best in the heat, according to Hitesh. 'We don't have to eat everything all the time, respecting the seasons is a part of eating well,' he said. He had once hoped to be in a proper 'job', but is now completely immersed in selling one of Gwalior's favourite foods.

There is no signboard for Chhotelal Kachoriwala in Patankar Chowk, but every auto rickshaw driver can take you there. 'I'm not sure when exactly this business began, but I am the fourth generation,' Lakhan Kachoriwala says. Chhotelal is famous for kachori and samosa and also some of the best imarti—fat, golden and juicy—you'll taste in Gwalior.

Agarwal Puri Bhandar in Naya Sadak has a vintage air about it. It's small with just four tables inside. Santosh Agarwal mans the counter and also gets up when an order comes in to fry the puris in ghee. The business was begun by his grandfather Namakram Agarwal decades ago. The puri thali comprises seven small puris, a fantastic aloo sabzi and a light boondi raita. There's a paratha thali as well. We told him how much we loved the puri-sabzi. 'It's a very old shop,' he smiled, leaving unsaid, 'we've had enough time to perfect what we do.'

The fame of Bahadura's signature sweet, the ladoo, extends far beyond Gwalior and we had heard much about it. It's made in an ancient shop, with fluted pillars and trellis work, in Naya Bazaar. The space is spotless and Vikas Sharma seated inside keeps a watch over the making of his famous ladoos. The shop was begun in the early 1900s by his grandfather, Bahadur Prasad Sharma, who had learned the art of sweet-making in Allahabad. Preparations for the day's ladoos begin at 4 a.m. when the coal is fired up and the ghee

in huge karhais heated. A mixture of gram flour makes it into the ghee in tiny droplets. These are lifted out, soaked in sugar syrup, and then hand-rolled into golden balls. No colour is added, no fruits or nuts embellish the ladoo. It's softer and moister than any motichoor ladoo you will eat. Former Prime Minister Atal Bihari Vajpayee is said to have had a particular fondness for the Bahadura ladoo. 'There's no secret or magic to it,' Vikas Sharma tells us, matter-of-factly. 'It's just about using the right ingredients in the right proportions and making it in the proper way.' He makes it sound simple. But having had a taste of the ladoo, we know there's much more to it than simply sticking to the basics. Bahadura also makes a delectable gulab jamun. They used to sell kachori and jalebi at breakfast time, but that was halted after the disruptions caused by Covid-19.

The *chilla* or *cheela*, the thin pancake made of gram flour, isn't a common street food. But that is the signature offering at Hemu Cheela in Patankar Bazaar. It was begun in 1997 by Bhuvanesh Rathore, and his son Shubham Rathore now runs it with remarkable efficiency. The chilla is made by soaking and grinding moong dal to a super fine paste. It's spread thin on a tawa, filled with a spiced potato mixture, then a sprinkle of grated paneer is added and it's rolled up and served. This is as wonderful as a well-made masala dosa and Gwalior locals flock here for this satisfying snack.

Hemu is also popular for its gol gappe and you can choose from suji and atta puris. Seven pieces cost ₹20. The gol gappe is filled with spiced potato and the pani is served separately in a plastic glass. It's DIY here, possibly after Covid.

Not far away, near Ram Mandir, is a street cart known simply as Lal Pani. The gol gappe here are fabulous and, yes, the pani is red and spicy.

Gajak, that warming concoction of sesame and jaggery, was once a wintertime delicacy. Not anymore. For this sweet has been so commercialized it's sold in brightly lit shops with attractive display counters and is available all-year round. While Gwalior is known for its gajak, Morena, some 35 km from the city, is considered the home of gajak.

One of the oldest sellers of Morena gajak in Gwalior is Daulat Ram Gupta Morena Gajak Bhandar in Nayi Sadak. It was set up by Daulat Ram Gupta in the 1970s. Food history is often nebulous and the story goes that when Daulat Ram's guru asked him to give up his liquor business, he turned to his wife who was from Morena and she suggested making gajak. She also gave him a recipe for this sweet that requires much skill and expertise to perfect. Sesame seeds are mixed with jaggery and cooked to a treacly consistency. The mixture is then cooled and aerated by repeated stretching and folding till it acquires the brittle texture that is its defining quality.

We heard another story about Morena and Gajak. It is that when Arjun Singh was in power, he put in place a plan to rehabilitate dacoits from Morena. They were tough men and their muscle power was used in gajak making. Hence, the association of gajak and Morena. Ratiram in Nai Sadak is also a known name in the business and claims to be one of the oldest gajak makers in Gwalior. Mahendra Rathore, who was at the counter, told us his great grandmother Kesarbai started off selling sesame sweets at the qila a hundred years ago. Her son Ratiramji Rathore continued selling the gajak his wife

Bhogabai made at home. Now, the business is in the hands of the fourth generation and Mahendra said his son would take up the reins soon. 'You cannot make quality products without the complete involvement of the owners,' he added. Ratiram is a specialist in gajak, *revdi* and *chikki*, and its top-seller is the jaggery gajak.

Our last stop in Gwalior was the Dargah Hazrat Shah Abdul Gafoor Sahab. We drove through the bustling bazaar near Jama Masjid to get here. When we were there, it was calm and serene, and it was so on most days, a place to stop and say a prayer.

During the annual *urs*, the death anniversary of the Sufi saint, it is packed with the faithful. The occasion involves buying, sharing and eating balushahi, and it's made by Garg Mishtan Bhandar, a very modest stall. Squatting on the floor, Sunil Garg, third-generation owner of the business, says the speciality of the balushahi is that each one weighs a kilo. 'It used to be five kilos during the time of my grandfather, Munnalal, but people have become so wary of eating sweets, we began to make them smaller.' The balushahi is only available during the annual event.

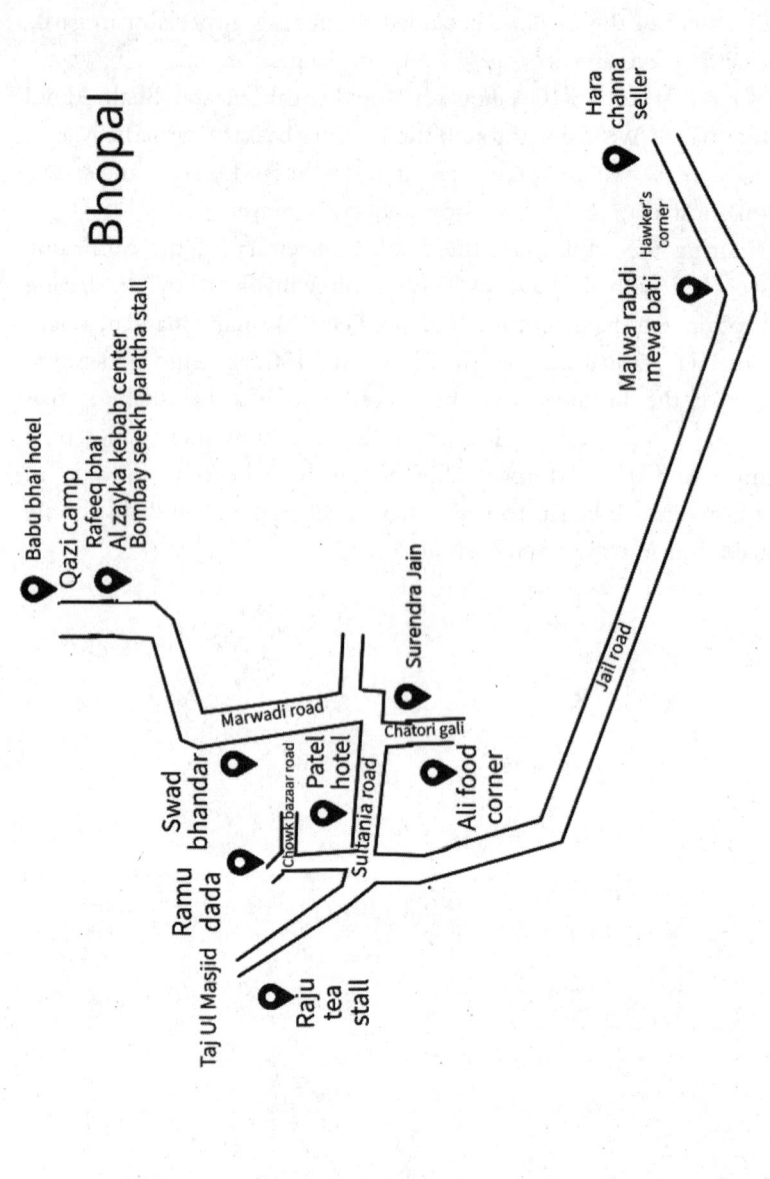

TEA IN THE WINTER, RASMALAI DONA IN THE SUMMER

Bhopal

*T*he vast expanse of the Upper Lake divides Bhopal into its diverse halves that together define its cultural fabric and character. To the north lies the old city with its graceful mosques such as the Taj ul Masjid, one of Asia's largest, the bustling, noisy Chowk and old streets through which young scooter-borne, burqa-clad women weave their precarious way, stopping at times at a kebab stall. These colourful, buzzing quarters, where you can catch glimpses of Islamic architecture, are a throwback to the time between the early nineteenth and twentieth centuries when the Begums of Bhopal held sway.

South of the lake, at the edge of which stands an imposing statue of Raja Bhoj, believed to have been the architect of this water body that is Bhopal's pride, is the modern city. The streets are wide, the buildings modern and the local foods—which are available in hole-in-the-wall eateries in the old city—are showcased in a hawker market, a *khau gali*, set up by the city authorities.

Bhopal shares its love of poha for breakfast with Gwalior and Indore in the region. But while the latter version is savoury and topped off with more spice, here it's a slightly sweet poha almost always eaten with a syrup-soaked jalebi or two.

It was 8 a.m. and the shops in the Peer Gate area were yet to open when we got there. But there was activity around the Swaad Bhandar, an unpretentious shop near Chintaman Chauraha, off Itwara Road. The first set of workers, Mohan Kumar Jain and Kamal, were already at work. A pile of turmeric-tinted poha, garnished with coriander leaves and shiny pomegranate kernels, was kept warm over a pot of simmering water. The day's first jalebis were being squeezed out into hot oil and hit the syrup in minutes.

The business, owned by Kalyan Singh—it's known to locals as Kalyan Singh Jalebi Poha—and Mohan Bhai is a local landmark and its breakfast special, priced at ₹15 a plate, is hugely popular. As the day progresses, other items like samosa and kachori appear. Later it's chaat. The workers, each specializing in the making of a dish, turn up one by one. '*Woh hai do baje wala*,' Mohan Kumar says, pointing to the cook who'll come in at 2 p.m. There's camaraderie, staff and regular customers chat and drink tea from the adjacent stall, performing a Bhopali morning ritual.

Like all cities with old quarters, which are a step back in time and removed from the frenetic pace of the rat race, Bhopal makes a ritual of tea drinking. Tea stalls are scattered across the city. More than mere shops selling a hot beverage, they are gathering places, somewhere to meet friends and chat, to unwind even when there's only standing space, and watch the world go by.

Not far from the Taj ul Masjid with its long flights of steps and striking white domes is Raju Tea Stall. If you drive down Sultania Road, you'll recognize it easily; it's the large shop with a throng of people outside from 6 a.m. till midnight. Fareed Qureshi opened the business in the smallest way possible in 1987. 'I began with 5 litres of milk and 12 cutting glasses a day, selling on the street,' he told us, scarcely able to spare time from collecting cash and issuing tokens at the 'stall' that now serves nearly 1,000 customers a day. He set up shop at a counter that already had 'Raju' painted on it. Customers started calling it Raju Tea Stall and the name stuck.

This shop opens onto the street with some tables on the pavement and serves a top-quality tea, just one kind with no variants. Over the years Fareed, assisted by his son Farhan, has added samosas, kachori, bread pakoda and khoya jalebi to the menu. Ghujia is a hot seller as well. Regulars wait patiently for fresh batches of samosas to emerge

from the karhai. Politicians, film stars, TV actors and other celebrity visitors to Bhopal have all had a glass of cutting chai here.

Other landmark tea stalls in Bhopal include the 100-year-old Patel Hotel, serving Irani chai in Ibrahimpura, and Babu Bhai Hotel, also in Ibrahimpura, open 24/7 and known for its salty *namakwali* chai.

In Bhopal's scorching summer, there's something to lift the spirits of shoppers in Chowk Bazaar. That's the rasmalai dona, a cool, soothing confection served in a leaf bowl, a dona.

Amid the winding lanes of Chowk Bazaar, past rows of stationery sellers and bakeries, is Ramu Dada's shop, one of the original makers of this Bhopali cooler. Ramu Dada began the business a hundred years ago, selling crushed ice topped with rabri and drizzled with an unguent rose syrup. The three ingredients come together in amazing harmony and a spoonful had us smitten. The business then passed to his son, Ramesh, who lives above the shop. He's now indisposed and sons Sachin and Saurabh look after the business. When they have to step out, Ramesh's soft-spoken wife, Narmadabai, minds the shop. They also have a scooter they've rigged up as a mobile stall to sell their signature sweet and it's parked near the Jama Masjid. Winters and rainy weather aren't great for business, but when the mercury rises, there's a huge rush for the rasmalai dona.

Another famous seller of this sweet bowl is Surendra Jain, who sets up shop in Chatori Gali. Chatori Gali in the chaotic whirl of Ibrahimpura is your typical Muslim quarter and, of course, meat lovers come here looking for their kebab fix. This was once a vibrant night market with many stalls plying their wares while the tantalizing aroma of meat cooking over coal filled the air. Around 2019, the authorities evicted many of the vendors and Chatori Gali has lost some of its earlier liveliness. A couple of shops here specialize in typically Bhopali kebabs and meat dishes.

Ali Food Corner is a stall in the shade of the Meer Zaheer Ullah Masjid that comes to life every evening. Here, a father-and-sons enterprise turns out bun kebabs, shaping spiced, minced beef into tiny patties, cooking them on a tava and slapping them between sweet buns with a plop of green chutney. They also do a delightful anda vada, topping hardboiled egg halves with green chutney before they are dipped in a gram-flour batter and deep-fried. There are a couple of stools to sit on and tuck into your bun kebab. There are also burqa-clad girls who stop by for a quick takeaway.

A night food market that is flourishing is Qazi Camp. Historians say this was home to refugees from Kazakhstan in the 1920s and that its original name was Kazik Camp. Now it's a haven for meat lovers, where you can eat an array of beef, lamb and chicken dishes.

At Rafeeq Bhai's, *nalli* biryani is spooned out of massive handis and Anni Bhai ki Biryani has won fans in the ten years that it has been around. The Bombay Seekh Paratha stall serves up a greasy, hit-the-spot chicken champ, while crowds flock to the Al Zayka Kebab Centre for its seekh kebabs whose aroma entices even before you near the stall. Through the night, veteran bread makers roll out tava and roomali rotis to be cooked on wood fires. It's a daily drama of

BAZAAR BITES

fire, smoke, meat and bread. After the nighttime indulgences, a frothy tea at Babu Bhai hotel is the perfect finishing note.

Speak of the must-eat dishes in Bhopal and local foodies will definitely mention the *mawa bati*. To the uninitiated, this may look like just another gulab jamun, but Bhopal's sweet connoisseurs know otherwise.

One of the most recommended sellers of this sweet is the Malwa Rabdi Mewa Bati stall at the Hawker's Corner near Number 6 Bus Stop in the new city. It's at the entrance to this circle of food shops selling everything from pav bhaji to momos and dosa. Shahid Khan has been here from the time the Khau Galli was set up in 2004. His speciality is the mawa bati and he recommends you eat it with rabri, sweet on sweet, but the contrasting textures and temperatures adding to the enjoyment. The mawa bati is a soft version of the jamun and has dried fruit and spices at its melting centre. Eaten hot, it's a sinful indulgence, but one that Bhopalis keep returning for.

In winter, outside the hawker corner you'll find the hara-chana seller, roasting the tender green pods with salt. Like the mawa bati, it is not to be missed. We bought big paper cones full to eat on the train back.

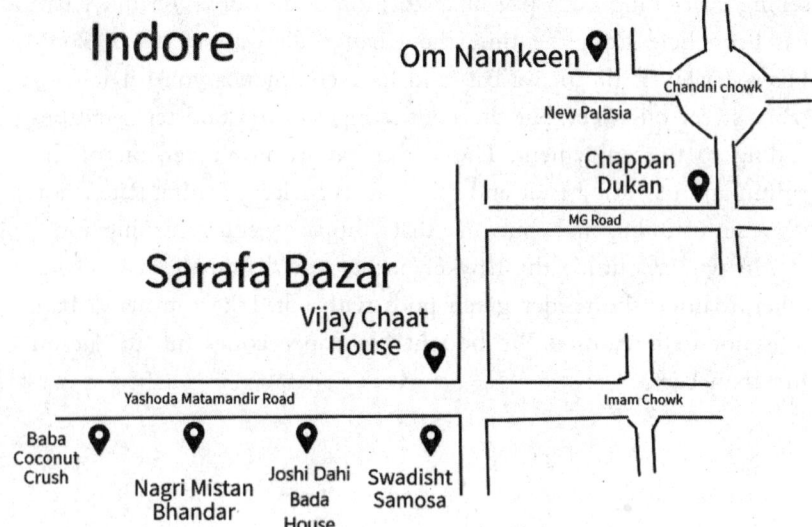

SARAFA BAZAAR AND CHAPPAN DUKAN

Indore

*O*ur first impression of Indore was how clean and tidy it was, even in the crowded bazaars in the old part of the city. The Khan River flows by this ancient quarter, with the seven-storey Rajwada Palace—under restoration when we visited—standing sentinel. The arresting edifice harks back to the time of the Holkar rulers of the region, among whom Rani Ahilyabai was the most renowned.

Indrapur, or Indreshwar as it was known then, was gifted to the Holkars by the Marathi Peshwa Baji Rao. The shared heritage of the Marathas and Indore is evident in many aspects of life here, particularly the food.

And how Indore loves its food, particularly the snacks, sweets and small meals from street vendors! No other city boasts of a night food market quite like Sarafa Bazaar behind the Rajwada Palace.

Here, street stalls serve *sabudana khichdi*—Indore locals swear it's better than anywhere in the country—and samosas, *pattice*, mithai, jaleba, chaat, kulfi-falooda and pani puri with the spicy water in many flavours like pudina, hing and jeera. Stirring to life at 8 p.m., the street buzzes with activity until 2 a.m.

Poets have spoken about the charms of Shab-e-Malwa, the evenings of Malwa, and they must not have alluded to the salubrious climate alone. Surely the pleasure of eating through the night adds joy to the Indore resident's day.

At the entrance to Sarafa Bazaar is Vijay Chaat House. As with all popular food shops, you can recognize it easily by the crowds milling in front of the counter. Also, there's Vijay Thaker presiding over the karhai in which *kopra* pattice bob about, in his signature white kurta, pristine without a single food stain. 'Our father, Dayashankar ji, who began the business in 1969, was a strict disciplinarian,' Vijay said, after we had managed to get his attention amidst the crowd of customers. 'Any clumsiness and a tiny drop of hot oil would land on your wrist. It was his rap on the knuckles. We learned quickly to combine skill and grace as we work in tiny spaces.'

Dayashankar began on the street in Sarafa Bazaar, setting up shop after the silver shops here shut down for the day. Indore was then a hub of cotton manufacturing and the little venture fed the workers from the mills. The shop owners were happy with the arrangement, for it meant there would be activity on the street at night and, therefore, safety for their wares. That is, in fact, how the silver bazaar became Indore's famous night food market. As a permanent shop, Vijay Chaat House first occupied a tiny space of 3 x 6 feet here for which Dayashankar paid a rent of ₹35 a month. He started serving pattice, one stuffed with coconut and dried fruit, another with fresh peas, *batla* kachori, also stuffed with peas, samosa and poha-jalebi. He had made his way to Indore from Surat and also began to sell Surti *khaman*, fry khaman with a crisp exterior, and *aamiri* khaman, a tangy crumble. They are all hot sellers, but it's the kopra and batla pattice that are iconic to this store. With their crunchy golden exterior, soft potato centre and filling of fresh and desiccated coconut or fresh peas, they are a real treat.

'We do not compromise on quality,' said Jatin Thaker, also, like his uncle, sporting spotless white. Along with his cousins, he manages the outlet in Chappan Dukan. 'We use only the best groundnut oil for frying and top-quality ghee for the jalebi.' Dayashankar's sons, Vijay, Niranjan and Keertibhai, run the business. 'Our father created the legacy, we simply need to preserve it,' Vijay said.

After tucking into the Vijay Chaat House pattice, we went looking for another Sarafa Bazaar icon. It was a shabby shop and likely hadn't received too many fresh coats of paint since it opened nearly

80 years ago. But Indore locals don't care about the setting as they line up for what is undoubtedly the city's best dahi bada.

The Joshi brothers now run the time-worn shop begun by their grandfather. The elder is a showman. Frequently, an instagrammer will pull out her phone and ask him to do his thing. Joshi places the large, fluffy vadas that have been pre-soaked in a foil dona. He ladles in thick, creamy dahi and then a swirl of sweet date chutney. Then he performs his 'magic' trick. He picks up all the masala powders together with the tips of his fingers and then sprinkles them one at a time onto the dahi bada: first salt, then chilli, black pepper, cumin and ajwain. The best is yet to come. He tosses the dona into the air, catching it as it lands neatly in his palm without a drop of yoghurt spilling. The crowd applauds and Joshi smiles.

'You don't go to a class to learn this,' he told us. 'It's what I've been doing for 40 years.' We ask him his full name; '*Ghulamon ka koi naam nahi hota*,' replied the entertaining food vendor. According to him, the customer is king and he is at their service. Besides the dahi bada, Joshi's is also famous for its *bhutte ke khees*, an Indore speciality. Fresh corn is grated and cooked in milk with lashings of ghee and spices. A little sweet, soft and warm, it's a winter indulgence.

Chappan Dukan is just that; it's a stretch that once housed 56 shops. Many are still there and, besides Sarafa Bazaar, this is one of Indore's buzzing food hubs. Shops open as early as 6 a.m., serving up Indore's favourite breakfast of slightly sweet poha and jalebi. Some of the city's most popular sweet shops are here.

In this stretch that's best known for its vegetarian street foods, there's one that stands out with its 'hot dogs'. Johny Hot Dog, now in its 40th year, is at the entrance to Chappan Dukan, a tiny shop owned not by a Johny but by Vijay Singh. 'I had to give the shop a name, and Johny seemed as good as any other,' he told us smilingly. The Johny hot dog is in fact a bun filled with omelette, a veg or mutton cutlet. The buns are soft and are warmed at the edge of the tawa in which the cutlets are fried. A spoon of green chutney and tomato ketchup are smeared on the hot buns, the filling is slapped between, and that's the 'hot dog'.

The omelette one is delicious and satisfying in its simplicity. Here they call it Egg Banjo. 'Bread and eggs get called many things, omelette pav, anda bun, bread omelette… It was the students of SGSITS who christened it egg banjo here. It avoids confusion and the name has stuck,' according to Vijay. A single product with just three variants allows this entrepreneur to ensure quality and makes his unpretentious shop an Indore landmark.

Indore must surely eat vast quantities of namkeen. It's part of festivals and rituals, served to guests who drop in unexpectedly, and an everyday, anytime snack. When they don't have vegetables at hand, Indori housewives toss up sev tamatar sabzi; sometimes it doesn't even require tomatoes. Namkeen shops are ubiquitous in the city and carts at street corners are piled high with different types of sev.

While everyone has their favourite namkeen vendor, Om Namkeen is one of Indore's oldest and most popular places to buy these salty, spicy, crunchy snacks. The business was launched in 1984 by Dhanpat Bothra with 56 varieties. Now, Om Namkeen stocks a mind-boggling 400 products and has received an award from the Federation of Sweets and Namkeen Manufacturers for this achievement. Dhanpat's son, Anurag, has also entered the business and is responsible for modernizing certain aspects of it. The namkeen, though, is still made the traditional way, even if there are now innovations like diet namkeen: roasted bajra oats mixture, roasted alsi and plain permal, salted rice puffs.

But the greatest demand is for the classics such as the Ratlami laung sev, and there's the IT mixture, inspired by a combination of different nuts, grams and namkeen that officers from the nearby Income Tax office would ask for. The original shop—there are now five outlets in Indore—is at a stone's throw from Chappan Dukan and customers can sample every single product from tasting trays that are set out. They can also tuck into a plate of paneer samosa or kachori from the counter outside while they wait for their namkeen orders to be packed up.

Walk down Pipli Bazaar, just off Sarafa, and you'll see a line-up of shops specializing in mawa. The mawa bhandars display small mountains of the reduced milk solids, creamy and white, waiting to be crafted into the sweets that Indore loves.

One of the first vendors to open shop in Sarafa Bazaar every evening is Somesh Giri's sweet stall. He squats on the street, his confections on display. Somesh's father, Shiv Giri, started the business 45 years ago on this very spot. He sells malpua steeped in syrup, rabri and kalakand, which, incidentally, originates from the village of Kalakund near Indore. Some of the sweets are seasonal, Somesh says. The gajar ka halwa, which uses vast quantities of Indori mawa, and the warm moong ka halwa are winter specialities. It's the season when the best carrots are in season and the weather is just right for warm moong halwa oozing ghee. In summer, these are replaced by shrikand and rasgolla, both at their best when eaten chilled. Come winter or summer, Sarafa Bazaar's vendors keep Indore's sweet cravings sated. Another thing to try here is the super-sized jalebi known as jaleba.

If you ask for a glass of *shikanjvi* in Indore and expect sweet lime juice, you're in for a surprise. Shikanjvi here is a lassi-meets-thandai drink, rich, cooling and scented with saffron.

Sarafa Bazaar's most popular shikanjvi seller is Nagori Sarva Phalahari Mishtan Bhandar, a 100-year-old establishment. Here, the younger generations continue to run the business started by their great grandfather, who came from Nagore in Rajasthan. Originally a mithai shop, the shikanjvi was introduced later here and is now a must-have for most people who step out to shop in the Rajwada area on a warm summer afternoon.

A popular cold drink vendor in Sarafa is Baba Coconut Crush, another uniquely Indori concoction. Tender coconut water, malai, ice and sugar are whizzed in a blender to make the popular crush that beats a can of cola any day. Launched by Akash Tanwar ten years ago, this place also attracts its share of Indore celebs and a flexboard depicting them sipping their coconut crush serves as the backdrop to this roadside stall.

Winter is pleasant in Indore. It's awaited eagerly also because of the abundance of seasonal produce, such as sweet peas, red carrots and crisp radish. Then there's *garadu*, the local taro. It's parboiled, cubed and deep-fried, dusted with sharp spices and served up in a paper cone. If you taste these crunchy squares with their soft centres, the mellowness of the yam complemented by the masala mix, you won't enjoy French fries very much anymore.

Garadu is available through the winter from food carts all over the city. When in Sarafa Bazaar, you can buy it at Swadisht Samosa, a smoke-stained shop right at the beginning of the food street.

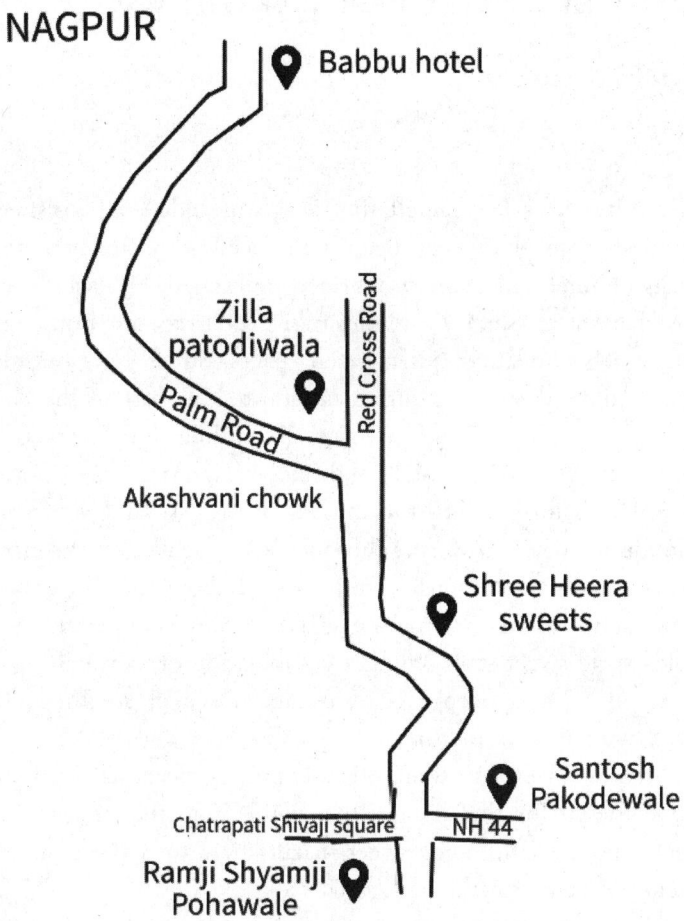

A HUGELY POPULAR PAKODEWALA

Nagpur

The city that's considered the centre of India—all distances are measured from here—has been influenced from many directions and its cultural and culinary fabric is multihued. The winter capital of Maharashtra, Nagpur's administrative quarters are housed along wide streets and amid quiet, green spaces. Street carts outside the public buildings serve up dishes unique to this part of the country.

The old parts of the city are all bustling, loud bazaars, amid which are scattered food stalls and bhojanalays, which feed locals for cheap. Delve further into the innards of the city and you arrive in Mominpura, where towering mosques stand guard over the crowded, chaotic streets. Here small eateries like Babbu Hotel specialize in biryani and Muslim-style non-vegetarian dishes. Shoppers also stop by at old-world sweet stalls selling a combination of halwa and paratha, the bread a huge, deep-fried disc, bits of which are torn off and served with the warm paratha.

Nagpur loves its sweets—Haldiram's is headquartered here—and is known for the oranges that come from the orchards amidst which the city is located. Sweet makers here turn the oranges into deliciously zesty barfis.

We flew into the city very early and headed for breakfast. At 6.30 a.m., more than a hundred people were milling outside a modest eatery on Wardha Road, not far from the Radisson Blu. It would seem that Nagpur locals don't bother with cooking breakfast and are happy to head to Ramji Shyamji Pohewale to jostle with the coriander to give it a dark-green colour, it's sold at small stalls and carts across the city.

One stall that's hugely popular is the one at Civil Lines. The nameless stall is known simply as Zilla Patodiwala since it's near the administrative office buildings. Now in its 50th year, this business was begun by Omkar Prajapati, who came here from Rajasthan. It's now managed by his son, Ashok, who mans the one-table stall, from 8 a.m. to 7 p.m. every day. The patodis are prepared in a karkhana (factory) nearby and transported by cycle to the stall. The patodi is broken up and topped off with a ladle or two of kadhi to make one of Nagpur's favourite street foods. 'We've been here before the new zilla building came up,' Ashok said, 'and some customers have been coming every day for years.' Ashok's regulars are many and he knows how exactly they like their patodi-kadhi. 'If the stock is going to be delayed, I have to call and let them know,' he said as he served us a hearty plate of his speciality.

Pakodas are the generic calorie-laden, hit-the-spot fried snack that all of India loves. Nagpur likes it made with moong dal and fried in marble-sized rounds, and likes it even more when it's made by Santosh Pakodewale.

A massive flexboard announcing the name with a photo of the owner stands at the front of a three-storey building that's the backdrop for this business. They needn't have taken the trouble. For the crowd on the pavement and spilling over onto the road at the stall opposite South Point School on Manewada Ring Road is announcement enough that you're at the city's most popular maker of pakodas.

Santosh had no idea the small street-food business he began in 2002 would grow to this size and gain such popularity. Now, he's a limelight-loving entrepreneur, gold bracelet and massive jeweled rings on his fingers announcing his success. 'I was working elsewhere and decided it would be good to be my own master,' he told us, inviting us into his office in the building behind the stall. 'At the time, I would make pakode from 500 gm of moong dal and sell from the footpath.'

crowds. The *tarri* poha, Nagpur's favourite way to kickstart the day, is the speciality here.

Begun by Tribhuvan Nath Pande 30 years ago, it was named after his identical twin sons Ramji and Shyamji. They now run the place, along with two other brothers. The day starts long before dawn for them and the shop opens at 5 a.m. We watched while Ramji stirred up one round of poha. The flattened rice soaking in recycled oil cans is strained and emptied into basins in which you can bathe a baby. Soyabean oil is heated in a massive karhai and in go mustard seeds, peanuts, sliced onions and turmeric. Ramji lifts up the heavy basin with ease and lets the poha drift into the bubbling oil with its condiments. Cubes of boiled potato and the contents of a pack of frozen peas are also added and it takes some heavy-duty stirring before the poha is ready. It's moved to the counter and served topped with tarri, the dark, super spicy brown-chana gravy that's the preferred accompaniment. Customers can ask for spicy or medium, and the quantity of tarri will be adjusted accordingly. The plate can be topped off with *chivda* if you like.

Carrying their plates, several customers head to a table holding a pile of peeled onions. Knives and cutting boards are provided and each one chops up some onion to add to the tarri poha. 'We put the onions out there, whether they cost ₹100 or ₹25 a kilo,' Ramji said. 'By letting the customers chop onions for their plate, we save on labour.' The customers don't seem to mind one bit and some come here several times a week for breakfast. There are office-goers on their way to work, students, salesmen, senior citizens after their morning walk, all of who have been eating at Ramji Shyamji for many years now. 'It's the quality of the ingredients and what we serve that makes them come back again and again,' Ramji said. 'We use the best poha, and only soyabean oil for cooking it. Everything is done in sight of the customers. There are no shortcuts or compromises and that encourages them to eat here as they would in their homes.'

A street snack little known outside Nagpur is *patodi*. A deep-fried pastry stuffed with a mixture of besan, dal and enough fresh

In the next 15 years, his pakode earned a massive following and business flourished. Santosh was able to get his own place in Naren Nagar and establish himself firmly on the food map of Nagpur. More recently, he's had to move from there to the present address, where he's acquired a building that serves as store room—he now uses up to 100-plus kilos of moong dal a day—and prep area. This is where the dal is soaked and ground in massive quantities.

At 4 p.m. every evening, three huge karhais are fired up, each manned by two people, shaping the pakode and deep-frying them. They emerge crisp and golden, to be served in paper cones topped off by a green chutney that has blobs of yoghurt in it. 'Our chutney is our speciality,' Santosh said. His stall uses up 250 litres of yoghurt for the chutney every day. Besides the pakode, bread pakoda and hot masala doodh—of which they sell 50 litres every evening—are other specialities here. Santosh now employs nearly 20 people, all in uniforms with the Santosh Pakodewala logo embroidered on them. 'I don't hire professional cooks,' said this enterprising street-food vendor. 'I go looking for people who are lost in life, recovering alcoholics, people on the fringes of society, and I hire them. They find purpose. Food transforms their lives.' If this stall sees Nagpur locals queuing up every evening, the crowds swell further in the monsoons, for the pakoda is essential rainy-day food. '*Barish mein toh maja hi maja hai*,' as Santosh put it.

In a city that's famed for its oranges, it's no wonder the fruit is celebrated by sweet makers. Among the most famous is Shree Heera Sweets, a 35-year-old establishment. The original shop is in Gokulpeth and there's a more modern outlet just down the road. Its crusty owner, Atmaram, says santra barfi was introduced some 20 years ago and it's now become the best food souvenir to buy in Nagpur. The orange harvest is at its best in the *mrig bahar* (November to March). Atmaram buys the oranges for his santra barfi at the local auction, often bidding for a tonne or more. Since the oranges are seasonal, the fruit is turned into a pulpy, sweet marmalade and stored for production through the year. A largely female workforce

then turns this stock into Nagpur's signature barfi that is a delicious mix of creamy texture and zesty flavour. It's an apt confection for a place that calls itself Orange City.

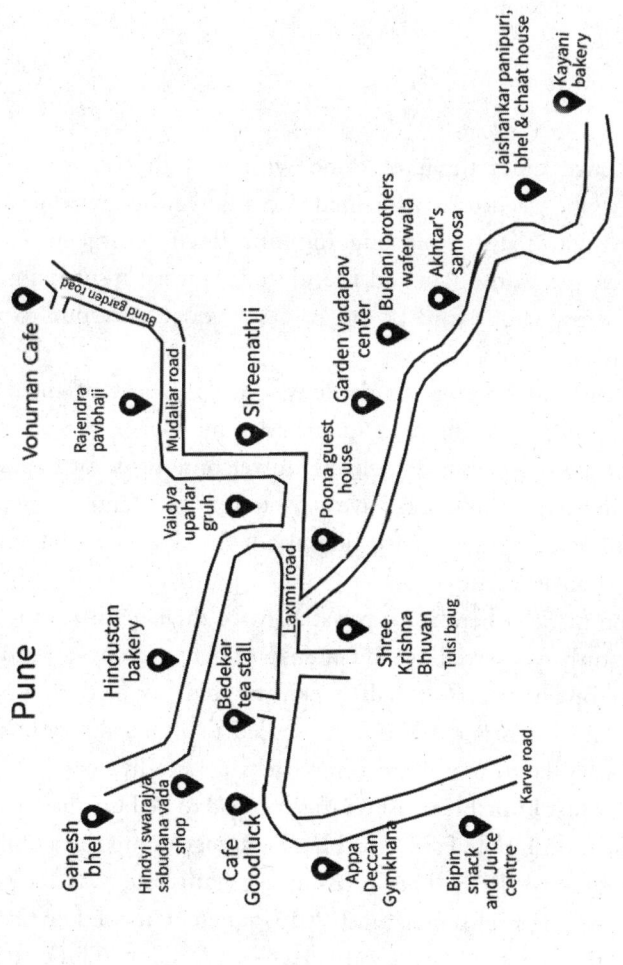

PERFECT MISAL AND PARSI BAKING

Pune

The once quiet town of Pune with its pleasant weather and a laidback vibe has now transformed into an urban sprawl, the landscape scattered with massive and ongoing infrastructure projects. There still are green spaces though, and the old educational institutions, which gave the city its 'Oxford of the East' sobriquet, continue to nurture a vibrant youth culture.

In the old quarters of the city, once the seat of the Peshwas, there are ancient edifices, including Mastani Mahal in Shanivarwada, the separate quarters in which the unwelcome bride of Bajirao lived. These historical landmarks have attracted more attention since Sanjay Leela Bhansali made a lavish film about the doomed love of Peshwa Bajirao and Mastani.

The markets here are captivating with their textiles, shops selling *pheta*s (turbans), jewellery and utensils. There are street vendors and small shops, many over half a century old, to feed shoppers and locals. The Parsis and Iranis, long settled in Pune, also contribute to its culinary culture and are throwbacks to another era.

Our first Pune breakfast on this trip had to be bun-maska and chai. Vohuman on Dhole Patil Road has been serving up this combination to Pune since 1978. This unassuming Irani café was located next to the Jehangir Hospital until 2015, when it moved to its present spot—after wrangles over property—near Ruby Clinic. It's still a basic eatery, with bun, bread and jam in various combinations: one slice butter, two slice butter, bun butter, bun butter jam, toast butter, toast butter jam, toast butter cheese, in the true quirky sense of Irani cafés. The buns are soft and sweet and have a cherry embedded in them. The butter is Amul, kept softened in a large bowl near the cash counter. As orders come in, buns are slathered with the butter and served sliced. Soft, sweet, enriched with generous amounts of salted butter, a bun and a cup of tea is an affordable, satisfying breakfast or pick-me-up.

The omelette, especially the cheesy version, is also a hot seller at Vohuman. Hormuz Irani ran a restaurant called Light of Asia in Mumbai's Colaba. He moved to Pune to set up this café. He became a much-loved figure among his regular customers, being called 'Uncle' and 'Bawaji'. After his passing in 2016, son Sarosh Irani took over and continues to enjoy the affection and loyalty of his customers.

Older than Vohuman is Café Goodluck, established in 1935 by Hussain Ali Yakshi. It opens just before 8 a.m. and all tables are occupied within minutes. With its checked tablecloths under glass tops, tea served in white cups and saucers by efficient, if brusque, waiters, this is the quintessential Irani café. Customers come here at breakfast time for the bun maska or bun omelette with tea. Kheema-pav is frequently ordered too. More recently, Café Goodluck has begun to serve egg curry, biryani and even tandoori chicken. 'It appeals to students, who are a majority of our customers,' said Abbas Ali, manning the counter during the breakfast rush. Café Goodluck is in an old building and the junction at which it is located is called Goodluck Chowk. 'It was granted by the government, we've done nothing. It's our customers who've made us famous,' said this old-timer.

Sabudana (sago) khichdi served with kakdi—a sweet raita with grated cucumber and thin yoghurt—is another much-loved breakfast in Pune. Bipin Snack and Juice Centre, a hole-in-the-wall operation on Karwe Road, is a success story, going by the crowds thronging it, jostling and shouting out their orders: khichdi-kakdi, pohe, patties, vada-chutney, idli-sambar and sheera. The famous khichdi-kakdi is served with a scattering of sev and is very, very good. We also loved the 'patties' which is a slice of bread topped with potato masala, dipped in bhajia batter and deep-fried. It has a topping of coriander, onions, grated coconut and a squirt of sweet chutney.

The sabudana khichdi at Appa, situated near the Deccan Gymkhana, also has a huge fan following. It has survived, thanks to the pull of nostalgia a young man felt for the place. Sangram Deshmukh used to frequent the Gymkhana and eat at the clubhouse where 'Appa' used to serve khichdi-kakdi, pohe and idli-sambar. When he aged and fell ill, the eatery was set to close. Sangram felt he couldn't let that happen. 'I approached the staff and asked them if we could recreate the experience.' They agreed and he set up his no-frills outlet just down the road from the Gymkhana. 'I've kept the original concept intact, but introduced a few dishes, such as *kothimbir* vada,' he tells us, greeting and serving customers with a bright smile. And, yes, the kothimbir vada is very good. Go here for the pohe as well.

Sabudana dishes are a defining aspect of Maharashtrian cuisine. They come into their own in Pune's street stalls and small shops. The very best sabudana vada we ate was at Shreenathji in Ravivarpeth. Here, Rohan Gadekar, clad in jeans and white linen shirt, mans one of the busiest food carts in the area. He started vending these vadas from a cart in 2003. He's been at the same spot ever since, amidst a busy market. An assistant shapes and drops the vadas into a massive karhai and the crowds begin to gather. They wait patiently, for the fryer will not be hurried. He keeps turning and shifting the vadas till they are completely crisp and golden. Piping hot, they are served up with a green chutney and sweet cucumber raita. The cart operates from 11 a.m. to 9 p.m. 'I do just this one thing and it's worked,' says Gadekar.

Hyndavi Swaraj also has a reputation for its sabudana vadas. This is a large street-food business with a line-up of carts selling the signature vadas, plus pohe and other items.

Misal, the soupy dish of potatoes, legumes and spice, topped off with something crunchy, and served with sliced bread or pav, provides everyday sustenance to a vast number of Punekars. Its origins in

BAZAAR BITES

Pune make for captivating culinary history.

In the early part of the twentieth century, a young man, Raghunath Ramachandra Vaidya, left his home in the Konkan region and came to Pune to earn a livelihood. He started off practising the family tradition of conducting pujas and rituals. During the time, he stayed with a family in Shanivarwada who ran an eatery. That became Vaidya's inspiration to enter the food business. At the time, eateries were few and far between in Pune. Many operated outside the auditoriums where plays were staged. Vaidya decided to choose another location.

A hundred years ago, Bagade Road was a busy arterial road. Traders, vendors and shoppers thronged the area with its vegetable market, goldsmiths and grain merchants. Vaidya rented a building belonging to one of the Peshwa generals. He opened shop on the day of Hanuman Jayanti in 1910. At the time, there was a well-known eatery, Santosh Bhuvan, serving a dish consisting mainly of leftovers such as the potato mixture from batata vada and the crisp bits of batter that remained after frying bhajias. Vaidya served a similar dish, but used freshly cooked potatoes, shev and chivda. The masala for the *rassa*, gravy, was made with a paste of green chillies, ginger, garlic and coconut. Tamarind was used as a souring agent. It was only in 1928 that tomatoes appeared in markets and green tomatoes made it to the dish that came to be known as *misal*.

The crowds that flocked to Bagade Road ensured Vaidya's little shop flourished. Initially, misal was served with puris. Bread only became an accompaniment after a Hindu bakery was established in 1938. Until then, orthodox Punekars would not eat bread baked by other communities. The business then passed to Vaidya's son—who did not have sons—and then his granddaughter.

Deepak Joshi, who gave up a career in computer science, now looks after the business he inherited from his mother. 'It is more than a business,' he tells us. 'My grandfather told me Vaidya Upahar Gruh is not just our livelihood. It must also be responsible for those who work here.' If Deepak Joshi is the fourth generation running this iconic eatery, his staff are also fourth generation. 'They all come from a small village, Pangnoli, near Mahad,' Joshi says. This continuity is both the charm and quintessence of this famed misal vendor. To step into the shop is to go back in time. Everything from the furniture and sepia-tinted photos to the framed mirrors and, of course, the recipe for misal, have remained unchanged for 100 years and more.

Another immensely popular misal shop with waiting crowds is Bedekar Tea Stall. It started off as a chai ka *tapri*, selling tea along with shev and chivda. Owner Dattatreya Bedekar then set up a small eatery and, in the mid-1950s, introduced misal to the menu. His son and daughter-in-law Damodar and Sushma Bedekar continued the family business, creating along the way the misal that has become a Bedekar signature now. The misal has vegetables, including potatoes, brinjal and cabbage, tamarind and jaggery, and gets its distinct spiciness and aroma from *goda* masala, the Maharashtrian spice blend. 'No two misals are the same anywhere,' said Amogh, who entered the business along with his cousin, Tanvi. They are the third generation, and have plans for expansion. 'Ours is a misal from a home kitchen, not a restaurant.' Customers tell him they have been coming here since the 1960s. 'It is a responsibility to fulfill every day, keeping them happy and satisfied,' Amogh said.

For more misal from a vintage-era restaurant, go to Shree Krishna Bhuvan in Tulsibaugh. It was begun in 1942, has been passed down the generations, and is now run by Atul Sudhakar Joshi. Besides the misal that comes with *sada*, medium and *theeka* rassa—indicating spice levels—this place also serves bhajia, *sheer* and poha.

A lunch treat we thoroughly enjoyed was *thalipeeth*. Maharashtra's multigrain roti is nutritious, tasty and deeply satisfying. And the very best, those in the know tell us, is at Poona Guest House in Budhwar Peth in the old city. While it isn't a street-food business, it's old, unpretentious and affordable, and we had to include it in this collection. Walk past rows of shops selling fabrics and salwar kurtas, and take the stairs up to a clean, spare dining room. Besides the thalipeeth, crisp and spicy and served with minuscule katoris of garlic chutney and yoghurt, Poona Guest House also offers a typical Maharashtrian thali, missal and dahi ke pohe. Sharmila Sarpotdar manages the place begun by her husband's great grandfather, Nanasaheb Sarpotdar, in 1935. 'He was in the business of making silent movies,' she tells us. 'Realizing it was a fickle industry, he decided to branch out and start this so he could have a steady source of income.'

Mumbaikars are likely to be riled, but Pune's pav bhaji is in a class of its own. We went to Supreme Corner where Sanjeev Patel sits at the back of the shop collecting cash and keeping an eye on the business he began in 1979. He began at the same spot, then operating from a shack that was just 5 x 4 feet.

'I had seen that Bombay and Surat had pav bhaji and it was popular. It wasn't available in Pune, so I decided to start a business,' Patel said, when we chatted with him after our very satisfying pav bhaji dinner. 'Initially, there were days when I sold just one portion and walked home alone, but I hung in there,' he said.

Patel has a simple formula on which his now flourishing business is based: 3 dishes, 4 hours of operation and 6 days a week. Supreme Corner's menu has just pav bhaji, pizza —the premade base and Amul cheese kind—and tawa pulav. We went at 10 p.m. and there were still customers waiting for a table. The pav bhaji is excellent with just the right amount of butter. Sanjeev Patel tells us Supreme is the second largest buyer of Amul butter in Pune after Kayani bakery. The pulav, served piping hot, also hits the spot. This no-frills eatery is open only for four hours every evening and is closed on Tuesdays, 'because even restaurant staff need a day off,' Patel says. His mantra for success? 'No shortcuts,' he says. 'Every ingredient is fresh; the masalas are made in-house.' The popularity of Supreme Corner has come with attendant problems and copycats have cropped up. Patel took one offender to court and won the case. 'I'm now semi-retired,' he says with the contentment of someone who's created something good in food.

Rajendra Pav Bhaji also comes up when you ask for pav bhaji vendors of repute in Pune. It was begun in 1992 by brothers Dilip and Ravindra Kamte. Second-generation owner Varun Kamte tells us

the regular pav bhaji is the top-seller here, even though they have several variations on the theme. An expansion plan to start five outlets didn't deliver the desired results and they were shut down. So, it's just the one place now.

You cannot say vada pav in Pune and not hear Garden mentioned right after. The batata vada is flat, perfectly spiced, and cooked to a golden crispness. It fits snugly into soft pav and is served with the crisp edges of batter that coats the vada and chutney. Garden Vada Pav, named after the location where it operates in the Camp area, was begun in 1970 by Kashinath Naiku. While the business has grown into a shop, the cart remains. Akshay Naiku of the third generation minds the shop while his brother mans the cart, thronged by people waiting for their vada pav fix. The vadas are mixed, shaped, battered and fried in full view of customers. Masala tak, a thin sweet-salty lassi on which float bits of boondi and shev, is another speciality at Garden.

Vada pav isn't the only hot-selling evening snack in Pune. Akhtar's Samosa rests on the success of serving a single, perfectly executed product. To indulge in these exceptional samosas, head to Saifee Street in Camp. It's a mini khau galli with shops selling kebabs, chicken pulao and juice.

Akhtar's Samosa is a tidy little shop with stylish signage and efficient staff. There's a reason why this shop draws such a crowd. The samosas are of the best quality: the covering is thin and crisp and the non-vegetarian fillings are superb. The prawn samosa, ₹20 for one, is packed with juicy prawns in a green masala and is not just delicious, but is great value for money.

The business that began in 2002 goes back six decades and more, said Akhtar Abdul Shaikh. 'It's a family tradition. My grandfather made and sold samosas—the filling was only vegetarian then—to theatres and small eateries. I've heard it said that they would make and sell close to 4,000 samosas in a day.' After Akhtar's grandfather's passing, the business withered away. 'I had worked in hotels and restaurants and had moved to Dubai,' he said. 'I couldn't let such a tradition just die. I came back and relaunched it in a slightly modernized format, adding on non-vegetarian fillings.'

His delectable samosas are affordable because, he says, he works on small margins and large volumes. 'This is a blessing from my elders. I just do the work, God puts flavour into this food,' he said, echoing a sentiment we heard owners of several other small food businesses voice as well.

Misal, vada pav, pav bhaji and even idli-sambar rule the street-food scene in Pune. Still, you can stumble upon some most enjoyable chaat at some places.

Jaishankar Pani Puri, Bhel and Chaat House in Babajaan Chowk, which stands across the road from the dargah, is one of these. It began as a humble cart operated by Motilal Devnani in the mid-1950s and is now run by Sanjay Prabhakar Yande and his wife Jayashree. She was manning the cash counter when we went to get our fill of pani puri. 'Everything is made in-house,' the pleasant Jayashree told us. 'The puris are a mix of maida and sooji and the chutney is made of dates.' Besides the excellent pani puri, Jaishankar is also known for its Dilli chaat. 'Lots of celebrities have come here,' Deepak, who has been working here for 25 years, told us.

Punekars also rate Ganesh Bhel highly. This is no longer a small operation; the outlets are sleek and there are branches across the city. At Ganesh Bhel, you can also buy packaged products and even bhel puri chutney in squeezy packs.

Around a temple dedicated to the family guru, sprawls the business of Budhani wafers. Arvind Budhani manages what he says is the oldest of the four outlets that make up this complex of wafer shops. It was set up in 1955 by Motilal Budhani, who came to Pune from Bhuj. He worked elsewhere before that and used his last salary of ₹110 to begin the business with his brothers. 'We were a large family and resources were often scarce,' Arvind Budhani said. 'The women of the house helped with making the wafers. Often, at home we ate only the edges of the potatoes left over from slicing them for wafers.'

The business has grown to an impressive scale and other outlets are now managed by Arvind's cousins. The product range has also increased. 'We have some 3,000 SKUs,' Arvind told us. The process is entirely automated and chips are exported in modern foil packaging. Punekars, however, buy their plain or cheese wafers, the top sellers here, in paper packets. The freshness of these wafers is hard to match. The manufacturers also assure customers they are free of additives and preservatives.

If Madurai has its jigarthanda, *mastani* is Pune's very own cool drink. Dozens of mastani parlours are scattered across the city.

The original is Sujata Mastani at Sadashiv Peth. It was begun by Sharadrao Kondhalkar, who started off selling hand-churned ice cream. Later, he introduced the drink that has now come to be known as mastani. Ice cream parlours of that time were serving what was called ice cream cold drink, cold milk with ice topped off with ice cream. Kondhalkar blended the ice cream into the milk, and the rich cooler that is famous in Pune was born. The mango mastani is the best-selling flavour here. Over the years, various other flavours, from guava to fig and gulkand, have been added on.

Food-loving visitors to Pune will invariably carry back the Shrewsbury biscuit the city is known for. While it's made by several bakeries here, it's Kayani that's synonymous with this buttery biscuit, believed to have its origins in the eponymous English town.

We also went to the Irani bakery on East Street in Pune's cantonment area and were met with a long queue of customers waiting for their turn to buy the famous biscuits. They are made of Amul butter, flour and sugar—eschewing the eggs the original recipe called for—moulded by hand and baked. Kayani is also known for its vanilla cake and cheese papdi. Set up in 1955 by Hormuz and Khodyar Irani, this traditional bakery is now in the hands of Rustom Irani, of the third generation. The lockdowns in 2020 and 2021 hit this family-run business hard. Through these periods, even while they could not make or sell their wares, Rustom Irani went to the bakery every day to kindle the wood-fired ovens. Pre-Covid Kayani was selling 500 kilos of its famous biscuits every day. The sight of waiting customers assured us they would soon return to that.

Less hyped than Kayani, but no less respected, is Hindustan Bakery in Shanivarpeth. Begun by Vinayak Mehendale in the 1950s, it's now run by his son, Sanjeev Mehendale. With its tiny storefront, it is popular for its bread and biscuits. But it's best known for its vegetable pattice, crisp and flaky with a mixed vegetable filling that packs a punch. We walked through the back-end where the ovens were diesel-fired and most processes were still carried out manually by skilled workers.

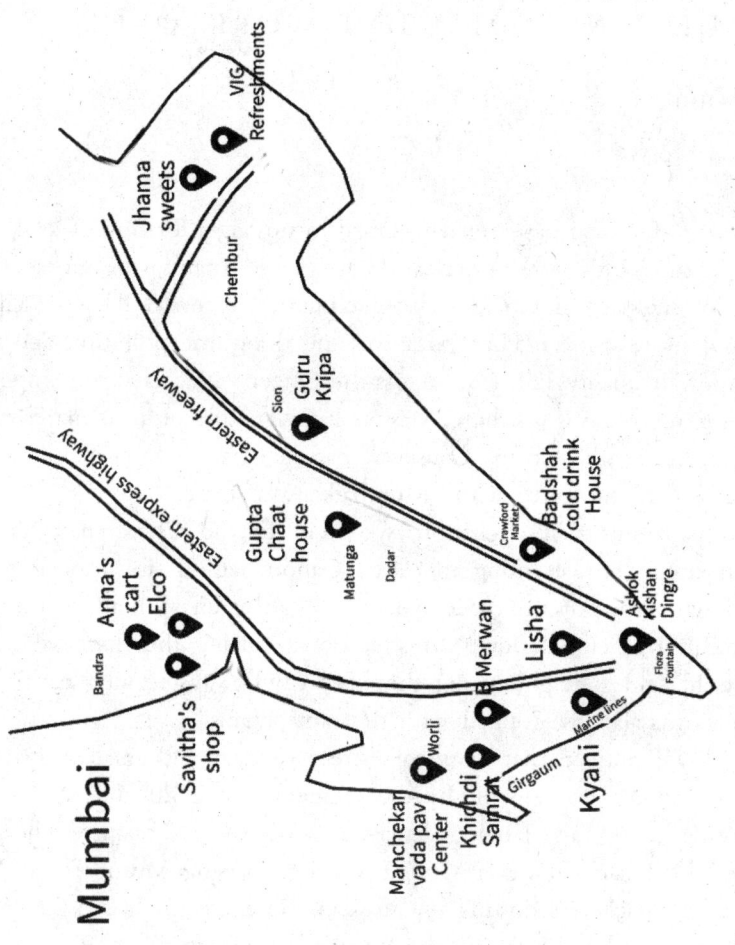

FUELLING A MASSIVE WORKFORCE

Mumbai

*M*umbai has been enveloped in nostalgia for one of us. Priya spent a decade here in her salad days as a journalist. On our last trip, after the second Covid wave, maximum city evoked less nostalgia and more distress. There was, for one thing, the pollution and the poor air quality. The view across the Queen's Necklace, remembered as gorgeous, was just haze. Massive infrastructure projects marred the landscape. Still, Colaba Causeway had kept its seedy charm and the never-say-die spirit of the Mumbaikar was intact.

On our first afternoon, we went to the Chhatrapati Shivaji Terminus area wanting to eat at Canon, famous for its pav bhaji downtown. But the place where we had eaten so many late-night meals had closed down. 'It shut down during the first lockdown itself,' said a neighbouring shopkeeper who was serving pav bhaji, plus masala dosa topped with the same bhaji.

We noticed that Mumbai's street vendors and small shops had been more severely hit by the pandemic of 2020 and 2021 than other cities. Sad at being deprived of Canon pav bhaji, we headed to the Khau Galli near SNDT College, passing Mumbai's aspiring young cricketers dotting the maidan. Here, we had a satisfying pav bhaji at Lisha, which has stood in the same place since 1971. Momo stalls, desi-style pizza outlets and chaat vendors also serve Khau Galli customers.

Perhaps because of the size and population of Mumbai, every downtown pocket and suburb has its street-food hubs and these have a certain sameness about them. Every hub has the dosa vendors, panipuri-walas, bhelpuri sellers, sandwich shops—all the dishes that represent the street-food culture of the endlessly bustling city. We decided, therefore, to track down some exceptionally good or unique dishes and also simply to traipse through various quarters of the city, stopping now and then to taste something or to chat with shop owners.

While downtown, we had to go take a look at Flora Fountain, the graceful edifice and heritage structure. We strolled down Rustom Sidhwa Marg, at the end of which was a cluster of street-food carts serving office-goers in the area.

Ashok Kishan Dingre has been selling sandwiches here since 1976. It's the uniquely Mumbai sandwich: Wibs white bread, tomato, potato, onion, cucumber, beetroot and green chutney. You can have it toasted over coal in a handheld toaster and with cheese if you want. Ashok told us about surviving the lockdown. 'I sent my staff home just before the first lockdown and they came back in September 2020. It's hard to find and keep efficient staff and I'm glad my boys are back.'

A visit to Crawford Market was a must and so was a drink at Badshah Cold Drink House. Begun by Meherban Irani in 1905, it's now run admirably by his 85-year-old daughter Yasmin Irani. The must-have here is the royal falooda, with rose syrup, sabza, vermicelli, milk and ice cream. Purists are likely to look askance at the chocolate, butterscotch and black currant variants that have come later. A Badshah falooda hits the spot after a shopping spree in Crawford Market.

Later, we went to Girgaum, taking in its old-world air, past shops selling traditional attire, brassware and jewellery. We went to Khichdi Samrat, which has remained largely unchanged in appearance since its inception in 1950 by Brij Kishore Agarwal. Now run by Mahesh and Atul Agarwal of the third generation, the Kathiawadi Khichdi is a speciality here. 'All the masala are made in-house,' Atul said, playing gracious host and urging us to eat some more. Khichdi Samrat serves

FUELLING A MASSIVE WORKFORCE

16 varieties of khichdi, all of them scrumptious and comforting.

While the internet has reams on 'Mumbai's best vada pav', we went to some of our old favourites. Aram opposite CST seemed this time to be merely resting on its past glory —the shop was begun in the 1940s—as did Shree Krishna Vada Pav in Dadar of similar vintage.

Our recommendation for some really good vada pav would be Manchekar Vada Pav Centre at BDD Chawl in Worli. Santosh Manchekar mans the small streetside shop started by his grandfather in the late 1960s. The freshness of his vadas—nicely spiced potato in a gram-flour batter, slapped piping hot onto soft pav—makes this a satisfying treat.

Also in BDD Chawl is a little kebab business that seemed to be of another time and place. It's not easy to find, occupying a courtyard tucked away between chawls no. 103 and 104. There is no shop nor stall or signboard. Every evening Shanti Mohan Unkeri, seated on a makeshift platform, sets out his wares—tiny cubes of mutton on skewers—and begins to grill them over coal. His wife, seated on a charpoy alongside, applies green chutney on pav and the grilled meat is placed on it. 'Eat it hot, otherwise there's no mazaa,' Unkeri said, handing us this humble snack. Keep inquiring for Mohan bhai kebab if you want to get a taste of it.

Bade Miya is, of course, the brand that made slumming it and eating *baida* roti standing on the street a cool thing. Now, it's grown to four sit-down restaurants in Colaba and we cannot but lament the drop in quality. Somehow, Mohan Unkeri's effort seemed far more laudable.

Another such nondescript venture we stumbled upon was in the pleasant residential areas of Bandra. Here, on Chimbai Road, the narrow front of a house becomes a buzzing counter serving hot breakfast from 7.30 a.m. to 10.30 a.m. every morning. It's known simply as Savitha's shop. Savitha, wearing a nightie and assisted by the women of the family, rolls out tiny puris, selling 12 of these with a potato curry for a mere ₹15. 'People can eat their fill for a small price,' she tells us. The business this enterprising and caring woman began in 2000 also sells poha, upma and vada.

In Bandra, we decided to drop in for a morning pani puri at Elco, with a long-established reputation in the chaat business. It's been around since 1975. Owner Parshu Bhagnani told us the pani puri here is made in the Sindhi style; the sweet and sour pani is ice-cold and the filling of the puri is a combination of potato and moong sprouts. Wandering about Bandra, we stopped at Anna's cart near Amarson's. Like countless South Indians who arrived in the City of Dreams seeking a fortune, Ganapathy, whom the locals know only as Anna, came here from Pudukottai in Tamil Nadu. His vada, served with two chutneys and sambar, sold from a mobile cart is as good as you'll eat anywhere in Tamil Nadu. True to the script, Ganapathy lives in Dharavi. 'I've been selling idlis and vada since early 2000. I've been pretty much in the same spot, moving across the road sometimes or few metres this way or that. And, yes, paying off the cops is an everyday thing,' he said matter-of-factly.

Matunga, with its flower stalls and South Indian condiment shops, is also great for exploring. The second-hand books for sale on the pavements around King's Circle can throw up gems.

In this suburb, where the lanes are still tree-lined, is Gupta Chaat House. Owner Vijay Gupta's story is a typically Mumbai rags-to-riches tale. 'I had a difficult life, struggling since the age of 15,' he told us with candour. 'I was your average Mumbai vendor, selling everything from corn to underwear. I drove rickshaws for a time.' He began the chaat business on the street in 1995, then moving into a garage that he had to give up for redevelopment. In 2013, he opened the shop with its colourful menu boards listing nearly 150 items: besides chaat, there are sandwiches, pizzas and frankies in all sorts of combinations.

Vijay Chaat House's specialities, though, are sev puri and bhelpuri. Experimenting with the ingredients at hand, Vijay Gupta came up with a toast sevpuri that, he says, brought him fame and attention. His customers now include Bollywood film personalities like Mahesh Manjrekar. 'I'm in a good place now,' Vijay Gupta said. His success is a nod to the entrepreneurial spirit of Mumbai. We could take or leave the much-hyped toast sevpuri, but the pani puri here was very good.

Guru Kripa in Sion also draws chaat lovers by the hundred. Founder Vishindas Wadhwa's family had come to India as refugees. In 1975, he began selling Sindhi-style snacks from a basic stall. In time, the business grew and it's now a massive operation with counters for chaat, sweets, packed snacks, including pani puri as a DIY kit. It's the samosa chhole that earned most fame for Guru Kripa and there was a time before multiplexes and popcorn when this eatery supplied thousands of samosas to movie theatres. And for an entire generation, an aloo samosa from Guru Kripa and a chai during intermission completed the movie experience, much as caramel popcorn does today.

Mumbai is so vast, you could live here for years and yet not know its every aspect. That's how the trip to Chembur became such a discovery. This is where most of the refugees from Sindh Pakistan came and settled after Partition. So, the food culture has a distinctly Sindhi flavour.

We went to Jhama Sweets, which was begun in 1947 by the Jhamamulla family. They sold their now famous Karachi halwa, pista barfi, gulab jamun and gajar ka halwa to begin with. Now there are dozens of confections and 13 branches spread across Mumbai.

Down the road from this landmark sweet shop is Vig Refreshments, which has been in existence since the 1960s. Eating their popular tikki chhole we chatted with owner Praveen Arora, whose maternal grandfather Sevaram started the business. 'He was from Karachi and sailed to Mumbai,' Praveen said. 'After my grandfather's passing, my mother and father ran Vig and now I've stepped in.' Besides tikki chhole—a crisp potato cutlet, topped with spicy chickpea curry and sweet chutney—Vig is known for an array of Sindhi snacks, including dal *pakwan*, a crisp fried bread served with chana dal. 'Taste and quality depend on a skilled staff,' Praveen said. 'This isn't a cookie-cutter café, there are no formulae. The quality of what we serve

depends on the hand of the cooks.' He prides himself on retaining staff even in trying times. 'Our youngest staff has been with us for 15 years, the oldest for more than 40.'

Valuing staff is another thing we saw and appreciated in many small food businesses. Other eateries worth checking out in this belt of Chembur are Gopal's Mutton and Chicken for their Sindhi meat dishes, and Satu for its decadently rich jalebis.

Since nostalgia was the theme of our Mumbai sojourn, we had to go to our favourite Irani cafés and bakeries.

Our first stop was Kyani at Marine Lines for a breakfast of *akuri* and pav. It was founded in 1904 by Khodram Marzeban. The Parsi-style scrambled eggs, kheema and *sali boti* are more recent additions to the menu. For the longest time, it was bread, biscuits and cakes that Kyani specialized in. To linger over strong, sweet Irani chai here is to experience a rapidly disappearing and once quintessential part of Mumbai's food culture, the Irani café. So these places are more than just eateries; they are heritage spaces valiantly staying afloat in turbulent times.

FUELLING A MASSIVE WORKFORCE

The other Irani business holding on similarly is B Merwan outside Grant Road Station, which has been serving bun maska and mawa cakes to three generations of Mumbaikars. Begun in 1914 by Boman Merwan, it is now in the hands of the third generation and Sharosh Nowshir told us about the changes the pandemic had caused at this vintage bakery. When we went after the pandemic, Merwan was offering only takeaways and customers had to stand behind a rope tied across the front of the shop to pick up their orders, served wrapped in white paper and tied up with string.

Sharosh let us cross the rope and enter the empty café. The chairs, imported from Czechoslovakia, were stacked up in a corner. The Italian marble-topped tables at which students, families and couples sat and ate veg puffs were stored away. Mirrors in lovely frames still adorned the walls. The baking continued to be done in old-fashioned ovens, but they churned out far fewer items than in pre-Covid times. 'How can I open for dining?' Sharosh asked. 'The average spend here is so low and without enough customers, we won't be able to meet the overheads.' He added that the prices had been fixed so everyone could afford to eat here. We were deeply touched when he said, 'Blessings are more important than money.' And then, 'I'm sorry I'm not even able to offer you a cup of our tea.' Many things had changed, but not the hospitality here.

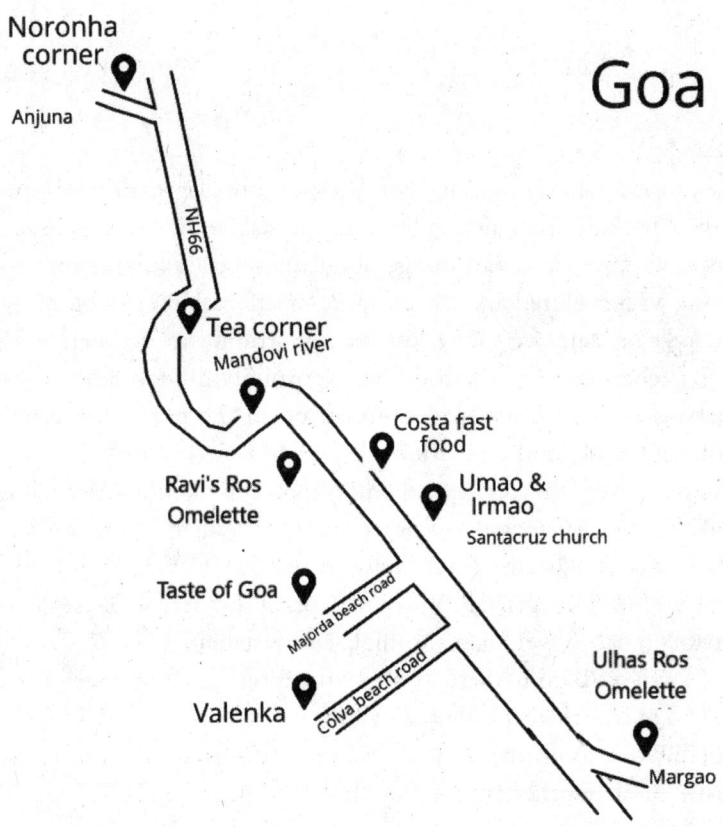

WHERE THE LOCALS GO

Goa

The seaside state is one big holiday spot, popular with everyone, from backpacking foreigners harbouring nostalgia for the hippie era and upscale travellers who lounge about its super-luxury resorts, to domestic visitors lured by the prospect of affordable alcohol and a surfeit of bars. And we rarely lose an opportunity to go there.

Goa's charms are many, from the opportunity to grab beach time to soaking in its laidback-ness, summed up in the phrase 'sussegad', and of course its food and drink.

It has, over the years, become home to stylish restaurants specializing in gourmet fare from everywhere. Then, there are the beach shacks which are 'shacks' only in name, for at these you can eat everything from grilled lobster to Goan fish curry at prices that aren't too much lower than the high-end restaurants.

Far removed from these tourist attractions are the street carts known as *gaddo*s, rickety little stalls and hole-in-the-wall shops selling uniquely Goan foods that not all visitors to the state discover. These are truly local hubs, often coming alive for only a few hours every night, where Goans gather for their street-food fix. Their offerings can be more substantial than the snacks and chaats that make up the street-food repertoire elsewhere. This is especially because the stars of Goan street food like *ros* omelette and cutlet pao are built on bread.

Goa's bread-making tradition goes back to its Portuguese colonial ties. New Christian converts, particularly in Salcete, learned the technique from the Jesuits. It helped that members of the Chardo caste in the area produced the *sur* or toddy that gives Goan breads its characteristic rise and flavour. Today, fewer and fewer *poders*, the neighbourhood bakers, are using toddy, but their breads continue to be celebrated and are at the core of many street-food businesses.

Meat and chorizo, another ingredient that goes back to colonial times and European sausage-making traditions, also feature prominently among street-food stall offerings.

The cultural distinctions that influence Goan culinary traditions are also visible in the realm of street food; the Hindu vendors specialize in eggs and chicken, while the Catholic entrepreneurs serve beef and pork. On the unique street map of this sunny state they exist in perfect harmony.

We drove through the dark, winding roads of Colva to meet Caetano Tavares. He used to be a tiatrist, playing comedy roles in local theatre. He is now a vendor of food, but has lost none of his love of the theatrical. Chatting with him, we ask him what time Valanka, his shop on the Colva beach road, shuts down. He pulls out a white board leaning against a wall and turns it over. 'Sorry, Sausage Bread is Over', it reads, reflecting the quirkiness of the place that is one of the area's most famous *choris* pao makers.

The choris pao is the quintessential Goan snack, combining two of the state's most loved food items, served in many forms across the board and even inspiring innovations such as chorizo kulcha. In its pure and basic form, it is choris, the Goan sausage cured with vinegar and spices, served between fresh pao. 'From Canacona to Mapusa, this is the best choris pao,' Tavares declares, with pride, not arrogance. His acting job didn't pay enough and in 1993 he decided to sell choris pao. A well-wisher lent him a cycle and he plied his wares on the beach and near schools.

Now, Valanka, named after Tavares's teenage daughter, is an extension of his home, a sprawling building with a large front yard. The stall is decorated in an unselfconscious style that is pure kitsch. The limited seating is made up of park benches. The entire wall is covered in pictures of religious icons, a massive footballer cutout,

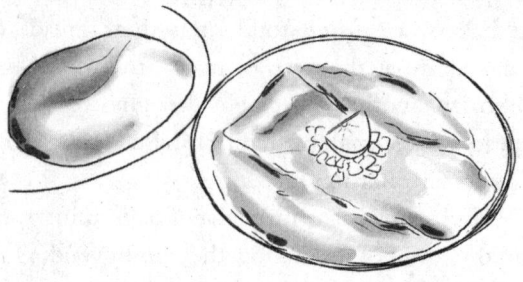

and scenes from some of Tavares's plays from the past. A candle burns before a small altar. Fairy lights are strung up and the menu lists just three items: Sausage Bread ₹50, 100 Sausages for ₹450, and Coca Cola (that comes in old-fashioned bottles).

Valanka, then, is the ultimate specialist focusing on a single offering and making it with a focus on quality that is surprising for so modest a venture. Caetano and his wife Santana make the choris at home, buying the pork from the same trusted butcher for years. He points to the food safety certificates he has hanging on the wall. The pao comes from the local poder. It's served warm and fresh, with a generous serving of the spicy, pungent choris inside. Caetano attends to customers and manages parking for the vehicles that draw up outside. Santana serves the choris pao from their home, through a grill-covered window. We certainly thought their offering was top-quality, and so do Valanka's loyal customers. Goans living abroad pack up and take vast amounts when they go back after a visit, to satisfy their choris-pao cravings when far from home.

Given the popularity of his fare, Caetano has been asked why he won't expand his business—perhaps put up some umbrellas in the front yard and become a tourist attraction. 'I have enough, maybe no money in the bank, but I don't want more,' he said. This is another sentiment we find echoed by small food vendors who are proud of what they do and have found contentment in that.

Signs for ros omelette can be spotted at eateries across Goa, as common in tourist spots as they are in busy hubs frequented by locals. It's simple and satisfying, using basic ingredients, eggs and curry. Some say the dish probably emerged from a clever recycling of leftover *xacuti*, a distinctly Goan gravy, velvety with a signature spice blend and coconut. An omelette, spiked with onion and chillies, is cut up into large bits and soaked in this gravy, the ros, and you have this street-food star, always served with Goan bread, either pao or poi, the latter made with wheat and bran.

At 8 p.m. on a weekday night, Ravi, owner of the eponymous Ravi's Ros Omelette in Panjim, is busy, working at machine-like speed. Earlier, he served up his famous plates from near the majestic Immaculate Church. Now he's moved to a grimy lane close to the new Municipal Market. It's one of Panjim's little khau gullies and the *gaddo*s line both sides.

At Ravi's, fresh omelettes are made on a large tava and the pao is warmed on it as well. The crowds jostle around the tiny cart, ordering plates of ros omelette or pao with chicken gizzard. Ravi takes orders, dishes out the food, collects the cash, and waves hurried greetings to customers, many of whom appear to be long-time acquaintances. He also gives instructions to his two assistants. When a ros omelette order comes in, the omelette is placed in the plate and the gravy is ladled in from a massive vessel—it's topped off with finely chopped onion and a wedge of lime and served up with bread.

Some customers pick up the stainless-steel plates and occupy the plastic tables behind the stall, others take the food away, mostly on their way home from work. Nearly all are regulars. One of them told us he now works in Bangalore and the ros omelette lures him back to Ravi's stall every time he returns to Panjim. According to Ravi, who has been selling ros omelette for 25 years, it's the unvarying flavour and the quality that keeps his customers coming back.

'You won't find ros omelette anywhere except in Goa and I am happy and proud that my customers keep coming back,' he told us as we vied for his attention amid the steady stream of customers. Ravi makes the ros at home with the help of his wife. 'The garam masala is important and we roast the spices at home and have it ground. The coconut is another key ingredient. His menu board also lists egg *bhurji*, chicken xacuti and bread omelette, but the ros omelette is the obvious money-spinner. On any given day, Ravi sells 300-plus plates of one of Goa's most loved dishes. He's closed one day in a week. When is that? Any day I feel like, said this hugely popular street-food vendor, summing up the easy way of Goa.

Taste of Goa at Majorda is another place that's famous for ros omelette and a hit with locals of that area. If you are in Margao, try the fare at Ulhaas Ros Omelette Centre near the Bank of Baroda.

Drive towards the football ground in Santa Cruz, a short distance from Panjim, on any given evening and you cannot miss a gaddo around which gathers a crowd, some waiting for their orders, others tucking in, seated on the few plastic stools alongside. Avilino and Nancy Costa have been running this business, known simply as Costas, for 10 years. Their special is the cutlet pao, another of Goa's favourite gaddo offerings. Fillets of meat, both chicken and beef, are marinated in Goan vinegar and a distinct *jirem-mirem*, cumin and pepper, spice mix. The Costas do this prepping at home and bring the meat to their stall. There, it's dipped in egg and *rava* and shallow-fried to golden brown. Then it's slipped between a split pao, topped with some shredded cabbage and served with no other adornment. Customers can ask for a spoon of gravy, chicken or beef, to moisten the bread before the cutlet is placed on it.

When we went to meet the Costas, the shy and soft-spoken Nancy was chatting with one of her regulars, Mabel. The young working professional told us she lives in the next village and makes it a point to come here twice a week for the cutlet pao. 'When I worked in Dubai for a while, this is one of the things I missed most about home,' she told us. 'It's the best, including the pao, which is a special one for cutlets.'

This loyalty, even affection, that Goans feel for their local street food and those who make them was a recurring theme during our travels in the state. It's certainly what keeps these small enterprises running and allows them to survive the vagaries of business. They are also unique in the way that families participate in the making and serving of the food. At Costas, Nancy preps at home and takes orders and collects the cash, while Avilino mans the frying station, flipping hundreds of cutlets through the evening. Besides the cutlet pao, Costa also serves fish croquette, chicken lollipop and beef chops, from 6 p.m. to 10 p.m. every day. Such is the popularity of these, most items are sold out by 8 p.m. Under the shadow of the white-walled Santa Cruz church are two other gaddos, Umao and Irmao, big brother and small brother, which also sell cutlet pao and other snacks, besides *sorpotel* from a massive aluminium vessel.

In North Goa, a food truck run by the Noronhas on the Anjuna Mapusa Road enjoys popularity with locals and tourists in the area. So much so, the spot where the truck is parked is known as Noronha Corner. You can order cutlet pao, beef croquette, sorpotel and other Goan dishes here.

Goan sweets stand apart in the world of Indian sweets. They rarely use milk or milk products or dry fruit, and most have been handed down from Portuguese culinary traditions. *Bebinca* is probably the best known of these, but stocked in the unassuming sweet shops of Goa are dozens more, few familiar to those outside the state. There are *bolinhas*, crunchy-soft coconut cookies, and *bolo de batica*, a semolina and coconut cake, which can also be baked in a pastry shell. Others have more earthy flavours, such as the *shivroli*, rice-flour strands topped with jaggery, and *doce de grao*, known simply as doce. It's a fudge made with chana dal and sugar, with a gorgeous texture and flavour. *Perad* is guava cheese with a fruity intensity and *pinaca* is shaped from toasted rice that's powdered and mixed with jaggery.

One of the places to buy them all at one go is an unpretentious shop called the Tea Centre, near the old Municipal Market in Panjim, just around the corner from the fish market. It was started in 1966 as a store selling tea and coffee powder by the father of Floyd Pereira, who now runs the shop. At 9 a.m., even before the shutters go up, a crowd begins to mill outside Tea Centre. It's a grocery store and the shelves are lined with canned products and spice powders. But it's the fresh savouries and sweets that most of the morning customers are here for. Interestingly, the Pereiras don't make any of the items. They all come from different suppliers, each specializing in one thing. They arrive one after another in cardboard cartons: bebinca, packets of bolinhas, individual servings of shivroli, and dark, sausage-shaped pinaca.

'Wait for five minutes,' Floyd tells a customer. 'Fresh batica is on the way.' This small business runs on the principle of a supportive community. 'Our suppliers support us and we look after them,' Floyd tells us. Many supply their homemade wares exclusively to Tea Centre. Besides the popular sweets, prawn *rissois*—seafood encased in a soft, crumb-fried crescent—beef samosas, chops and croquettes and chicken pan rolls all fly off the shelves within minutes of arriving. This tiny shop, its signboard intact from the 1960s, plays an important part in keeping the sweet traditions of Goa alive. Few people make these at home these days, but they can always enjoy a square of doce with their morning tea as long as stores like Tea Centre continue to source and sell it, taking pride in the specialities of Goa.

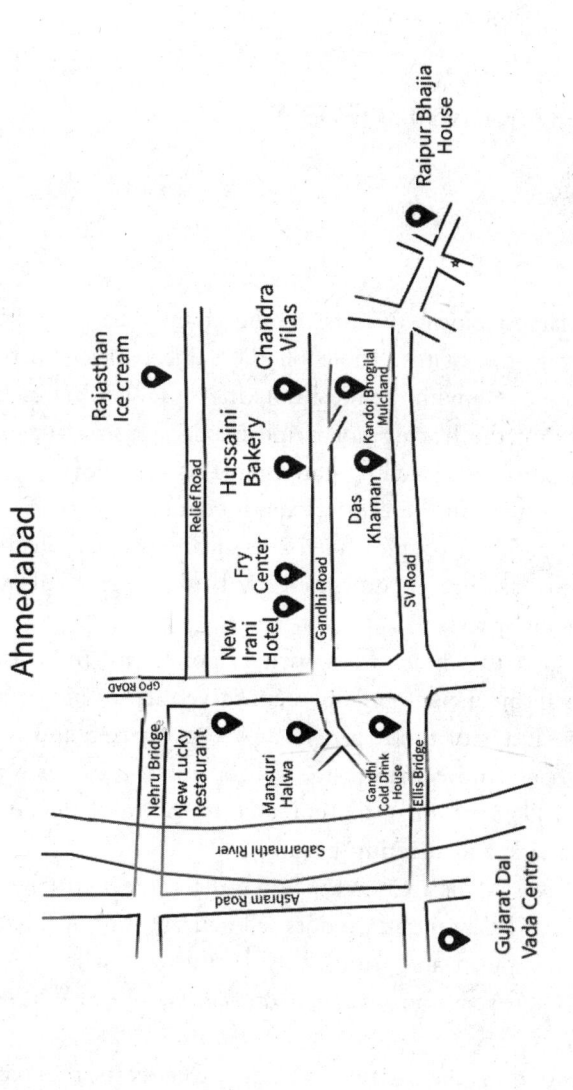

JALEBI FAFDA AND BUN MASKA, CHAI: THE BREAKFAST ICONS

Ahmedabad

Gujarat's largest city is the first in the country to get UNESCO World Heritage site status. While on the subject of superlatives, it's also possibly the one with the most honking-obsessed drivers. Bracing ourselves against the blaring horns and maniacal traffic, we explored the city's old quarters, catching glimpses of its past glory scripted by Sultan Ahmed Shah in the early fifteenth century. Sellers of spangled clothes and sparkling bangles filled the square, part of Bhadra Fort, a complex which once encompassed royal palaces, graceful mosques, gates and open spaces.

We stopped to admire from various points the Indo Saracenic architecture of this ancient settlement, its carved arches and latticework windows. A cluster of food carts occupy one quarter, and a narrow lane leads to an entire market for kebabs, mutton samosas and fry centres. Teen Darwaja, once the entrance to the royal square, is now a local landmark and meeting point.

Beyond it is Manek Chowk, the jewellers' street that becomes a street-food market by night. Vendors sell generic pani puri and chaat, pav bhaji, tava pulav and fruit 'shots' in the city where alcohol is prohibited. There's also an Asharfi Kulfi stall, by one of Ahmedabad's oldest kulfi makers.

Towering over the maze of Manek Chowk is the old Stock Exchange, its colonial architecture somewhat incongruous amidst the *pols*, gated residential streets. The building is now abandoned and at its gates vendors sell *chawana*, Ahmedabad's street snack of spicy *farsan* served with shreds of raw papaya.

The 'revived' Sabarmati River divides Ahmedabad into old and new, the latter a sprawl of bungalows, shopping centres and high-rises. Serving residents here are hundreds of fast-food outlets and street carts, more modern than in the old city. This, we realized, often means gussying up traditional dishes with Amul cheese, mayonnaise and peri peri sauce. The Sabarmati Ashram, founded by Mahatma Gandhi, is situated on a tranquil stretch here. Whether or not on account of his advocacy of vegetarianism, it is practised by a large number of eateries in the city. We were also impressed by the range of non-vegetarian food that is available in the city, connecting it to its past when it was the hub of a thriving Sultanate.

For our first breakfast in Ahmedabad, we went to Chandra Vilas on Gandhi Road, not far from Rattan Pol. It's famous for its jalebi-*fafda*. It is a Dussehra tradition in these parts to eat fafda and jalebi. Nowhere is the clamour for this gram-flour savoury and the syrup-soaked sweet more evident in the city than at Chandra Vilas. This 120-year-old eatery claims the credit for introducing this combination, now a cliché for Gujarati-street breakfast, to Ahmedabad.

Chandra Vilas began life as a teashop when, at the turn of the last century, Chimanlal Joshi began to sell tea and snacks. His entrepreneurial spirit saw the business soon become a little restaurant in this part of the old city, which was then a bustling commercial hub. Chandra Vilas served a basic Gujarati thali, affordable to all, as also the now famous fafda and jalebi. Later generations of the Joshi family continued to preserve the legacy of a humble eatery which had hosted Sardar Vallabhbhai Patel and catered to Raj Kapoor whenever he was working in Ahmedabad.

Communal riots in 2002 saw Chandra Vilas burn down. While the shop reopened to sell snacks and tea, it would take another 10 years before it could be fully refurbished. Step in here now, and the chequered floor and smoke-stained interiors would have you believe this is how the shop was several decades ago. It is such a piece of

Ahmedabad's heritage now that food walks and cultural tours almost always bring people here for the signature breakfast. While we were there, we spotted a group, clicking away at the food on their plates. The fafda, made from a simple besan paste, takes skill to be turned into long thin strips that shatter at a touch. Bits of the soft dough are pressed and spread by hand on a wooden board, then lifted out deftly and slipped into hot oil. The jalebis are made at the entrance to the restaurant, an assembly line of golden swirls that move from oil to waiting sugar syrup. The fafda is served with a sweet *kadhi*, a small mound of shredded raw papaya and fried chillies. Chandra Vilas is the most famous place for this much-loved breakfast combination. But you can buy fafda in farsan shops across the city.

Vying with fafda-jalebi for Ahmedabad's favourite breakfast is another combination: bun maska and strong, sweet tea. It happens also to be the city's favourite evening snack, going by the crowds at New Irani Hotel on Salapose Road, near Teen Darwaja. It is no longer new, having been in existence for over 60 years. Reminiscent of Mumbai's Irani cafés, this one was born from the friendship between Yakub Patel and his Iranian friend. This popular café is now run by Moin Patel of the third generation. During the first lockdown, he oversaw a major renovation of the place; thankfully he retained its vintage charm. The demand for the bun maska is evident from the fact that one worker has been assigned only to slice and butter hundreds of buns at quick speed. He stops from time to time to sharpen his knife and then goes about slicing the soft, sweet buns in half. He then dips into a large stainless-steel drum holding white butter that's whipped and light, the maska, and liberally slathers both sides of the bun. It's then cut into four fat slices and served to customers who throng the place. Many of them dip the bun into their cups of tea. Besides bun maska, New Irani Restaurant is known also for its unpretentious but excellent mutton *bhuna* and other non-vegetarian dishes to be eaten with butter chapati.

Another place, also in the old city, known for its bun-maska and chai is New Lucky Restaurant in Lal Darwaja, a short distance from

BAZAAR BITES

Sidi Saiyyed Mosque, with its much-photographed jali or latticework. Lucky, haunt of journalists and minor politicians, sells everything from milkshakes to sandwiches, but its top-selling items are the bun-maska and chai. It's something M.F. Husain enjoyed whenever he came to the city and he showed his love for the place by leaving behind a prized painting, which occupies pride of place on one wall. Fun fact: New Lucky Restaurant has been built on, or rather around, a burial ground. Owner Krishnan Kutti learned this only after he acquired the land. He chose to spread his restaurant around the sarcophagi, each surrounded by a low steel fence. Every morning, the staff place fresh flowers on the tombs draped in bright cloths. It's now part of the café lore of Ahmedabad.

Gol Limda is a well-known landmark in the old quarters of Ahmedabad. Das Khaman at this busy circle enjoys similar fame. This is the original and the headquarters of a street-food brand that has grown to become a chain with eight outlets in the city. It's come a long way since Pitambar Das began the business of selling Surti khaman from a *khomcha* in 1922. Today, a TV screen at every outlet plays a glossy version of the history of Das Khaman with shots of celebrity chefs tucking into the fluffy squares of steamed gram flour. Also, true to the Gujarati spirit of innovation and entrepreneurship, Das Khaman now sells toast khaman, green fry khaman and *tam tam* khaman, along with Chinese samosa and *patra*. Pitambar Das sold only the traditional khaman, made with the help of his wife Nanduba, from hand-ground gram flour. His product came to be known as Das Kaka nu khaman, hence the present name of the brand. The mobile vending business became a shop in 1950 at Gol Limda.

Now in the hands of the fourth generation, Das Khaman is run by Hemal Thakkar and Kunal Thakkar, who have led the modernization and expansion. Scaling often dilutes the experience of revered brands. But Das Khaman still manages to be the top seller of khaman in Ahmedabad. The Gol Limda outlet we went to gets so crowded there's a token system in place. Das Khaman's popularity is justified. The classic version is excellent, especially when eaten hot, soft, perfectly seasoned, with just a hint of sweetness. We enjoyed our plate of sada khaman very much.

If you enter the Bhadra area, your nose will lead you to Bhatiyar Galli. It is lined with stalls and small eateries selling chicken, mutton, fish and organ meats, grilled over coals, deep-fried in dark karhais and curried in vast handis. The smell of cooking fills the air as dusk falls on the old city. The owners of these businesses claim theirs is a 600-year-old heritage, their ancestors, the *bhatiyar*s, who were innkeepers and cooks, moving here when Ahmed Shah came to build his magnificent city. Some of these stalls deal in the *barah* handi, lining up mutton and chicken dishes in 12 large vessels. The 'fry centre' is another Ahmedabad fixture, and they serve kheema, brain, *gurda-kaleji*, all tawa-fried in copious amounts of oil and masala, served with rotis or buns.

We went to Bhatiyar Gali in search of the original Bera Samosa. As is the case with well-known brands that spawn lookalikes, there are several Bera outlets across the city. We were assured that this one in the depths of Bhatiyar Gali was the original, by Anish Shaikh, who managed the business begun by Ibrahim Bhai Shaikh 90 years ago.

'As the family grew, it was agreed that various relatives would begin other branches,' he says, in between shouting out orders for kebabs and samosas, the two items the grubby eatery serves and is famous for. One bite of the samosa, with its crisp shell encasing minced mutton spiced with onions, green chillies and coriander, and we realize the fame is well deserved. It's a truly delightful samosa and in normal times Bera would cater anything between 500 and 1,000 samosas for weddings and other large gatherings. The mutton kebab, a deep-fried kofta spicier than the samosa, is the other speciality here. Anish Shaikh says spices ground in-house and the best quality of mutton bought every day from the Municipal Market in Mirzapur are the keys to Bera's success and reputation. The samosas are made in small batches through the day, ensuring freshness. Customers, us included, are willing to wait while a new batch is fried. The vegetarian counterpart of this is a similarly crisp samosa stuffed with spiced potato. They are called Navtad samosa, taking their name from Navtad Pol, the old residential quarters, where they were first made and sold. These small and delicious samosas are now sold across Ahmedabad, but customers still make their way to the old city to buy from vendors all occupying one stretch of a street.

Bapu, Thakkar and Darbar are some of the prominent names here. Darbar is the pioneer, says Sunil Bhai, as regulars refer to him. His maternal grandfather Mojilal Umeedram, a theatre artiste, began making and selling these samosas, believed to have their origins in Surat. As his business grew, others followed suit and the samosas got their name.

Darbar also sells Punjabi-style samosas and Jain kachori, which contains no onion or garlic. But the Navtad samosa, accompanied by a sweet chutney, is the hot seller with people coming to buy them by the kilo. They can also be bought uncooked to be fried later. Given this popularity, it would be tempting to scale and grow. 'Why take on those headaches?' Sunil Bhai asks. 'It's good to look after this shop, meet every single customer, and make sure the samosa is of the best quality.' It's a sentiment we often heard echoed by vendors of street food who seem to have found complete contentment, no matter how small their business.

Bhatiyar Galli is packed with stalls that all sell fairly similar

JALEBI FAFDA AND BUN MASKA, CHAI: THE BREAKFAST ICONS

dishes: seekh kebab, bhuna gosht, fried fish and tawa-fried offal. Eat in one or the other, there isn't too much to choose from. But A1 near Teen Darwaja has a unique offering. This is the *silli* gosht; it's meat on a stick. The meat is marinated in a spice mix, skewered and crumbed. At the time of serving, it's dipped in egg wash and deep fried. The meat is tender and the egg coating gives it a pleasing, crunchy texture. It's a hole-in-the-wall shop and the frying happens in a mobile cart outside it. The business has survived and thrived ever since Haji Unnat Bhai started it 40 years ago. Now it's run by his descendants, including Shabbir Husain Shaikh. Besides the silli gosht, A1 also serves the elegantly christened *nargisi* kofta, fragrant minced meat wrapped around a morsel of hard-boiled egg and deep-fried. A1's offerings are served with a slightly sweet bun and a thin, green chutney. It's a hearty, affordable snack or meal for those who come to shop in this vibrant bazaar.

Gujarat must surely be one of the largest consumers of vadas and bhajias in the country. We didn't see these deep-fried delights being sold by weight in too many other places.

One of Ahmedabad's most-loved bhajia vendors is Raipur Bhajia House. It stands at a busy traffic junction over which towers the heritage Raipur Darwaja, one of the gates into Ahmed Shah's city. It's a small street-food hub now, with several carts selling *chorafali*, another popular snack in these parts. These are light and flaky strips of gram flour, similar to fafda, scattered with chilli powder and spices. The enterprising Somabhai Motibhai Patel started the business of supplying fried snacks to the travellers who passed this way in the early 1930s. Mill workers in the area also made up a large segment of his customers. It is now run by his descendants, Subhash and Mahendra Patel, who went ahead and trademarked Raipur Bhajia House—possibly a first in these parts for a small food business—in a bid to thwart the countless imitations that have sprung up across the city. They've chosen to keep the legacy alive and many of the old practices as well. The bhajias are still fried on coal fires. The gram-flour batter is made fresh several times in a day by skilled workers, while others man the massive karhais. This is one place that does not serve any chutney or condiments with the bhajia. Customers buy paper-wrapped mixed bhajias by weight. For residents of Ahmedabad, picking up 100 grams of bhajia from here is a comforting ritual.

Sabarmati Jail is another destination for bhajia fans in Ahmedabad. Inmates run a canteen that serves some very good-quality bhajias.

The Gujarat Dal Vada Centre in Lal Darwaja is an unassuming vending stand. Rickety tables and plastic stools allow customers to sit and tuck into their plate of dal vada served with chutney. The shop, started by Kamleshwar Omkarnath Mishra, has been managed by loyal retainer Salim for several decades now. The vada is made from finely ground moong dal, seasoned and fried into small golden rounds that are crunchy and soft. A 100 grams cost ₹40.

Fried snacks extend beyond bhajia and dal vada. Farsan is a vast world in Gujarat and can encompass all manner of fried snacks, usually crafted from gram flour, the spicing and shaping making each different. These have names like *phoolwari*, *farsi puri* and *vanela gathia*. The first is a soft-centred stick, enlivened with pepper and other spices. Farsi puri is Gujarat's *mathri*, a favourite accompaniment for masala chai, and the vanela gathia is made from dough twisted into a rope. We watched a seasoned gathia maker roll these fresh and drop into the waiting oil at Manek Chowk. To buy these speciality farsans in Ahmedabad, head to Bhavnagari Farsan House in the old city.

Ahmedabad has a long tradition of Western-style baking, possibly acquired from the British occupation of the area. Sweet buns, known as *naan* here, are the commonest accompaniment for meat curries and kebabs. Biscuit-making was, similarly, well-developed here, and the reason why there's a Biscuit Gali in the old city.

Now, most of the bakeries along this stretch have shut down, but Hussainy Bakery soldiers on. 'We don't know the exact year when the business started, but we are the fourth generation running it,' said Mohammed Ashraf, dressed in white, calmly manning the counter. 'We live nearby, as was the tradition, and are able to be here all the time.' Hussainy bakes an array of biscuits, buns and breads, but their all-ghee *nankhatai* is what they are most famous for. And very good it is, too.

Ahmedabad also has a century-old association with ice cream. In 1907, an enterprising Vadilal Gandhi opened a soda fountain in the buzzing Teen Darwaja area. At first, the ice creams were made in a hand-cranked machine. Two decades later, he imported ice cream-making equipment. The business is now in the hands of the third generation. The name Vadilal has become a corporate entity and brand; but the original soda fountain remains.

If you want to taste ice cream still made the old-fashioned way, head to Rajasthan Ice Cream near Padshah's Pole in the old city. The small shop wears a vintage air, and is clean and tidy. It was started in the 1960s by Kanhaiyahal, who came here from Bhilwara in Rajasthan. An ageing Ratanlal, who now manages the place, told us the ice creams, using nothing other than milk, cream, sugar and natural flavours, are still made in a 'kothi', the traditional churn for ice creams. The freshness and goodness of the ice cream is unmistakable and we tucked into our *sitaphal* and jamun ice creams with joy. Devi Singh served us with the air of an old retainer. He has been working in the shop for 50 years. 'We never sack anyone or ask them to leave,' Ratanlal told us. The ice cream is excellent, and so are the values underpinning this resilient business that came up with an immunity-boosting ice cream during Covid.

Ahmedabad's ice cream love finds its way into the city's many falooda parlours. The oldest is Gandhi Cold Drink House in Bhadra. Rohan Gandhi mans the counter of this small shop started in 1913 by his grandfather Saifuddin Gandhi. The classic falooda comes with vermicelli and basil seeds drowning in rose syrup, topped with milk and ice cream. Stir it and it turns into a glass of pink that cools and refreshes. Gandhi says they've been able to flourish because of the quality of ingredients they use; the flavouring syrups are all made in-house. A falooda at Gandhi Cold Drink House is the perfect way to round up a tour of Bhadra.

A whole street in old Ahmedabad is occupied by *kandoi*, the traditional sweet makers. Bhogilal Mulchand is a leading shop on this stretch. The business took shape in 1845.

It's now in the hands of the seventh generation who have modernized and expanded. In a tribute to their beginnings, a sepia-tinted photograph of the second-generation sweet makers adorn one wall. 'It was taken with a government-owned camera,' we are told. Bhogilal Mulchand now stocks a mind-boggling array of sweets; its signature confection is the *mohanthal*, rich with ghee and a pleasing gravelly texture. We could only guess at the many things that must go into this sweet and the skill it takes to craft it.

Mansuri Halwa, also in the old city, is another reputed sweet maker specializing in halwas. Now there are flavours like pineapple and strawberry. You'll have to decide if you like these innovations or prefer the traditional doodh halwa and kesar pedha.

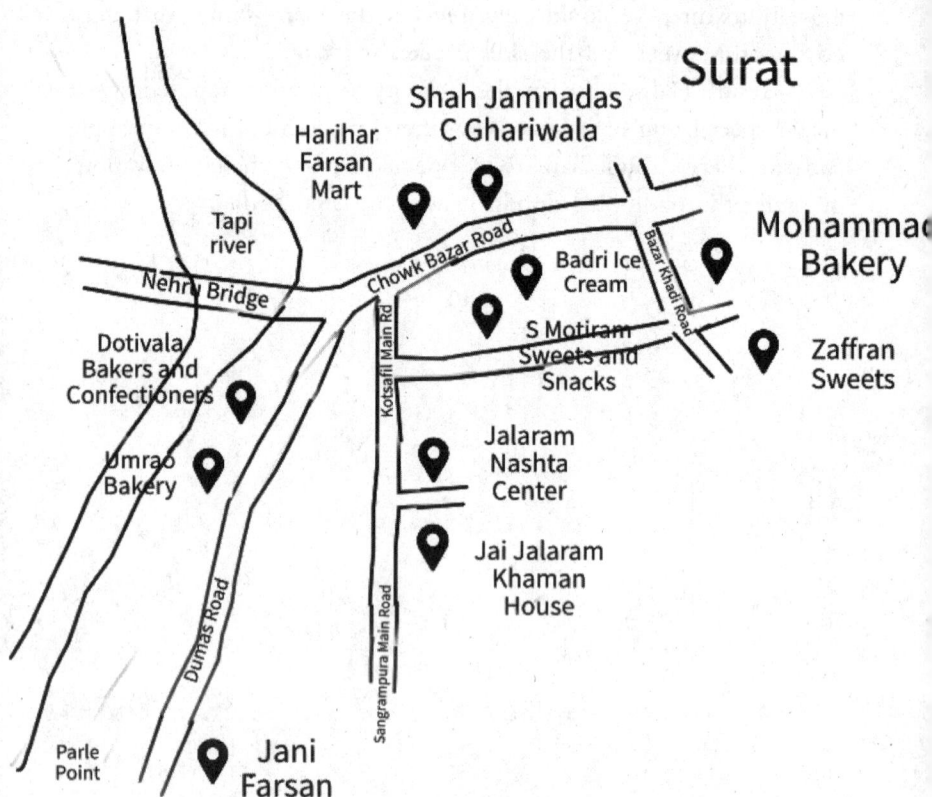

LOCHO: FROM FAILED ATTEMPT TO A SIGNATURE SNACK

Surat

It could be the affluence resulting from the diamond and textile trade that have a long history here or the work done under the 'smart city' scheme. We noticed modern Surat wears a sheen. Its high-rises could give those in Mumbai a complex. Buses use dedicated lanes lined with greenery. There are no electrical wires passing overhead and the drinking water is of a very good quality. Public parks and green spaces dot the urbanscape. Fast food outlets serving sandwiches and vegetarian pizza abound. Tea stalls shaped like teapots attract millennials in the city where there are no bars. As is the style in Gujarat, everything gets enriched with cheese and mayonnaise. Traditional foods get tweaked with flavours called Mexican, Szechwan and peri peri.

For more atmosphere, away from the dazzle, there are the old quarters such as Gopipura and Zampa Bazaar with its Arabic university, Aljamea-tus-Saifiyah. Walk through the residential quarters in these parts and take in many-layered histories—the Mughals, the Marathas and European colonizers have left their impact here—that are woven into the architecture. We wandered about Zampa Bazaar, stopping to take in whiffs of kebabs, *chaap* and naan and saffron-tinted biryanis, vowing to return here during the month of Ramzan. It is a world far removed from the malls, glitzy office blocks of modern Surat and four-lane highways leading to Hazira port. But all of it comes together in the melting pot that is Surat.

It has been repeated often enough to become part of local food lore. Someone attempting to make dhokla failed at it. They said *locha ho gaya* ('things have gone awry'). Thus *locho*, Surat's signature snack, was born.

We hit the locho trail and found the best at Jai Jalaram Khaman House in Sagrampura in the old part of the city. The modest store run by Sunny Tailor—sewing was the original family trade—is only 16 years old, but has the air of an old and respected place. The locho here is the traditional one; you can choose between oil and butter variants. 'We were firm on not adding cheese, mayonnaise and tomato sauce. That kills the purity of flavour, in my opinion,' Sunny said.

They grind chana dal and cook it to a soft consistency. That's the base of the locho. It is then ladled out, seasoned oil or butter is added, and the mixture goes through a deft process known as rolling. It's then topped with sev, also made in-house, and served with a green chutney that contains crumbled khaman and coriander. Eaten hot, the soft-fluffy locho with its spiced oil and crunchy sev makes for a delicious small plate. The quality of the ingredients they use and the skill with which each of the items on the small menu is made is their USP, according to Sunny. Jai Jalaram has regulars who come here for their locho fix every single day. Alongside, the shop also makes khaman and idri or idada, a white dhokla not unlike the idli.

Jani Farsan at Parle Point is another, trendier spot for locho and other Gujarati snacks. It's now run by Pratik Jani of the third generation and the menu is packed with innovations and variations on the theme. Locho can now be Italian, tandoor, Szechwan or peri peri, with the additions of cheese, mayonnaise, Chinese condiments and sauces. We preferred the traditional style, but there's no denying the attraction of these innovations.

Bhajias and dal vadas are ubiquitous in Surat. But the street-food trail in the city is dotted also with small and reputed places serving unique items from the wide world of fried snacks.

Harihar Farsan Mart at Chauta Pul in Bhaga Talav has customers coming here just for its pattice. These are little rounds of mashed and spiced potato filled with a mixture of freshly grated coconut. Brothers Harishbhai and Kailashbhai now manage the business begun by their father Chaganbhai in 1960. At first, he sold his tasty snacks from a vending cart. The modest shop came about in 1988. 'Most days we use up 50 coconuts, grating them fresh every morning,' Harishbhai said, prodding us to have another nariyal pattice and another. They are served with *kadhi* and fried chillies. The shop also sells various other farsan. 'It's the pattice we have a monopoly on in Surat,' Harishbhai told us. 'We are hands-on in the business, that's why quality is assured and our customers are never disappointed.'

The khaja is another unique Surti creation. We tasted the freshest at S Motiram Sweets & Snacks on Ambaji Road in Bhagal Char Rasta. It's made from maida with plenty of pepper, shaped into thick discs. Pressing by finger to create indentations helps the khaja to cook and crisp up, while giving it its trademark shape and look. 'I don't really know the year when the business began, but I'm from the fourth generation, so you have an idea,' said Himanshu Sukhadia. Traditionally, khaja was made only in the monsoon, when eating it with aamras was a custom. But with demand all year round, Motiram's khajas are available at all times. Still, it's best to enjoy them as a seasonal delicacy, say old-timers.

As the monsoon recedes and winter approaches, new produce hits the markets. In Gujarat, this means the arrival of *ratalu*, purple yam. It frequently finds its way into *undiyo*, the winter delicacy. On the streets, it's turned into ratalu puri, which is a sliver of the yam, dipped in batter and deep-fried. It emerges with crisp coating and a soft, starchy centre with the earthy flavour of the tuber.

Jalaram Nashta Centre in Navsari Bazaar in Putli is a street cart parked opposite a fading three-storey mansion and tossing up a range of fried items. Along with the batata vada and dal vada, Chandrakant, who manages the cart with his son, also serves this seasonal delicacy. The fried items are served with kadhi poured from a plastic jug. 'I've been here 30 years, doing the same thing,'

LOCHO: FROM FAILED ATTEMPT TO A SIGNATURE SNACK

Chandrakant said. His customers, and there are plenty of regulars, don't want that to change.

Surat's most popular egg dish business calls itself Bhai Bhai. 'We happen to be located between the Hindu and Muslim quarters. People from both communities would eat here, side by side,' explained Sanjay Shahu, the dynamic manager of the business. His father, Iswarbhai Babubhai Shahu, started selling egg dishes in the mid-1970s from a vending cart and it has flourished since, thanks to constant innovation and enterprise. There are over a 100 egg dishes on the Bhai Bhai menu: from omelettes to *ghotala*, egg pulav and things we'd never heard of before, like egg *kachu* and *bhul bhulaya*! Many of the signature items use copious quantities of green garlic and that's a speciality here, informed Sanjay. He told us also that the number of eggs consumed per day in Surat exceeded the population. You'd be tempted to believe it, going by the number of three-egg dosas Bhai Bhai sells. 'Surat is a food and egg-loving city. People will come in their Mercs to eat here,' he said.

In a region where even savoury dishes tend to take on a little sweetness, it's not surprising traditional sweet shops have acquired iconic status. One of the oldest and most reputed is Shah Jamnadas C Ghariwala. The *ghari* is the top-selling item and the signature sweet here. The ghari is of Surti origin. Legend has it that a priest instructed a sweet maker to create this to provide energy and strength to the freedom fighters in the mid-nineteenth century.

The Jamnadas version is also said to have been wrought through similar intervention. Manoj Ghariwala of the fourth generation who now runs the business told us that his great grandfather's spiritual guru instructed him to make the ghari with mawa, different from the original semolina. It is now a rich and decadent sweet, mawa and dried fruit are encased in maida, deep-fried, and then glazed with a silken sugar coating. It deserves all the hype it has generated. The *ghewar* at this sweet shop is also famous and different from the Rajasthani version. This business now has three branches in Surat, the oldest being at Chauta Bazaar. The shops are sleek, well-lit spaces

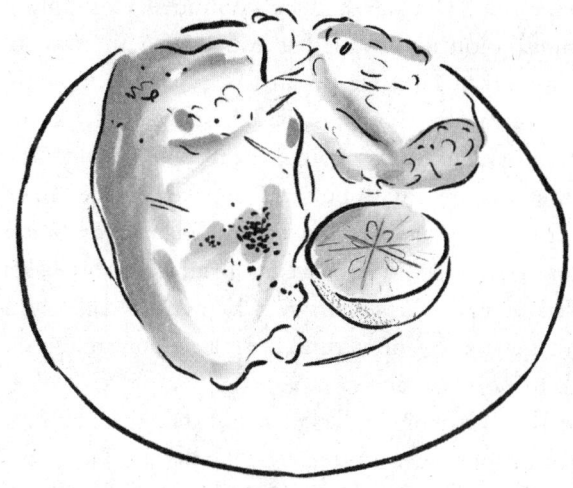

catering to the modern customer. But the sweet-making traditions are old and time-honoured.

No Bohri wedding in Surat is considered complete unless guests are served the sweet with the curious name of *sagla bagla*. It was concocted in Mohammadi Bakery in the Zampa Bazaar area over 100 years ago. Its special status in the world of Surti sweets is well deserved. This is a work of art, delicate filo-like pastry enfolding a rich mawa-based filling enriched with nuts and scented with cardamom. In the time of mechanized sweet making, this must still be painstakingly crafted by hand. And it is the women who are engaged in this task. Khalidbhai is the fifth-generation owner of this business and his son Aiyaz also works here. Mohammadi Bakery has now opened an outlet, Zaffran Sweets, exclusively for its sweet confections and the sagla bagla rules here. Each piece comes in a specially crafted triangular box to keep this delicate sweet intact.

Nankhatai, *khari* and *makhaniya* are Surat's favourite biscuits and scores are made in the local bakeries every day. The oldest is Dotivala Bakers & Confectioners. The bakery traces its origins back to the Dutch occupation of Surat. Some Parsis were employed by them to make breads. When the Dutch left, they handed over the ovens to Faramji Pestonji Dotivala and he continued to supply breads to the remaining colonials. Bread that was drying up was sold cheap and found a market. Dotivala began to dry bread in ovens to crisp them. That became the Irani biscuit. These were recommended for anyone who was ill and was unable to eat regular food. Doctors also suggested they eat them with butter. The baker decided to add butter to the mixture and that became the makhaniya or butter biscuit. The nankhatai is also said to have its origins in this bakery when they decided to bake the local sweet known as 'dal'. Cyrus Mistry of the sixth generation now runs the place, continuing a tradition going back to colonial times.

Umrao is another big maker of nankhatai, khari and makhaniya. It is old, too, having been started by Pitambardas Devchand Umrao in 1945. He had learnt the art of baking from the British in pre-Independence times. The bakery has now become a multi-outlet business with most processes modernized.

Rubbing shoulders with shops selling ornate bridal wear in Zampa Bazaar is King Quality Centre. Don't be fooled by its faded façade and plain interior. For this is one of the best ice cream makers in the region. It was begun in the 1930s and now Nadir Badshah manages it. His friends who come to chat and have a scoop of ice cream—for the place seemingly doubles as an adda—joke that his surname is fitting as he is indeed the king of ice cream. 'You could say it's in my blood,' Nadir said. 'Other younger members of the family have gone abroad, but I'm still holding the fort.'

King ice creams are a must-have at every wedding feast in Surat. They are made from milk, cream and sugar, and the flavour comes from the best, fresh ingredients. We happened to taste a seasonal mulberry ice cream and were completely wowed by the goodness of it. 'It's food, we are putting it into our system. You have to be ethical in its making,' said Nadir Badshah. It's an old-fashioned way and one that certainly ensures King rules the ice cream market here, perhaps not by numbers, but by the trust it evokes in customers.

Badri on MG Road is an equally respected place for falooda

and cold drinks. It began in 1929, selling soda and ice. Raj Badri of the third generation now manages the outlet in a busy hub of Surat. He's proud of keeping the quality consistently good, especially with the wonderfully cooling falooda and the cold cocoa that uses high-quality chocolate.

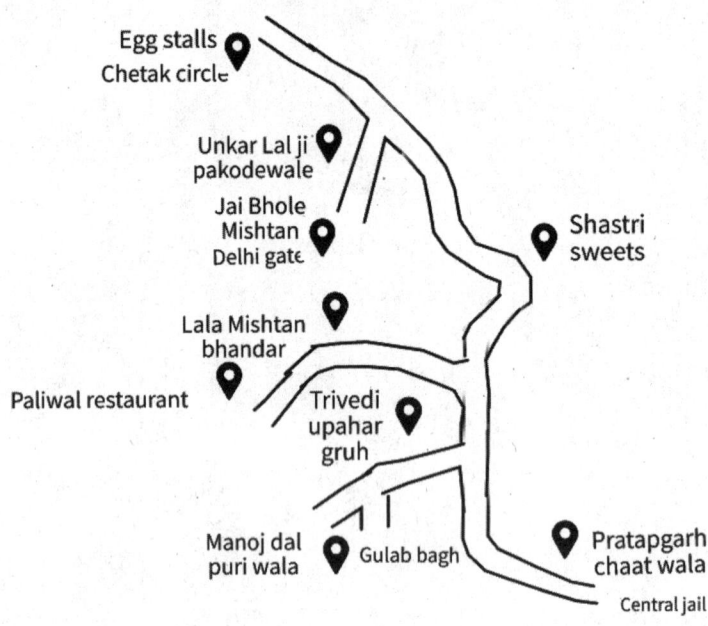

KACHORIS GALORE

Udaipur

Even the most seasoned traveller cannot but succumb to the charms of Udaipur. It's a place from the past, its royal heritage scripted all over the landscape. The city that nestles amidst the Aravalli range is all gleaming white palaces and lakes upon which the sunlight dances like so many scattered diamonds. Some of these magnificent edifices are situated on the lakes, like some floating fantasy. A few are now uber luxurious hotels, but you don't need to stay in pricey digs to enjoy Udaipur's lakes.

Fateh Sagar serves as a gathering place for the city and you can walk along its shores and stop for a crisp, spicy bread bada and ginger chai at one of the many food carts parked here.

The City Palace, a complex of several palaces on the shores of Lake Pichola, impresses with its architectural finesse and its beautiful peacock motifs. Sloping streets lead away from the palace to the old city, its narrow lanes lined with silversmiths, shops selling trinkets for tourists and, of course, some of the best food in Udaipur.

Like elsewhere in Rajasthan, the kachori rules the street-food scene here. Invariably, kachori makers also specialize in samosas. One of the most loved vendors is Paliwal on Jagdish Mandir Road in the old city. This nondescript shop that occupies a narrow space was begun in 1980 by Mangilal Paliwal, who came from nearby Rajsamand. His three sons, who live above the shop—continuing an old practice in businesses of this sort—now run Paliwal. The kachori here is filled with dal, generously laced with asafoetida, and keeps well for three to four days, unlike the aloo and pyaaz kachoris. But it's best eaten hot and regulars who know that line up waiting for fresh batches to be fried up. 'I have been coming here ever since I was old enough to go anywhere alone,' a customer told us. 'You can't beat the flakiness and flavour of this kachori.'

The samosa is equally a winner, crisp with a delicious filling, also heavy on the asafoetida. They are delicious on their own, but you can have them with the sweet tamarind chutney and the green chutney, which, along with the mint and coriander, also includes a little spinach.

When we went there, 'smart city' work was underway and the road outside Paliwal was a dug-up mess. It didn't seem to stop the regulars who evidently loved the restaurant and its genial owners. 'I've seen tongas and tribals selling firewood pass this way. Now it's getting white-topped,' said one of the Paliwal brothers. Some things change, but others remain the same. And the fantastic food of Paliwal is among them. 'We are Brahmins, we don't have too many other skills, so cooking it is for us,' they said. Just keep cooking, is what their regulars and devoted fans of this little shop say.

A few stores down from Paliwal is Lala Mishthan Bhandar. It is 150 years old. On the wall of the small shop hangs a photo of Diwali celebrations in 1955 in which the brothers who owned the shop then are reclining, resplendent in their silk kurtas and turbans, with their sweets spread out in a feast between them. The shop is named after Lalla Narayanji, who started the business during the time of British rule. 'I came to work here at the age of 10,' said his grandson, Kishan Lal, now 70 years old. 'My job was to master the making of gulab jamun and makhan bada.'

The emphasis on skilled sweet-making at this venerable institution is evident in the gulab jamun, warm and soft with its caramel milkiness flirting with intense sweetness. Specialists in seasonal sweets, Kishan Lal makes us taste the hara chane ki barfi, made with the fresh, green chickpeas that come into season in winter. There is also the urad dal ki ladoo, made by making boondis out of urad dal batter, soaking them in sugar syrup and shaping them into large balls that provide warmth in the cold months. Gajar ka halwa and moong dal ki halwa, widely acknowledged as among the best in Udaipur, are other winter specials. 'In summer we shift to cooling shrikand and rasmalai. Also aam burfi when the fruit is at its best,' Kishan Lal said. 'In the monsoon, it's another range of sweets, such as rabdi ki malpue.' While trendy restaurants are now speaking of local and seasonal, this reputed sweet maker has been relying on this ancient wisdom for decades in its quiet, unhurried way.

The other reputed place for kachori in Udaipur is JMB. There are several outlets under the name in the city—Jagdish, Jayesh and Jai Misthan Bhandars—all run by the same family. The oldest is at Surajpole where Vijay Bajaj began the business in 1964. His parents, Govindibai, who lived till 103, and Radhamalji Bajaj, had come to Udaipur from Jakmabad in Pakistan during Partition and made and sold food to make ends meet.

Vijay Bajaj, too, started off by selling tea, namkeen and lemon soda in the mid-1950s. Later, he set up a proper shop in the very place that the Surajpole branch of JMB now is and added on the Jodhpuri favourites of kachori and mirchi bada. An array of sweets is also available now at this shop, including malai barfi, besan ki chikki and malai *ghevar*. It's seemingly a favourite with celebrities who visit Udaipur and there are laminated photos on the wall confirming the visits of Usha Uthup, Imtiaz Ali and Kartik Aaryan, among others.

There is the kachori and there are the myriad ways to serve and eat it. It can be cut up and soaked in a tangy kadhi, slightly crushed and drizzled with green and sweet chutney. And it can be made into chaat. Which is what the Pratapgarh chaatwala near Udaipur Central Jail does. The cart, now manned by Vinit Agarwal, has been at this spot since 1981, first rolled there by his grandfather Jagdish Lalji. For the kachori chaat, Vinit makes a dent in the kachori, much like a pani puri, and fills it with yoghurt and chutney. Besides the hugely popular kachori chaat, he also whips up dahi bada, papdi chaat and pani puri. The signature touch here is the heeng jeera pani

KACHORIS GALORE

he serves for free to anyone who eats chaat at his cart. It's excellent for digestion after indulging in chaat, say regulars. 'I have customers who call me and ask me to keep a litre and more of heeng jeera pani for them,' Vinit said.

Aloo sabzi with puri is a common combination across the North; in Udaipur, however, puris are frequently served with *gatte* ki sabzi or dal. Without doubt, the most famous dal puriwala is a street cart near Gulab Bagh, not far from City Palace. 'You will not get a meal like this anywhere else,' our auto driver told us. 'I've been eating here since I was a child.'

Manoj Prakash has been running this business since the 1980s, opening as early as 7.30 a.m. and closing up just before 6 p.m. His customers flocked back once the lockdown ended. 'It's a fulfilling meal they get for ₹30,' Manoj said. He serves up five fresh puris on a square of newspaper with a foil bowl of the dal—it's chana thickened with *makkai* ki atta, unique and very tasty. The other item he sells is dal *baati*, the same dal served with baati that's boiled and then fried. 'I sometimes wonder what drives me to do this hard job—on my feet, day in day out,' he said to us. 'I think it's being able to feed so many people for so little. I could raise prices, but then many people won't be able to afford it. I'd rather serve more people at these prices. In fact, when I started off, I would charge just ₹5 for the same portion.'

Manoj Prakash's business may operate from a humble cart, but his ingredients are always fresh. 'If there's leftover dough, I take it to Dudh Talai and feed the fish,' he said. Any leftover puris and baatis are given to the monkeys who arrive unfailingly at 4 p.m. every day. 'If I don't have leftovers, I make a fresh batch to feed them,' said this cook who follows a zero-waste policy and has little knowledge that his humble cart is such a green outfit.

The jalebi could vie for Udaipur's most eaten sweet, whether with breakfast or as an accompaniment to the night-time hot milk that is an everyday practice here. Serving this traditional and hugely popular combination is Trivedi Uphar Gruh at Surajpole, a busy part of the city. It was started in 1947 by Hari Vallabhji Trivedi. Now his son, Digvijay Singh Shreemali, looks after the business. 'This was part of Mewar in those days,' he told us. 'And in all of six *jillas*, we were the only ones making this quality of jalebi in desi ghee.'

Nothing has changed in the intervening years, he assured us, adding, 'We make no compromises.' Which may be the reason why generations have been coming here for the kachori, the mithai and, of course, the doodh jalebi. 'We have senior citizens who come with their grandchildren and tell them "I came here first when I was your age." That sort of connection makes what we do special,' said Digvijay.

Trivedi Uphar Gruh is also known for its urad dal ki ladoo made only in winter. 'This is different from urad dal ladoos you'll find elsewhere,' he said. 'We use *gondh* and dried ginger and send it across the country during this season.' This small shop opens as early as 6 a.m. and Digvijay himself mans the jalebi karhai from which emerge the spirals, thin, crisp and syrup-soaked. 'I gave up a government job to come and look after this shop,' he said. 'This place means everything to me. To neglect it would be akin to abandoning one's ageing parents.' And he tends to it with the love of a child for a frail parent.

Udaipur residents are divided over who makes the best jalebi and Jai Bhole Mistan, a row of shops facing the street at Delhi Gate, is high up on the list. Vinod now oversees the business begun by his grandfather Sukhlalji in 1962. He started off selling patasi, Vinod told us. 'He then tried various other businesses: groceries, milk and yoghurt, mithai. Nothing really flourished. His guruji then asked him to sell rabdi-jalebi and that's what he did, laying the foundation for what you see now.'

Vinod's father Ghanshyam then expanded the range on offer. Jai Bhole is now also known for its huge variety of namkeen, besides aloo bada and mirchi bada. 'I've been coming to the shop since I was a child and began to work here from the age of 18,' Vinod said. There are five adjacent shops that make up the business now. One sells jalebi, imarti and gulab jamun, and the largest throngs of people are in front of it. Another serves up kachori, samosa and mirchi bada. The other three make and serve a vast array of namkeen: heeng sev, boondi, *ghatia*, fafda and mathri.

Udaipur's love of all things batter-fried is evident in its street-food shops and carts. The bread bada lines up after kachori, samosa and mirchi bada. A spicy potato filling is used to sandwich two slices of bread, it's cut in triangles, dipped in besan and deep-fried, becoming all sorts of hot, spicy, crisp and utterly satisfying.

We had a piping-hot one at Shastri Sweets at the eponymous Circle. The shop is 48 years old, begun by Keshav Das Veerwani. He was a fan and follower of Lal Bahadur Shastri and decided to name the shop after him. A portrait of the former prime minister has pride of place on the wall here. Keshav Das's son Ravi now manages the shop, which has two sections: one stocking sweets and the other serving *nashta* and snacks such as the fabulous bread bada we had. 'My father began with a tea shop and worked long and hard to make this brand that's now well known in Udaipur,' Ravi said.

A more modest bread bada business is the Panditji cart run by Kamlesh Vaishnav at Fatehsagar. He's been at the same spot since 1992, arriving at 9.30 a.m. every day and closing shop around 10 p.m. His bread badas are also spectacularly good and so is the chai, simmered with fresh ginger he pounds in a pestle and adds to every cup. A stroll around beautiful Fatehsagar is made better with a stop at Kamlesh's cart.

Pakode may be a ubiquitous snack, but Unkar Lal ji Pakodewale at Delhi Gate in Udaipur has a huge fan following for its wares. It was started by the fast-talking Jitu Gupta's grandfather over 50 years ago. 'I'm the third generation in the business,' he said, doling out dozens of leaf katoris with pakode and chutney. His pyaaz pakode is famous, as is the sabudana *tikiya*. You can order an assortment. The pakodas are fried fresh, tossed in a spice powder and then served doused with chutney. Another speciality here is 'segari' pakode to be eaten during fasts. These are made with *rajgira* or water chestnut flour.

Chetak Circle is Udaipur's egg-bhurji hub. There are carts and small shops with names like Egg World, Egg Point and Egg House. Here, Jamnalal Sahoo's egg business, which he runs from a cart around which are scattered some plastic stools, is 25 years old. He has a pile of hardboiled eggs in their shell. When an order comes in, he peels two eggs and chops them up roughly. Onto the tawa go chopped onion, tomato, green chillies and spice powders. Also, interestingly, a glug of tomato ketchup. The chopped eggs are tossed in and stirred about to get coated in the masala. Jamnalal then serves it up with a stack of sliced bread. It's cheap, it's satisfying, and it's very good.

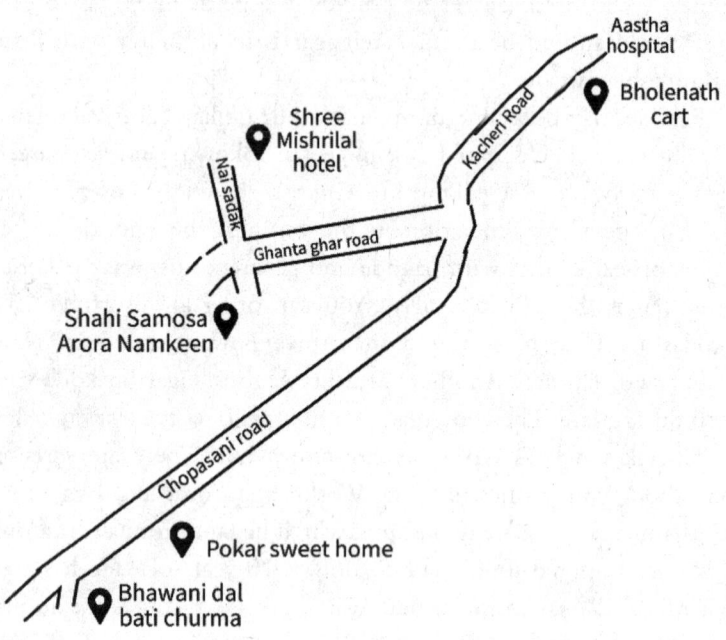

DOODH BHANDARS: WHERE MILK IS A CELEBRATION

Jodhpur

The city at the edge of the Thar Desert is all that the travel brochures promise. There is the majestic Mehrangarh Fort where we spent a morning, taking in its burnished red sandstone beauty and admiring the views from above. The fort is one of the most awe-inspiring in the country, towering over the maze of narrow streets that make up the old city.

On one side there are houses painted in shades that lend Jodhpur its sobriquet of Blue City. Tucked away in winding alleys are havelis, some well over 200 years old, not unlike the riads of Marrakesh. Inside there are courtyards with gnarled lime trees, sparrows hopping about the boughs.

Many of these once splendid homes—we stayed at one that had been converted into a hotel—have fallen into disrepair, but you can still stumble upon a beautiful miniature adorning a niche or an ornate jharoka that makes you stop and admire. There are buzzing markets selling bangles and costume jewellery piled up in mounds of bling, the point-toed shoes the city is also known for, and the vividly coloured fabrics of Rajasthan—ethnic wear tailored for tourists who flocked here before the pandemic and also sarees, dupattas and swirling skirts.

We went to Jodhpur after the lockdown and the city amazed with the speed with which it had bounced back to some form of normalcy. '*Idhar Covid nahin hain*,' a shopkeeper said, and you would be tempted to believe, giving the press of people, especially in the ancient quarters around the clock tower, a landmark and gathering place. And around it is some of the city's best-loved street food.

It was 11 a.m., the hour between breakfast and lunch, and there was a crowd milling in front of Shahi Samosa, which lies in the shadow of the Ghanta Ghar. It was the time of the pandemic, but no one seemed to care about social distancing. At the back of the shop, workers were stirring up vast quantities of the potato masala, the signature filling here—finding its way into the shahi samosa, mirchi bada and bread bada that are the hot-selling items at this smoke-stained store. Others were kneading dough, rolling it out, shaping it into cones and stuffing them with the masala to make large, fist-sized samosas. At one time, some 200 of them go into a vast karhai holding groundnut oil and emerge golden brown, so crisp the covering shatters at a touch, the masala spicy with a distinct sourness.

Krishna Arora, nephew of Anand Prakash Arora who started the business in 1984, was minding the shop when we went there. 'You don't need chutney for this samosa,' he said. 'Everything is in the filling itself.' That it certainly is, and this is one of the very best samosas we tasted on our travels. Of course, he was loath to part with what exactly went into it. 'We make all our spice powders, no commercial masalas here,' he said proudly. 'All the making is in the open, there's nothing to hide.' Grandson of Anand Prakash Arora, Deepanshu now runs the store, which lays claim to introducing the shahi samosa to Jodhpur over three decades ago. 'Everyone in Jodhpur knows this is *the* place for samosa,' Krishna says. There are lots of shops calling themselves Shahi Samosa in Jodhpur, underlining the power of the original brand.

Rajasthan's cities run on kachori. Each will claim theirs is the best. In Jodhpur, Pokar Sweet Home in Sardarpura has earned a solid reputation for its version, besides an array of other dishes unique to the city. Anand Bhati Thakar, exuding a sense of calmness, sits at a low table in the large shop with its time-worn air about it. His father Pokar Ramji began the business in 1962, first as an itinerant vendor of pyaaz kachori and then selling his wares from an empty train bogey. Later, he bought the space where Pokar Sweet Home now stands. Behind the restaurant is a maze of corridors and rooms where masalas are ground and pickles stored in massive drums. Pokar is also famous for its mango and lime pickle. Besides kachoris, which can also be served as a chaat in the form of a dahi kachori, topped with yoghurt and sweet and hot chutneys, Pokar's other specialities include puris served with gatte ki sabzi and a malai curry, an amazingly soft dahi vada topped with a blob of white butter and an array of sweets, the ghevar being particularly fabulous.

During the lockdown, Anand Bhati Thakar packed nearly five lakh packets of puri-sabzi and mithai for health workers and those in quarantine. 'We are committed to quality, whether it's the ingredients or the way we cook,' he told us. He has no ambitions to expand. 'We did not start with anything. This place has given us everything. I would rather nurture it,' he said, with all the wisdom and sagacity of a man who has seen the ups and downs of life. His son, Manish, also manages the business now. Anand Bhati Thakar is a picture of old-world hospitality, urging us to try this dish and then another. '*Raat ko zaroor aana*,' he said. A late-night glass of warm milk with jalebi or *fini*, the winter speciality, is a Jodhpur ritual. Pokar opens as early as 5 a.m. and goes on till 1 a.m., serving its delightful milk-and-jalebi to those who seek this sweet comfort at a late hour.

Another place that's popular for kachori in Jodhpur is Surya Namkeen at Jalori Gate Circle. Started by Ram Babu Arora 35 years ago, the old shop is popular for its pyaaz kachori, plump mirchi badas, a potato stuffed chilli dipped in batter and deep-fried, and *mogar* ki kachori with a dal filling. Customers stand at street level while the shop is at a height and have their snack handed down to them. A recorded message blares, warning customers to beware of pickpockets.

The kachori is the star of the street-food menu of Jodhpur. There are numerous takes on how it's served. The kadhi kachori is among them. The Bholenath cart opposite Aastha Hospital in Paota is a 10-year-old specialist. Lalit Jagdish Malik, the owner, learned the

DOODH BHANDARS: WHERE MILK IS A CELEBRATION

art of kadhi kachori in Ajmer. When you order a plate, he takes a kachori and cuts it with scissors into triangles and puts it into a small foil bowl. The kadhi is kept warm in a large container and he spoons generous ladlefuls onto the kachori pieces. Green and sweet chutneys are swirled on and chopped onions are scattered on top. It's a comforting dish, especially on cool winter mornings, providing a medley of flavours and textures: the slightly sour kadhi, the spice from the green chutney, a hint of sweetness, and the crunch of the kachori.

In the time before Internet, guide books pointed travellers to the sights and experiences of a city. 'Forty years ago, we were on Lonely Planet's list of top things to do in Jodhpur, alongside Mehrangarh Fort and Umaid Bhavan,' a proud Sandeep Arora said, sitting at the cash counter of Mishrilal Hotel in Jodhpur. His great grandfather, Mishrilal Arora, began this business in 1927 at the very spot where it stands now, in the crowded square around Ghanta Ghar, the clock tower. This was in pre-Independence India and Mishrilal sold rabri and kachori under a licence from the British rulers. He also dealt in sherbets, the syrups for these coming down from England. His son Radheshyam took over the business later and it was he who introduced the makhaniya lassi this store is famous for.

The lassi here is made with the thickest yoghurt and flavoured with cardamom and the lightest hint of kewda. Its crowning glory is a blob of white butter on the top which makes it makhaniya. This lassi is not your average cooler to be drunk from a glass. Rich and thick, it is to be eaten with a spoon. Rajendra Arora then stepped into the shoes of his father. Now, his sons Sandeep and Varun are keepers of this Jodhpur landmark.

On our travels, we've been utterly impressed by how young people are stepping up to work in a business that is so demanding in terms of time, long hours and sheer hard work, to preserve and continue a family legacy. That is certainly how it is at Mishrilal. Everyone comes here for the lassi, but there's also a line-up of sweets: kalakand, pedhe, gulab jamun, plus namkeen, mirchi bada and mogar kachori. Also, a fabulous rabri. 'It's not just a question of reducing or thickening milk, it's an art,' Sandeep told us.

If the kachori is Rajasthan's favourite small plate, dal baati is a much-loved 'main', a meal that is as satisfying as it is basic. Modest bhojanalayas across Jodhpur specialize in baati, the roasted wheat flour ball served with a simple dal. Chutneys and other condiments can be served on the side. One of the best known is Bhawani Dal Bati Centre in Sardarpura. It was begun in 1970 by Bhawar Singh. Now his son, Mahendra Singh, runs the small restaurant. The baati is made from a type of wheat that is slightly red, Mahendra Singh explains. It's ground into a coarse powder to give the baati its unique, crumbly texture. Some years ago, he introduced an electrified 'crusher'. The baati is slid into it and pressed down reducing it to a crumble that the waiter collects in a bowl and brings to the table. This is for lazy people. True baati aficionados still prefer to crush it by hand on the plate, have a large spoon of ghee poured on and douse all of it with the flavourful dal. Alongside, you can order a fiery red garlic chutney or a smashed green chilli condiment or both. If you are feeling indulgent, you can also have a *churma* ladoo, made with the

DOODH BHANDARS: WHERE MILK IS A CELEBRATION

crushed baati. A baati meal costs only ₹60. 'It's heavy and satisfying and that's why people love it,' Mahendra Singh said.

Jodhpur possibly has some of the best milk in the country. Few sweet makers use milk from commercial dairies, preferring instead to buy milk directly from farmers in the surrounding villages. Milk is so celebrated here that there are scores of doodh bhandars in the city, all just selling hot milk. It's boiled in wide iron vessels over wood fires, constantly stirred with long steel spatulas. Many come alive at night and stay open well into the wee hours. Apparently, a 2 a.m. glass of hot milk is not unusual here. Sometimes, there are jalebis to be had as an accompaniment. In winter, it's common to have hot milk poured over a wispy mound of fini. We tried this one late night and it was absolutely delightful. Pokar (mentioned above) is also a specialist in late-night doodh jalebi.

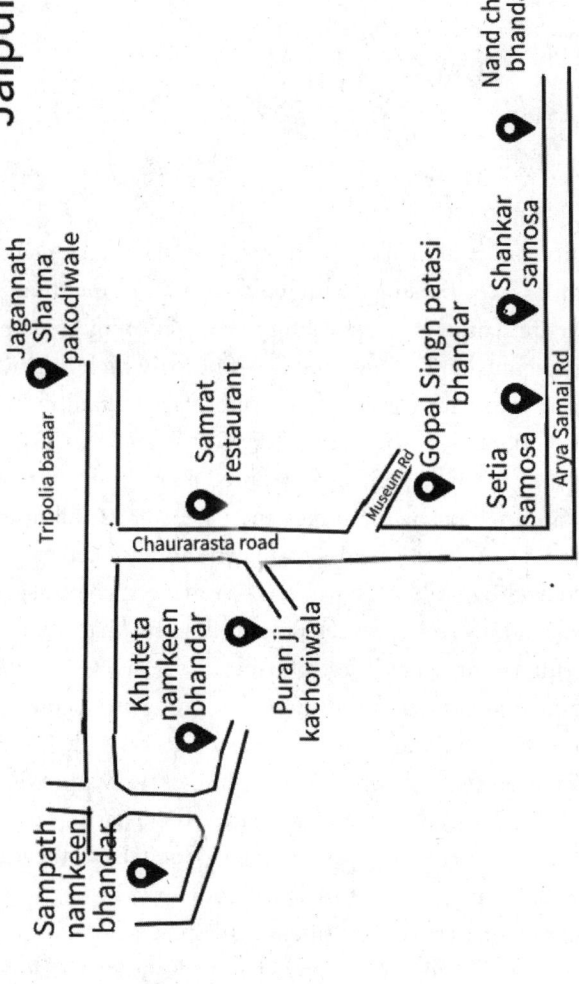

PATASI: JAIPUR'S TAKE ON THE PANI PURI

Jaipur

The city has it all: palaces, shimmering lakes, ancient forts astride hills, and bazaars bursting with colour, not to mention noise and chaotic traffic. Jaipur is an appealing juxtaposition of green parks, wide streets, museums and luxury hotels—one of which, Narayan Niwas, houses our favourite bar—and the old quarters, famously known as the Pink City, which now has UNESCO World Heritage site status.

The arcades with their pink-painted shops spill over with bright *bandhni* fabrics, bed sheets, mojris and silverware. Adding to the local colour and flavour is the food—namkeen shops tucked away in narrow alleys blocked by ambling cows, pakoda makers, chaiwalas with a fan following, and numerous sweet shops selling makhan bada and doodh ladoo, both Jaipur specialities. Outside the Pink City, too, lovers of street food find famous vendors tucked away in various places.

More recently, Masala Chowk, a food court that showcases all the iconic eateries of Jaipur, has been set up within Ram Niwas Bagh. It's a sanitized version and lacks the charm of the original outlets, but if you're short of time and don't have the stomach for eating off the street, then this is a good option.

The kachori, crisp discs filled with spiced potatoes or dal, must surely be Jaipur's most loved breakfast and anytime snack. There are shops in the Old City specializing in kachoris, and you can also buy them off carts across the city.

One of the oldest kachori specialists in the city is Sampath

Namkeen Bhandar in Chandpole Bazaar in the Old City. Anil Maheshwari is the third-generation owner of this business that was begun in the 1940s. The aloo kachori is the speciality here and, unlike in many other shops, it's served without chutney. One bite into the flaky kachori and its deliciously spiced filling, and you agree it doesn't need anything extra. The handmade masala for the potatoes is the secret and what makes this kachori special, according to Maheshwari. Sampath also sells 25 varieties of namkeen and the *noogre*, crisp little balls of gram flour, and sev are a popular combination. Chilli, cumin and a pronounced hit of asafoetida flavour these fried favourites. Maheshwari proudly proclaims you won't get the same quality elsewhere. He's here from 8 a.m. to 10 p.m. every day, clearly enjoying the making and selling of Jaipur's favourite snack. '*Yeh hamari nasha hain* (This is what gives me a high),' he said.

Another well-established kachori shop is Khuteta Namkeen Bhandar on a main street in Kishanpole Bazaar. Here, too, the aloo kachori is the top seller and is served on a square of paper with a spicy, runny green chutney.

Jaipur's kachori repertoire includes the hing kachori, stuffed with a mixture of dals seasoned with copious amounts of asafoetida, which gives the kachori its name. One of the best places to eat hing kachoris is Puranji Kachoriwale in Chaura Rasta. This, too, is in a narrow street and the famous kachoris are shaped and fried at street level. The business was begun in 1963 by Puranji Kachoriwala, and his grandsons Govind and Vishnu now carry on the tradition. The kachori here is seasoned with fennel, crushed coriander and cloves, making for an intriguing combination of spices. It's served with yoghurt and the owners take credit for introducing this combination. Puranji also makes mawa kachori, which combines Jaipuris' love of kachoris and sweets. The kachori is filled with mawa and dried fruits and soaked in a saffron-tinted sugar syrup.

Rawat Mishthan Bhandar, which claims to be the 'inventor' of the famous pyaaz ki kachori, also makes the indulgent mawa kachori. Right across the street from Puranji is Radhe Kachori Wala, run by another branch of the family. As often happens in old family-run businesses, there has been a split. The two shops coexist with no apparent conflict. But we found it wasn't always the case when we were on the street-food trail in other cities.

Samrat is an Old City landmark, occupying Shop No. 273 in Chaura Rasta. The food is prepared at street level and if you want to 'dine in', then you descend into a shabby space a few steps below. Samrat, now in its 65th year, serves all the Jaipuri favourites, from mirchi bada to pyaaz kachori. One of its most popular items is the laccha aloo tikki, made from grated—rather than mashed—and spiced potatoes. Think of it as an Indian hashbrown, if you will. This is an extra crunchy aloo tikki and the Samrat version comes with two chutneys. Nawal Kishore, who now manages the place, said his father Jugal Kishore who had sold puri-bhaji in Mumbai came to Jaipur and started off selling chai and kachori in the Pink City. Several 'nashta' items were added on and Samrat now, somewhat incongruously, also serves idli sambar and masala dosa. Coming from dosa country, we wouldn't venture to order those here. But the laccha aloo tikki is quite special.

Pakodas are the low-profile stars of the street-food scene, ubiquitous, but they rarely enjoy the attention most other dishes get, save in places like Santosh Pakodewale in Nagpur.

In Jaipur, Jagannath Sharma Pakodi Wale at Shop No. 162 in Tripolia Bazaar is a landmark. The façade is pink, but the inside is dark and smoke-stained. The shop opens as early as 6 a.m. and closes at 11 p.m. The batter for the pakodi is mixed in large vessels and deep-fried in even bigger karhais. The pakodis, mainly besan ka bhujia and moong dal pakode, are weighed out on an ancient scale and served to customers milling outside the store through the day. The besan ka bhujia is soft strands of gram flour seasoned with asafoetida; the moong dal pakode here are crunchy and spicy.

Overseeing the making of the pakodis is Neelam Sharma, her head covered with her pallu, her fingers tinted with mehendi. She married into the family of Jagannath Mishra, who began the business

70 years ago. Neelam and her husband Mukesh Sharma are carrying on the tradition. It's uncommon for women to run street-food stalls, but Neelam has been doing this for 25 years and is perfectly in command here. It's a Saturday and extra-large moong pakode have been made. She tells us customers to buy them to feed the monkeys in the nearby temples and the eagles that also frequent the place. That's after they've had their pakode fix for the weekend, of course.

The pani puri has travelled across the country, acquiring slightly different shapes and spicy flavours, its name varying along the route as well. The gol gappa of Delhi, the pani puri of Mumbai, the puchka of Kolkata, and the phulki of Haridwar are known in Jaipur as *patasi*. The puris can be made of sooji—these are often elliptical in shape, atta or urad dal flour. Jaipur's patasi is almost always filled with potatoes and nothing else. The default pani is the spicy, green one. The sweet, brown one will be served on request. Patasiwalas with their wares in baskets or glass boxes can be found at most hubs and outside parks and public spaces.

There are reputed shops, too, such as the 50-year-old Nand Chaat Bhandar in the bustling bazaar that is Raja Park. The patasi with spicy pani and the dahi papdi are the specialities at this chaat bhandar which sticks with a tiny menu. A plate of patasi with five puris is ₹20, making it an affordable evening treat for most people. Narendra Kumar Khatri took over the tiny shop, which still looks pretty much like it must have done five decades ago, from his father Bhoj Kumar Khatri. The puris made of urad dal are special, Narendra Kumar told us. He began at the age of 10, mastering their making in the last 40 years. 'You cannot switch on a fan even in Jaipur's summer while we are making the puris. It's hard work,' he said. A customer came up and said she ate patasi made by Narendra's father as a little girl and continues to patronize the shop. It must add joy to Narendra Kumar's physically demanding day.

Another much-loved patasi vendor is Gopal Singh, who only recently found a permanent space in the city where he must have sold several thousand plates of patasi. He began life as a street vendor around the time of 'azaadi', said the 90-year-old, clad in white, with a black waistcoat and a white Nehru cap. He began selling his wares under a tree in the green expanse of Ram Niwas Bagh.

'I couldn't afford the ₹24 per year to put up a khomcha or the ₹35 it would cost for me to have a thela (cart). I would be out in the open, running for shelter to the Albert Hall Museum when it rained.' But even the seemingly free space was snatched away when the PWD evicted all the vendors from the park. Gopal Singh gathered the strength to go to Delhi and make a representation to no less a person than Indira Gandhi. He remembers that Barkatulla Khan was chief minister of Rajasthan at the time and Sunderlal Khurana was chief secretary. The action of the vendors had impact and Gopal Singh was granted a 10 x 8 feet space near the Scout Headquarters within the park. The authorities would interfere with his tiny business again and he was ousted when, in 1993, Ramchandra Kasliwal, an eminent Jaipur lawyer, filed a petition seeking to rid Ram Niwas Bagh of encroachments, ergo street vendors.

In 2015, Gopal Singh and his son Surendra managed to open a small shop in C Scheme. Here they sell their famous patasi; you have a choice of atta, semolina or dal puris. The filling is cubed potatoes, lightly coated with green chutney. In 2018, as if in poetic justice, Gopal Singh Patasi Bhandar was chosen to be among the 35 stalls showcased at Masala Chowk in Ram Niwas Bagh where the nonagenarian seller of patasi had waged so many battles.

For patasi off the street, Mathurawale Lalaji ki Special Patasi in Tripolia Bazaar is a popular stop. It opens only at 7 p.m. and the patasis are a massive mouthful.

If Allahabad's samosa is small enough to be described as delicate and Delhi's is massive enough to be mini meal, Jaipur's version falls somewhere in between. Samosas, no matter their calorie content, are second only to kachori in the local favourites list and are to be found across the city. Some of the best places to eat a truly satisfying samosa are in Raja Park.

Setia Samosa is a father-son enterprise set up in the 1980s. The

modest shop opens onto one of the main streets in this market area. Dinesh Setia's father worked in the electricity board and started selling samosa, kachori, mirchi vada and bread pakoda as a side business. 'He planted the sapling and Dinesh-ji has nurtured it to become a tree,' said a regular. The samosas are excellent, with a super thin crust, and the filling is spicy, spiked with green chilli bits and an intense masala. Shankar Samosa is another popular samosa vendor in Raja Park, but for quality we'd pick Setia.

Kalkatta Chaat Bhandar does street food in the most modest way, from a mobile cart parked opposite Krishi Bhavan Secretariat in upmarket C Scheme. The cart comes to life at 8 a.m. and already there are walkers, hip young people and tourists gathering around it, waiting impatiently for the griddle to heat up. But the staff will not be rushed. A griddle heated to the right temperature is one of the keys to a great cheela, which is among the top-selling items here.

The cheela is made of mixed lentils; 'multigrain', the young man making these spicy pancakes grins. It's spread into a thin, sizzling disc and topped off with grated paneer, finely chopped onion and green chilli. Folded into quarters, the cheela is served with chhole, which also has black-eyed peas, yoghurt, a sweet chutney, green chutney and a fiery garlic one. Utterly delicious and a great value breakfast the cheela turned out to be.

This humble but popular business was started in the early 1990s by Ramji Lal Tiwari. He had earlier spent time in Kolkata where he learned the art of making chaat. That's why he named his cart Kalkatta Chaat Bhandar. 'That was my training ground after all,' he told us. Despite the popularity of his offerings, Ramji Lal has a tough time. 'The Nagar Nigam people harass us from time to time,' he said with both acceptance and resignation. But he goes on, serving the cheela and the massive dahi bhalla topped with yoghurt, chutneys and a ladle of chhole. His approach is to keep the quality high, never mind if the margins are low. 'Feeding people good food feels good,' he said.

If you're looking for a rags-to-riches story in Jaipur, look no further than Sanjay Omelette Centre. Sanjay is unabashed when speaking about his days in torn clothes when he worked in various eateries as a cleaner boy and a *masalchi*. 'I've known extreme poverty,' he said. On a whim, he decided to set up a food business of his own. One day, he happened to see an omelette maker with a big crowd around his tawa. He thought that might be something he could try. A Brahmin, eggs weren't even allowed in his home. Undaunted, he went forth. 'I knew nothing about eggs, leave alone omelettes,' he recollected. With a small stove and two dozen eggs, he began to experiment and started selling his omelettes from the late '70s.

At first it was from a cart, and the quality of his fare began to draw customers. Sanjay moved to a shop in Bapu Nagar. An innovator, he added variations, including an egg pizza—an omelette garnished to resemble a pizza—that became a big hit. Now, his menu includes 20 types of omelette, including a doctor omelette made with egg whites and a tandoori omelette which is finished in the oven with a copious sprinkle of cheese. Served with two slices of bread, these are truly satisfying egg dishes. One of the things that you notice here is the generosity of the street vendor. Whether it's butter or cheese, there's no stinting. Besides the omelettes, there's soup, chaat, rolls, sandwiches, main course curries, bhurjis puffs, Maggi and thali, all featuring the egg as a star.

'I have experimented so much with eggs, you can say I have a PhD on the topic,' Sanjay laughed. In Jaipur he now has four outlets and also branches in Mansarovar, Dehradun, Prayagraj, Indore and Bhilwara. He's looking to expand down South. The brand, popularly known as Sanjay Omelette, is now called Egg Dee. We ask him why. 'Didn't you know, it's my answer to McD,' he said. 'We are the desi answer to the American chain.' If Sanjay now looks to be sitting on a successful business, it has been a hard route he has travelled, along which he's taken many risks and beatings. His many Jaipur regulars, whose days are fuelled by the egg dishes here, will scarcely grudge him that success.

Hawa Mahal, like all A-list tourist attractions, is surrounded by shops selling overpriced gewgaws, and peddlers of turbans and Rajasthani puppets. We walked past them to Pandit Kulfi, now in its 75th year. There is no better way to round off a tour of one of Jaipur's most famous sights than to stop by at this kulfi specialist, and it's even better if it's a warm summer day. Third-generation owner Ghanshyam Sharma says the kulfi here is still made pretty much the way it was in the days of his grandfather, Badrinarayan Sharma. The milk is sourced from trusted suppliers. The kesar and pista for the top seller, alongside the malai kulfi, is hand-ground and the boiled and cooled milk is hand-churned as it freezes. All of this makes for a summer treat that hits the spot with its creamy texture and perfect sweetness. Pandit also comes up with seasonal favourites, such as mango kulfi in summer, but the malai and the kesar pista ones are evergreen, Ghanshyam says. We tasted it and know just why.

At 4 a.m. every day, Gulab Singh Dheerawat, right up to when he passed away at the age of 95, would walk to the shop he began in the 1940s. His first task was to feed the dozens of poor who lined up in the lane leading to Gulabji Chai Wale, tucked away at the corner of Ganpati Plaza on MI Road. They each got a cup of the shop's famous chai and a bun with butter.

When we met him a few months before his passing, Gulabji was clad in spotless white, including a white turban, and wore a chain of rudraksha beads. To his regulars and the many he fed, he was a saint of another sort. He had been doing this for decades now. It's just one of the many philanthropic acts he undertook through his long, rich life. '*Kaun kis cheez ko saath lete jaate hain* (Who is going to take anything away from here)?' he remarked in the softest tones.

Gulabji Chai Wale is the favourite tea stall for many Jaipur locals, and the tiny stall sees 1,000-plus customers on any given day. 'The people give me and I give to the needy,' Gulabji said. But you don't just go here for the feel-good factor. The tea is exceptional, perfectly sweetened with the slightest hint of ginger. The snack to try here is the bun samosa. It's his grandfather who introduced it, said Jayprakash, who sits at a table alongside the stall handling the cash. A whole samosa is placed between a generously buttered bun, cut expertly in quarters served on paper plates. This unlikely combination works strangely well together and is a perfect accompaniment to Gulabji's chai.

In the Old City, a basement tea stall that ambitiously calls itself Sahu Restaurant is a highly recommended place for tea. Indrakumar Sahu dropped out of school to help his father, Ladurang Sahu, who started selling tea in 1965. 'I'm a graduate in chai making,' he laughed. The secret to his top-quality tea is buffalo milk, boiling it over coals, and mastery over the brewing, he claims. The tea is served in earthen kulhads and the tea leaves are sent off to make fertilizer, making this as green a tea shop as you'll find.

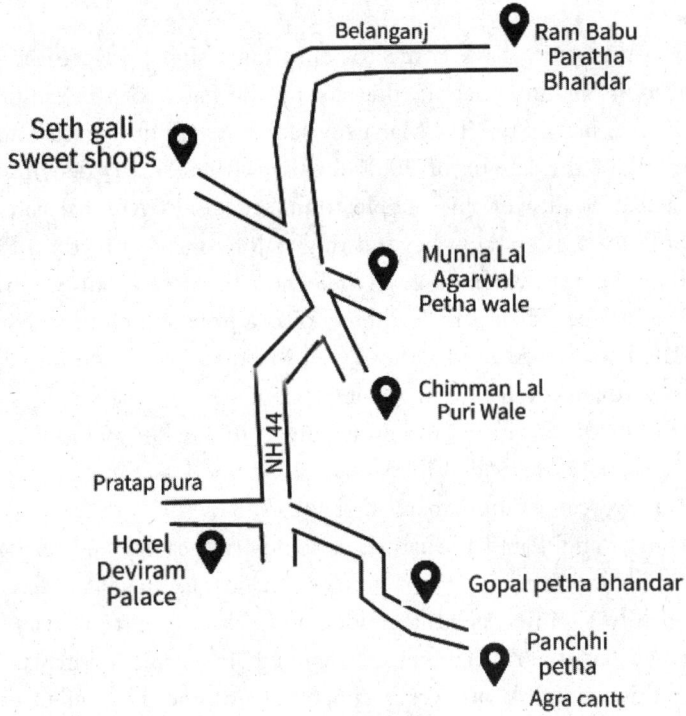

WHERE PETHA RULES

Agra

Few other cities have come to stand for a single edifice the way Agra does. For most people, the city on the banks of the Yamuna is simply the site of the Taj Mahal. Whether a monument to love or a symbol of the labour of 20,000 artisans, there is no denying the spectacular beauty of this marble tomb set amidst Mughal gardens.

Still, there is an Agra beyond this major tourist attraction. There are busy bazaars where a few cycle rickshaws can cause a traffic jam. Shops specializing in leather goods. Whole stretches of a street dedicated to sweets besides the petha. Mosques and more urbanized monkeys than you'll see anywhere else.

Part of the heritage arc connecting it to Lucknow and Varanasi, Agra isn't as closely identified with street food as those two cities are. But we came upon many delicious discoveries.

Ram Babu Paratha Bhandar is a no-frills eatery in Belanganj. You reach it passing a row of petha shops in Haathi Gate. Here, we tucked into a stuffed paratha, golden and crisp and utterly delicious. Later, we had Badri Khandelwal, manning the cash counter, tell us about this landmark on Agra's culinary landscape. He pulled out a red-and-gold menu printed for the golden jubilee celebrations of the Indian parliament in 2002. It was a curation of iconic dishes from various cities. Agra was represented by Ram Babu Paratha Bhandar. They served parathas stuffed with methi muttar, gobhi, mooli and aloo for the occasion. No wonder, then, that Ram Babu Paratha Bhandar is known as *Agra ki Shaan* ('The pride of Agra').

But there's no resting on laurels at this family-run shop that goes back to the 1930s. Badri, who now manages the shop with his brother Kishore, is completely hands-on, from buying ingredients to overseeing the making of the parathas. They inherited the business from their grandfather, Ram Babu, and continue to cherish it as a treasured legacy.

The parathas are made in impossibly heavy concave tawas weighing around 40 kg each. Each paratha is made fresh when an order comes in. One expert karigar stuffs the wheat dough with the chosen filling and rolls it with a *belan* weighing 5 kilos. 'It cannot be managed with slender rolling pins,' Khandelwal told us. The rolled paratha is then slapped on to the tawa and cooked, copious amounts of ghee being drizzled in. It emerges in quick time, crisp with a spicy filling. Parathas are served here with aloo sabzi, a brinjal dish, and a thin kadhi. Ram Babu is now a brand with five shops: two in Agra, one each in Vrindavan, Manesar and Jaipur.

Petha is to Agra what the caramel pedha is to Dharwad or khaja is to Puri, the one thing that's a must-eat and must-buy for visitors. And like any food that attracts so much attention, there is an abundance, even surfeit, of petha shops in Agra. Which is the oldest or which one sells the best petha are fraught questions in this town.

Panchi Petha is a signboard you'll see across Agra. We were told by those familiar with the petha industry here that it's believed Panchilal made the first petha in Agra in the 1920s. We went to a Panchi Petha outlet in Sadar Bazaar and were told it's the 'original' and that there are 10 branches of the brand in Agra. Panchi Petha now has 20-plus varieties of petha.

As to where to buy the best petha, the majority opinion seemed to weigh in favour of Munnalal Agarwal in Rawatpara. The shop, begun by Munnalal Agarwal in the 1930s, is now run by a taciturn Anil Kumar Agarwal. This is an old-fashioned mithai shop. It has no fancy display, no product innovations, though they have petha in flavours like rose and coconut. The traditional petha is just saada, white, or lal, red, the latter made using desi sugar. They cost ₹130 per kilo.

Continuing on the petha trail, we went to Noori Gate where most of Agra's petha is manufactured and sold wholesale. Large mounds of ash gourd, the base ingredient, for this sweet were piled up in stores. Many retail sellers buy their petha from here. Some of it may even be sold in shops that call themselves Panchi Petha!

Even if petha is ubiquitous here, there are other wonderful sweets to be had in Agra. Suraj Halwai in Sadar Bazar is now in the hands of the third generation and is known for its barfi, pedha and besan ladoo. Opposite it is another popular shop, Gopal Petha Bhandar.

Seth Gali is a colourful street with an entire line-up of traditional sweet shops. You'll find here shops selling *raj bhog* the size of avocadoes and sweet makers specializing in milk confections, including the exotic khurchan.

The spiced puri, elsewhere known as bedmi, is called bedai in these parts. It's one of Agra's most-loved breakfast street foods. The unanimous opinion is that Devi Ram in Pratapura serves the very best. While the 70-year-old business begun by Devi Ram has grown to acquire an upscale sweets-and-savouries shop right next door, the bedai and aloo sabzi, topped with a swirl of yoghurt, is still made and served in the old, smoke-stained shop. Breakfast is served as early as 7 a.m., and for Agra locals it's customary to wrap up this meal with a jalebi or two. In the evening, the offerings change to crisp, spicy samosas and mawa samosas, soaked in syrup. 'We are pretty famous, lots of TV crews have been here,' said Umesh Agarwal, who now manages the family business. His son, Priyank, dabbled briefly in the corporate world and has also entered the business now.

Food shops that are 100 or more years old are common in Agra. Chimanlal Puriwala near the graceful Shahi Jama Masjid is 200 years old. 'We are not sure when it opened, but I am the sixth generation running the place,' said a smiling Ravi Shankar Bansal. His son Neeraj is following in his footsteps. The puri and a simple aloo sabzi that hits the spot are the top-selling items at this shop that provides scores of customers with a satisfying meal that doesn't cost too much. 'We've been doing it for decades, you just learn the skill, knowing you have to continue a tradition,' Bansal said.

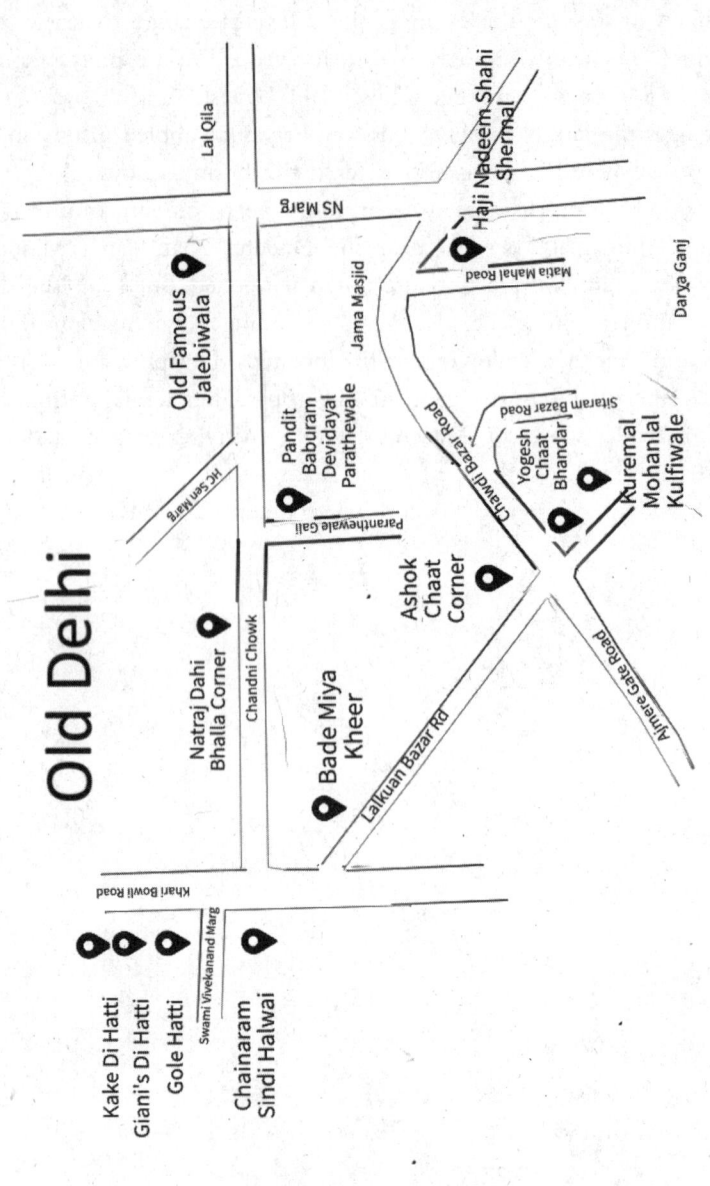

CHHOLE BHATURE TO MUGHLAI
Delhi

The traveller's first impressions of Delhi are bound to be as complex and variegated as the history of the capital itself. Its historical edifices such as the Red Fort and the Qutub Minar leave you awestruck; Raj Bhavan and India Gate announce loudly that this is indeed the seat of power; the Lutyens' bungalow zone, protected by green swathes from the Delhi where the teeming masses live and work, serves as a reminder of colonial rule.

The Old City, Purani Dilli, is the chaotic whorl depicted in travel posters and home to some of the city's most iconic street foods. Around the Jama Masjid, vendors grill kebabs and nihari simmers in vast pots, making a culinary connection with the Mughals who ruled Delhi, influencing everything from its architecture to its food.

The story, apocryphal or not we are not sure, is that when Shah Jahan moved his capital from Agra to Delhi in 1638, his personal physician warned that the water of the Yamuna here was not fit for consumption. To counter this, he advised that the food be made extra spicy. He also recommended the abundant use of ghee to tone down the effect of the spices.

This, then, is said to be the origin of the rich, spicy cuisine we now associate with the Mughals, the ubiquitous Moghlai fare of restaurants from Pune to Patna. The vegetarians, meanwhile, combined spice with sweet and sour elements and came up with chaat. Those who could not afford ghee began to slow-cook their meat, creating the nihari and similar dishes that are now an Old Delhi classic.

Elsewhere in the city, more recent history has shaped the street food. Migrants who came here after Partition set up various food businesses and some, such as a chhole kulche wala in Kamla Nagar, have become iconic. More recent migrants, such as the Tibetans who inhabit Majnu ka Tila, bring the flavours of their food to the city.

While the old and crowded parts of Delhi are where the best and most legendary street foods are to be found, the most exclusive colleges, the new market blocks and the areas outside the swank malls all cater to the Delhiite's fondness for street food. You are never far away from a dahi bhalla vendor or a plate of chhole kulcha.

Delhi is possibly the chhole capital of the country. Vast quantities of the dish, also known as chana—plump chickpeas bound in a dark spice paste—are eaten with *bhatura*, kulcha and rice. It is affordable sustenance for some, a guilty pleasure of grease and spice for others.

One of the best-selling chana bhatura dishes in the city is to be found in the somewhat seedy area of Paharganj. Past shops selling sexy, spangled dresses and next to Hotel Chanakya is the bustling business that is Sitaram Diwan Chand, a chana bhatura specialist. It traces its origins back to the 1950s when Diwan Chand wheeled a cycle laden with chana bhatura near DAV School. The tasty chickpeas and the fluffy bhaturas to scoop it up with became popular street food in the area. Sitaram then acquired a cart and began to sell his wares near Imperial cinema. His customer relations were as good as his chana bhatura and the business flourished. He was able to move to a permanent place in Paharganj. It's now a landmark on the chana bhatura map of Delhi.

Puneet Kohli of the third generation manages this vintage shop and displays the commitment and attention to detail that we noticed was a remarkable aspect of family-run businesses. 'We do just one thing, the iconic chana bhatura,' he says. That conviction and focus, in a market where customers are constantly clamouring for variety, is also how Sitaram Diwan Chand maintains such high quality.

The bhatura is soft and fluffy and the chana is dark and rich, but not overly greasy as in most places. Customers pay and get tokens

BAZAAR BITES

for half or full plates, pick up their food that arrives at the counter with assembly-line efficiency, and eat standing. A brisk takeaway operation is also in place here and Puneet tells us he's modernizing without losing the essence of the brand. Sitaram Diwan Chand's chana bhatura is so famous, cooks from this modest eatery travel across the country to cater to high-profile weddings, as well as to top industrialists and Bollywood stars. Catering demands also come from as far afield as France, and Sitaram Diwan Chand obliges.

In North Delhi's Kamla Nagar is an equally popular chhole bhatura vendor. Chache di Hatti has been catering to the predominantly student population of the area since 1958. Pran Nath, who hailed from Rawalpindi and migrated to Delhi after Partition, began to earn a living by selling Pindi-style chhole and bhatura. He pushed a cart around and eventually managed to find a permanent location, this tiny corner shop in Kamla Nagar. Pran Nath was known to locals as Chacha, hence the name of the shop. His son Kamal Kishore now manages the shop. He told us very little had changed at Chache di Hatti over the years. The shop sells plain bhatura and also a stuffed bhatura with potato filling. You can also buy chhole masala powder here and attempt a DIY version. But we'd say spare yourselves the trouble and indulge here in Pindi chhole.

Bhogal Chole Bhature Wala off Janpath is a nondescript stall tucked away in an alley, amidst photocopy shops and small offices. The chhole and bhature are made street-side and are a hit with the office workers and auto drivers in this area. Begun by Lala Bhogal, it's now run by Amit Bhogal. 'Old customers tell us they've been coming here since the 1950s, so we assume we've been around since then,' he said. The Bhogal chhole is quite greasy and spicy, and comes topped with a palak kofta and a small serving of *kachaloo*. This old eatery also serves chhole chawal and matar kulche. While chhole with bhatura or kulcha is the most common combination, chhole with rice is also a street-food staple loved for the carb satisfaction it yields.

Pawan Jain's 45-year-old shop, Atulyam Jain Chawal Wale at Shivaji Park in Connaught Place, is known for its many rice and gravy combinations. The chhole chawal is a hit. We ate the rajma chawal here, the plate topped with shards of crisp papad, and it was excellent.

Old Delhi, encompassing Chandni Chowk, the chaotic maze of Chawri Bazaar and the area around Jama Masjid, is the very hub of traditional street food in the city. Our trail began at Chawri Bazaar, the teeming market for everything from brassware to stationery. There are chhole kulche walas at every turn and several chaat stalls too.

Locals rate Ashok Chaat Corner at Hauz Qazi Circle to be among the best for gol gappa, dahi bhalla and a not-so-common *kalmi* vada, a crisp disc made of chana that's crushed and topped off with dahi and chutneys. The dahi bhalla we ate here is something special. Nearby is the New Ashok Chaat Corner, which appears to be an imitation. No wonder that Ashok Chaat Corner, which opened in 1948, has a board saying 'No Branches', and another more loaded one saying *Nakaldaaron se saavdhan*, 'beware of fakes'.

We then went to Sitaram Bazar Road, stopping to admire the occasional haveli, now fallen to disrepair. These must surely have been glorious homes centuries ago. For this part of Delhi was once Shahjanabad, seat of the Mughals in the seventeenth century.

We were looking for Kuremal Mohanlal Kulfi Wale, a shop that has been at the same spot since 1906. Mahiram Kuremal, who began the business, had only a small stall, two varieties of kulfi, doodh and kesar-pista, and an ice-filled earthen pot for refrigeration. His son Mohanlal then took over and introduced more varieties and the now-famous fruit kulfi, the frozen milk filled into apples, oranges, pomegranates and mangoes. We had a gorgeously smooth cream fruit kulfi, served with a flat piece of bamboo for a spoon. Nearby there's Kuremal Mahavir Prasad Kulfi, which does pretty much the same thing.

Also in Sitaram Bazar Road is Yogesh Chaat Bhandar, selling aloo chaat—there's a lot of that in this area—fruit chaat and fruit kuliya, which is often a mix of fruit filled into a hollow cylinder of cucumber.

It's a good idea to have a plate of chaat before you hit another landmark food shop here, the Old Kheer Shop also known as Bade Miya Kheer. It's on Kachcha Pandit Main Bazaar that connects Hauz Qazi to Chandni Chowk. Time slows down at this shop that traces its origins to 1880. The kheer, made from just milk, rice and sugar, is thick and luscious, acquiring a pale caramel tint from slow cooking. The owner, Jamaluddin, told us the milk was from their own dairies, not the market. You can have the kheer warm or cold and both are memorable.

On, then, to Chandni Chowk, which was redeveloped in 2021. It's less congested than before, with walkways for pedestrians and a ban on motor vehicles. The colour and vibrancy are intact and we enjoyed ambling along, stopping at some of our old favourites.

At Fatehpuri Chowk, at one end of Chandni Chowk, is Chaina Ram Sindhi Confectioners. The business began in 1901 as a modest enterprise and is now one of Delhi's most reputed mithai stores, best known for its Karachi Halwa.

In the vicinity of this popular sweet shop we came upon Gole Hatti, standing here since 1954, testimony to the entrepreneurial spirit of migrants who came here in the wake of Partition. Brothers Nathuram and Ram Kishan came to Delhi from Lahore in 1942 and struggled for a decade and more, until they began this modest eatery. Now run by Jajpal and his cousin Vinod, Gole Hatti is known for its chhole chawal palak and chhole bhatura. The chawal that accompanies the chhole is like pulao with subtle spicing and cubes of paneer, and is served in an earthen pot, a kulhad as it was in the 1950s.

Also in the area is another local favourite, Giani di Hatti, which has been around since 1956. The super-rich rabdi falooda is the hot seller here, a glass of falooda topped off with sinful reduced milk. Giani's also serves chhole bhature, chhole chawal and rajma chawal in one half of the store that's packed at all hours.

Next door is Kake di Hatti, calling itself the 'King of Naan'. The shop has been around since 1942. It looks rundown, but the parathas, tandoor-cooked and lavishly slathered with butter, are special and the curries like kadhai paneer and dal makhni are rich and delicious. The raitas have their own following, too.

The main street of Chandni Chowk is a string of eateries from lassi bhandars and sweet shops to lemon soda sellers and pani puri carts. There are also large sweet and namkeen shops like Tiwari Brothers and stalls selling Mumbai sandwich with paneer.

Shiv Mishthan Bhandar has a well-established reputation for its 'pure ghee preparations'. We stopped here for a samosa, which was microwaved for us and hence disappointing. This old shop also serves *nagori* halwa, a combination of semolina puris served with halwa, besides bedmi puri and jalebi.

Natraj Dahi Bhalla Corner occupies a prime spot in Chandni Chowk. This two-storey shop has been selling its signature product since 1940. The dahi bhalla is a moist pillow immersed in thick yoghurt, adorned with swirls of sweet, red chutney and sprinkled with a special masala. The aloo tikki, with a filling of spiced dal and a gorgeously crisp covering, is another best-selling item here and is served with red and green chutneys. The shop is now in the hands of the third generation and there's an efficient system in place to serve the crowds that mill around the shop. Pre-soaked bhallas, sprinkled with masala are placed on foil plates and stacked up. With each order, dahi is poured in and chutney is swirled on top. Customers stand, jostling on the street, slurping up the dahi bhalla. At the upper level of this corner store there is seating and a slightly more extensive menu. For most food-loving visitors to Chandni Chowk, the next stop after Natraj is almost always Paranthewale Gali, an entire curving street dedicated to parathas.

It's the lane adjoining the Kanwarji Rajkumar shop, which is known for its poori aloo, chana bhatura and gulab jamun, plus namkeen of which dal *biji* is the most famous. Food lore has it that Pandit Gaya Prasad first began selling parathas here in the 1870s. Three main shops—Pandit Babu Ram Devi Dayal Paranthe Wale, the first shop to the left, Pt Kanhaiya Lal Durga Prashad Dixit Parawthe Wala, and Pandit Gaya Prasad Shiv Charan Panthewala—continue the legacy, all claiming to have been in business since the late 1800s at least. They all have the same look and similar dishes on the menu. The parathas here are deep-fried in a karhai in plenty of ghee. While these are centuries-old food shops, there have been innovations aplenty and the parathas now come stuffed with everything from bhindi to karela, cashew and khoya. We baulked at the idea of a momo paratha!

Further down Paranthewale Gali is Jung Bahadur Kachoriwale occupying a hole in the wall. The shabby walls of this outlet are plastered with newspaper clippings about the place and there's also a sign mentioning the website. Jung Bahadur serves a flaky kachori, crushed, topped with a curry of potato and kachaloo, and then tamarind chutney. Also in the vicinity is Brij Mohan, whose family has been selling chaat here for three generations. He operates a small counter and his specialities are aloo tikki, aloo chaat and pav bhaji on the side.

Bishan Swaroop Chaat is a small kiosk on the main Chandni Chowk street which traces its beginnings back to the 1920s. The fruit chaat is the speciality here and you can have your mix of star fruit, apple, tomato, guava, watermelon and cucumber all tossed in chaat masala and served in a leaf cup, dona.

Shree Balaji Chaat Bhandar is one of the most popular snack vendors in the area. Run by Rakesh and Roshan Gupta, it is over 100 years old. The shop is curiously arranged with a street-level operation and one below, in a tiny basement where kachoris are fried and served. At the upper level are gol gappe, dahi bhalla and chaat, with the paapdi chaat being a hot seller.

A street-food tour of Chandni Chowk is incomplete without stopping at Old Famous Jalebiwala, occupying a corner kiosk on Dariba Kalan Road. We stopped here to eat the famous jalebis, plumper than is usual and absolutely delicious, and to chat with owner Abhishek Jain, whose forefather, Lala Nem Chand Jain, began this business in 1884.

Coming from a village near Agra, he arrived in Delhi with few resources and began to make and sell jalebis. It is claimed the same recipe is followed even today. The business was then passed down to

Lala Gyan Chand Jain, grandfather of Abhishek, and later his father Kailash Jain took it over. Abhishek is now hands-on, proud to keep a treasured legacy alive. For this modest shop has served the likes of former prime ministers Jawaharlal Nehru and Atal Bihari Vajpayee. Alongside the famous jalebi, this stall also sells samosas, one stuffed with potato and another with peas. They are smaller than the usual Delhi samosa and utterly scrumptious, as the crowds milling around this tiny shop prove. There must surely be the temptation to open branches or franchises, we asked Abhishek Jain. '*Kyun, do roti to khaani hai,*' he said with all the calmness of the monk. Contentment in what you do certainly equals excellence in the food business.

From Chandni Chowk, we headed to the imposing Jama Masjid. Matia Mahal Road, leading off the mosque, is a stretch of superlative food. In the evening, the aroma of kebabs grilling and nihari simmering in big degs fills the air. Outside some restaurants the hungry gather to be fed after the evening prayer. There are shops selling *wazwan*, masala for everything from korma to butter chicken, and shahi sheermal, a gorgeously rich flatbread, often embedded with nuts and dry fruit. Haji Nadeem Shahi Sheermal is one of the most famous, with stacks of sheermal displayed on the counter.

Our first stop on this vibrant street was at Al Jawahar, a large restaurant run by Mohammed Akhtar and Ikram. It was begun in the early 1950s and is best known for its nihari, which is commonly eaten with *khameeri* roti.

After Al Jawahar, we went to Aslam Butter Chicken. It was started in 1999 by Aslam Khan and is now run by Anwaz Khan. The signature dish at this small eatery has nothing in common with the chicken in a creamy, orange gravy. Here marinated chicken is grilled over coal. An entire packet of Amul butter is melted and poured over the chicken. It is a sinful indulgence and simply delicious.

At the distant end of the street is the Shabrati Nahari Shop, from an earlier time. It was begun by Haji Shabrati and serves only nihari, nalli or bone marrow cooked in vast pots to be eaten with roti.

We wandered further to Meena Bazaar. It comes alive at night

BAZAAR BITES

Rafiq Chicken Corner

with sellers of clothes, shoes, junk jewellery and rooh afza in large handis. The shops have loudspeakers announcing the benefits of this red, sweet drink. We took a quick look at Qureshi Kabab Corner, which is newer and quite popular with young diners.

Of course, there's excellent street food beyond Old Delhi, serving various neighbourhoods. One thing we would go back for is the bhelpuri made by a vendor known only as Uncleji. Sunil Sethi has a cart near the Patel Chest Institute on Chhatra Marg. He has been there since the late '80s. The bhelpuri is not a common street snack in Delhi, but Uncleji's version has a devoted following.

He tosses together puffed rice, papdi, sev, peanuts, cubed potato, boondi, chopped coriander and onions, finishing with two chutneys stored in large pickle jars. He makes these—one using tamarind and the other fresh coriander—at home. What goes into them, we asked. '*Issi ka sara khel hain*,' he said, giving nothing away and meaning that that was the key to his fabulous bhel puri.

Delhiites also rate high the chhole samose at Tilak Munjal-R sold from a tiny shop near the Pitampura metro station. Its origins lie in the business begun in 1947 by Girdhari Lal Munjal at Panchkuian Road; they also served jalebi and gulab jamun. The shop was called Frontier Samosa Shop and the signature dish came to be known as Panchkuian wale famous chhole samosa. After the original partnerships changed and the outlet shifted to its current location, the Munjals renamed the shop, but continue to serve the hugely satisfying samosa with chhole. Also on the menu are kachori with chhole, dry fruit samosa, dal samosa and gobhi samosa. You can also have a samosa in a bun here and wash it down with some very good Delhi-style lassi.

The capital's chaat lovers all have the one outlet they swear by. Prabhu Chaat Bhandar near UPSC Bhavan is one of these. Begun by Nathu Lal in 1935, it's now run by Prabhu Dayal of the fifth generation, and he told us that the recipes for the papdi chaat and dahi bhalla have been preserved over generations. The chaat bhandar is only a makeshift stall, but does roaring business from noon to 8 p.m. every day. Regulars come here for the dahi bhalla, generously swathed in sweet yoghurt and chutneys, the aloo chaat and the bharwan gol gappa. Ask Prabhu Dayal about the key to his success and he says, '*Sab ghuzaaron ke ashirwad*,' the blessings of ancestors.

You don't instantly associate pakoda with the street food of Delhi, but we discovered an excellent pakodewala at the Ring Road market in Sarojini Nagar. Khandani Pakodewale has been in business since the early 1960s when Balaram began to sell batter-fried vegetables. It is now run by Vijay and Om Prakash, the family being entirely hands-on, from marinating the vegetable mixtures to the making of the batter and frying these moreish morsels. There are over a dozen pakodas to choose from and we absolutely loved the lotus stem and the sweet corn ones. The mint and coriander chutney are the perfect complement.

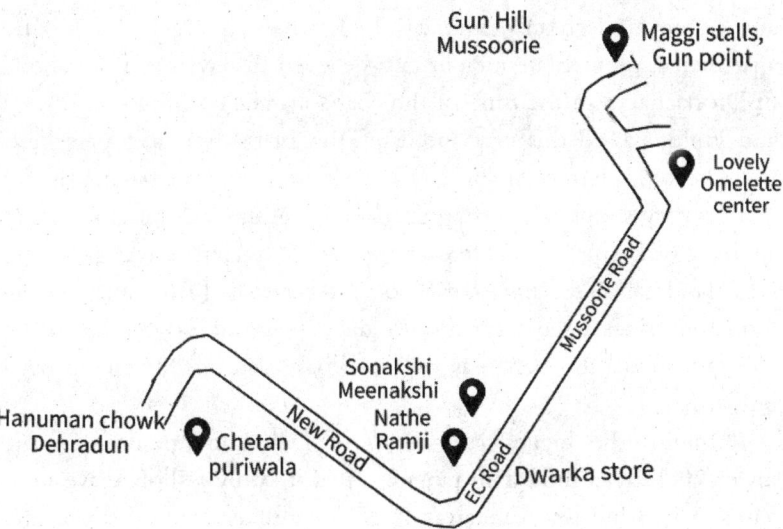

PURIS AND MAGGI POINTS

Dehradun–Mussoorie

At first glance, the capital of Uttarakhand may seem to be like any other modern city, with its high streets, malls and high-rise apartments. Yet, it is an ancient city, believed to have been the abode of Dronacharya in the time of the Mahabharata. Mahmud of Ghazni and Timur passed this way and, later, the British set up a base here.

The old quarters of the city are a trove of decades-old bakeries and grocery shops selling fragrant *kasuri* methi, Garhwal chillies and an array of Basmati rice. Here also are some ancient eateries that are local landmarks, serving puri-aloo and parathas. Dehradun's street-food trail is scattered with momo and *thukpa* shops—thanks to the Tibetan population here—as well as kebab carts and its much-loved bun tikki.

One of the biggest attractions of Dehradun, nestling in the lower Himalayan mountain ranges, is that it's only a short drive from Mussoorie, a hill resort getaway for Doon residents and for weekend trippers from Delhi. Chanawalas and sellers of roasted corn dot the steep streets, providing a tasty snack for tourists who come to ride the cable car and take in fetching views of the mountains.

Puris are an anytime meal in this part of the country. Chetan Puriwala at Hanuman Chowk in Dehradun is an iconic eatery, specializing in puris, known as kachori here. The small shop is grimy and cramped, with space for no more than 15 customers. Locals and tourists queue up patiently for a table or to take away. The wait is always worth it. This is one of the best meals we tasted on our

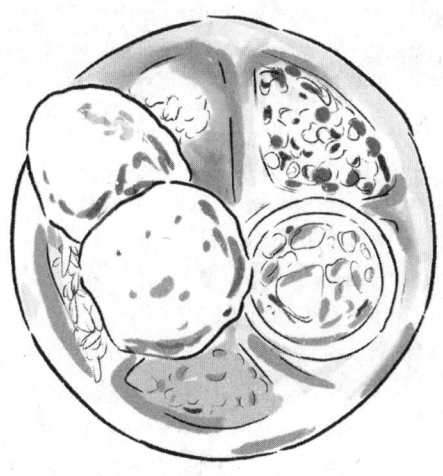

travels for this book. The shop opens at 8 a.m. and already the first customers begin to mill around the entrance. The massive karhai is filled with fresh oil and the dough, shaped into balls is brought out. It's in the style of a bedmi puri. A small amount of ground urad dal and spices such as chilli and cumin are kneaded into the dough, giving the puris extra crispness and flavour. The puris are rolled out and the first one is put into the fire with a prayer. Chetan Puriwala is set for the business of the day.

The puri is brilliant and the accompaniments even better. There's a dry sabzi, such as aloo methi, a delightful *raswala* aloo—we noticed they added dahi to the huge vessel in which it was brought out, a sweet pumpkin puree and chhole. A mound of grated radish and pickle is also placed on the leaf plate. Servers come around encouraging you to have another set of puris, more sabzi, and to taste some of the rice kheer, also a speciality here. This business was begun in 1973 by Chetan, and he now runs it with his son Ashwini. They are quietly efficient and welcoming, while wrapping up takeaway orders and managing the cash counter. It's a standout success story of a small food business that specializes in just one item. Compliment Chetan on the food and he points to the Hanuman Mandir next door, putting his palms together in a gesture of gratitude.

Dehradun enjoys pleasant weather for most part of the year, with temperatures dipping quite low in the winter months. It's the perfect excuse then to bite into something hot, crisp, spicy, which is what the city's much-loved bun tikki is all about. Bakeries abound in Dehradun and the soft bun is a key ingredient. Aloo tikkis are fried on a massive tava, while the bun is warmed up on the edges of it. The tikkis are slapped on to the bun, topped with zesty green chutney and you have the bun tikki, carbs on carbs, and so good.

The city's best-known vendor of this street food is near Dwarka Store at Chowk. It's been around for nearly four decades, run by Nathe Ramji and his son Vicky, who has now taken over the business.

There are several others, such as the Sonakshi Meenakshi stall, at the edge of a busy thoroughfare. This one is run by Balveer and his wife Sonam—she cooks the tikkis, while he takes the orders and handles the cash—and is named after their two daughters. The tikkis and chutney are made at home and they set up shop every evening. The frying medium is vanaspati, Balveer told us, because it makes the crispest tikkis. That and his other trade secrets make locals flock here every evening for their bun tikki fix. Who wants burgers, they ask.

Hill towns seem to have a particular fondness for instant noodles, specifically Maggi. Mussoorie takes this to extremes and the sloping streets of this pretty town are peppered with Maggi Points. Street vendors and small food shops have developed entire menus around instant noodles, offering it with onion and tomato, cheese, vegetables, egg and Szechwan sauce.

Riding the cable car to Gun Point is a touristy thing to do in Mussoorie. Up there is a stall selling Maggi and chai. With the mountain wind blowing cold and sharp, a plate of onion-tomato Maggi, served on a stainless-steel plate with a dented fork, is a welcome meal. The view of the snow-capped Himalayas in the distance is a bonus. Or, perhaps it makes mundane Maggi taste unusually good.

Can a business thrive selling just eggs? Yes, and Lovely Omelette

BAZAAR BITES

Centre on Mall Road in Mussoorie is proof. Starting life as an egg shop in 1918, it became a food shop in 1975 and is now known as one of the best places for an omelette in the region. A signboard outside this tidy, clean hole-in-the-wall announces that it's been recognized by Lonely Planet and rated the best omelette in India by *India Today*. Shahid Ahmed is the fifth-generation owner of Lovely Omelette Centre. He tells us Rajiv Gandhi has eaten here and Sachin Tendulkar, who owns a home in Mussoorie, is a fan. The omelettes are fried in Amul butter and there are packets on a shelf, alongside Amul cheese slices, which go into the popular cheese omelette. Onions and green chillies are chopped fresh for each session—the shop is open from 9 a.m. to 2 p.m. and from 3 p.m. to 9 p.m.—and Shahid was at the chopping board while he chatted with us. An unusual chocolate omelette is also on the menu and available only in January and February. Shahid says they use Lindt in this sweet-salty omelette. Whether it's this luxury version or a basic cheese omelette, Lovely stands for how good a simple thing well done can be.

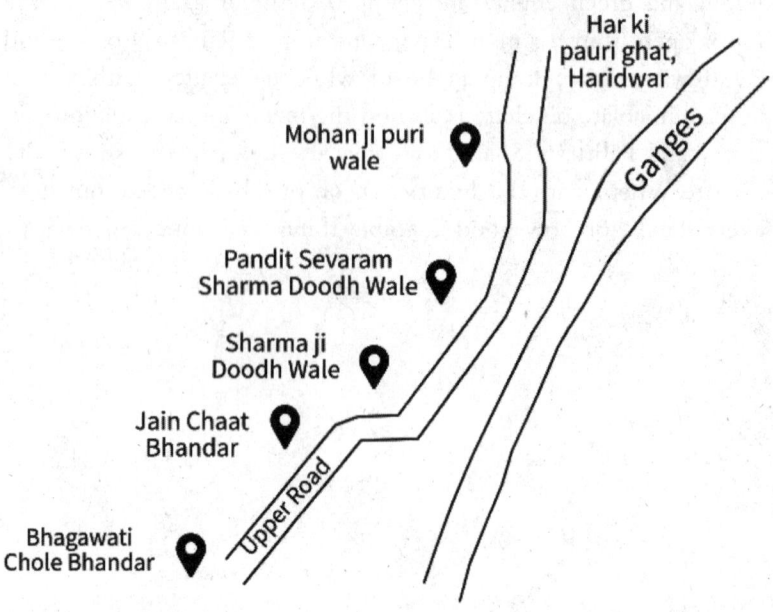

VEGETARIAN SPECIALS

Haridwar–Rishikesh

Haridwar captivated us, much like Varanasi did. Both towns revere the same river. But while the Ganga flows with a serene dignity by the Vishwanath temple, here, having left its Himalayan abode, it gushes and tumbles spiritedly. Haridwar is a key milestone on the pilgrim trail in Uttarakhand.

Like most temple towns, it is known for its vibrant bazaars and narrow lanes through which there is a constant flow of people. They shop for puja accessories, watch the daily spectacle of the Ganga aarti, make offerings in temples, and find food to fuel their perambulation.

The riverside ghats are buzzing hubs in Haridwar and the maze of lanes leading to the main one, Har ki Pauri, is lined with small, time-worn eateries, many specializing in puris and paranthas, milk vendors, tea stalls and sweet shops. Many are several decades old, handed down from generation to generation, operating from the same oil-stained premises.

The eateries around temple precincts serve only vegetarian fare and some shops pride themselves on their *sattvik* cooking that eschews the use of onion and garlic. There is a characteristic aroma—predominantly that of hing and roasted jeera—to the savoury street food here and could well be the taste of Haridwar.

Further upriver is Rishikesh, brimming with ashrams, the spiritual gurus at their helm and their followers. It has a distinct hippie vibe that grips you as you cross the massive Ram Jhula spanning the river flowing blue and clear here. A little way out of town is the ashram of Maharishi Mahesh Yogi, also known as Beatles Ashram, set in a wooded expanse. Now abandoned, it is part of the Rajaji Tiger Reserve. There are fetching views of the Ganges from the ashram and when you walk towards the pebbled banks, there's aloo chaat and *shakarkand* ki chaat to be had from a riverside vendor.

If the spiritual flavour of Haridwar and Rishikesh draws hundreds of thousands of people, the food to be found in various nooks in the ancient quarters of these twin towns certainly provides more mundane pleasures to the hordes of pilgrim and the locals.

It's a winter morning when we arrive in Haridwar and the clear ring of temple bells and rousing chants fill the air. There's yet another sound that's familiar to locals and visitors to the town—the sizzle of freshly rolled-out puris as they hit the oil at Mohanji Puriwale, which occupies a vantage corner overlooking the ghats of Har ki Paur.

The bazaars abound with shops bearing names like Gulati Vaishnav Bhojanalay and Shri Hari Ganga Shudh Vaishnav Bhojanalay, and puri is a speciality at these. Mohanji is among the oldest small food shops here. According to the staff, it's 100 years old, having been started by Mohanlal Modi all those decades ago. The dough for the puris is rolled in the tiny shop that has some seating at a rickety upper level. The potato curry comes from a 'kharkhana' as they call it, a rustic version of the modern central kitchen. Every order of puris comes with raswala aloo, a spicy chhole and a dry sabzi, all of it coming together in a hearty meal that tastes great in cold weather. Mohanji is also a specialist maker of suji and besan halwa, which combines beautifully with the puris as well. Prachin Mathurawale is another venerable puri vendor in this part of Haridwar and locals are divided on who is the better one.

There is a strong Punjabi influence and a sizeable population of Punjabis in Haridwar. The first Sikh Guru, Guru Nanak, is said to have bathed in the Ganges here and the Gurudwara Nanakwara commemorates his visit. The food of the Punjabis is also widespread here and that probably explains the popularity of chhole in these

BAZAAR BITES

parts. Chickpeas cooked with a typically dark spice mix is to be found in street carts and small shops here, served with bhatura, kulche or basmati rice from the Doon valley.

Bhagwati Chhole Bhandar is Haridwar's most famous chhole vendor, situated on Upper Road, in the vicinity of Har ki Pauri. Over 75 years old, it's now run by the third generation of the family that began the business. Gaurav Arora, in his mid-30s, has a jaunty air about him, as he manages the counter in the front of the shop where the chhole is kept warm and dished out in a steady stream. The shop is also known as Jeevan ji Chole Bhandar, in memory of Gaurav's grandfather who started it.

'I would not have this business and the satisfaction of feeding people if not for my grandfather and father,' Gaurav says. Their photos are up on the wall in the tiny space that seats about a dozen people. The chhole here is sattvik and is proof that Indian dishes don't always depend on the use of onions and garlic for deliciousness. There are many ways to eat the chhole: with long-grained basmati rice, deep-fried bhatura or kulcha, fluffy breads from a local bakery that are served toasted with butter. Bun Mix is a Bhagwati speciality, a sweet bun torn into a bowl of chhole and allowed to soak in all its spice and tartness. Business begins with a *kanya* puja every morning and little girls are fed before the first customers are served. It's a fitting gesture in a town abounding with pujas and rituals. Gaurav's tiny eatery certainly seems to have blessings from above.

On a narrow lane in Moti Bazaar in the Har ki Pauri area, squeezed between shops selling rudraksha beads and brassware, is a time-worn store that's famous for the simplest of things, hot milk. It was begun by Pandit Sevaram Sharma, whose name the shop bears. His son, Damodar Sharma, now runs the shop. He's not certain when exactly this small business began but thinks it's nearly a hundred years old. 'It's all I've ever known,' said the soft-spoken man. The family business involves sourcing milk from cows that graze the fields in Chandighat, a hamlet that lies at the edge of the adjoining forests. Every day, the milk is brought in and boiled in a vast, shallow vessel. It simmers through the day, the malai accumulating on the sides. Damodar serves the milk cooled by pouring it into and from a stainless-steel tumbler. You can have it sweetened according to your taste and have it with a serving of malai on top. A glass of warm milk in between shopping in the bazaar or a visit to one of the many temples in the area is a comforting Haridwar tradition. The Pt Sevaram Sharma Dudh Ghar also sells dahi and a limited selection of sweets, such as gajar ka halwa and til ladoos, which are seasonal winter specialities.

Chaat is among the stars of the street-food trail, particularly in North India. Haridwar has its versions. Walk through Moti Bazaar, past sellers of shawls and pickles, and you'll find Jain Chaat Bhandar tucked away into a narrow alley. *Gali ki sabse purani dukan* ('The oldest shop in the lane'), announces the red signboard. There's a counter facing the street and a few benches in the small space that serves as this legendary chaat shop.

Current owner Neeraj Kumar Jain's grandfather began the business in 1951 and it's been in the same spot over the decades, a place where locals drop in to eat pani ke patashe—which is what pani puri or gol gappa is called here—and to chat with the voluble owner. Thanks to social media, it now also attracts 'foodies' and tourists; Neeraj Kumar talks of the Youtube videos his shop has featured in. Publicity may have come with changing times, but the Jain Chaat Bhandar's offerings still follow ancient methods.

'People are adding all sorts of things to chaat and it has become equated with junk food,' Neeraj Kumar rues. His papdi dahi vada chaat is made with crisp papdis made in-house and vadas which have more moong dal than urad. He serves the chaat on *maalu ka patta*, a local leaf that's said to contain health benefits. Neeraj Kumar places two leaves together and tucks the ends in deftly to make a shallow container for the chaat. The papdi and vada are placed on it and smothered in creamy dahi. The chutney is just khajur, no tamarind, Neeraj Kumar tells us. On top of this arrangement, he scatters bright red chilli powder and roasted jeera powder, both made by him. That's all it is and it makes for one of the most delicious, fresh-tasting chaats we've ever had.

After you've eaten it all up, there's more. Neeraj sprinkles some of his in-house chooran, a digestive powder, over the leftover yoghurt and encourages you to *chat ke khana*, to lick it all up. 'Soon you'll be hungry for more,' he says. 'Chaat came to us via the hakims of Akbar's time. (The Mughal emperor was known to have had a particular fondness for the Ganges water of Haridwar). They are built with ingredients that are perfectly balanced and that are good for you.'

Another thing Jain Chaat Bhandar specializes in is kaanji vada, moong dal vadas soaked in sharp and piquant mustard water that is also known for its detoxing properties. It's available in large bottles, which you can take away. You'll probably need a detox after the indulgences in Haridwar.

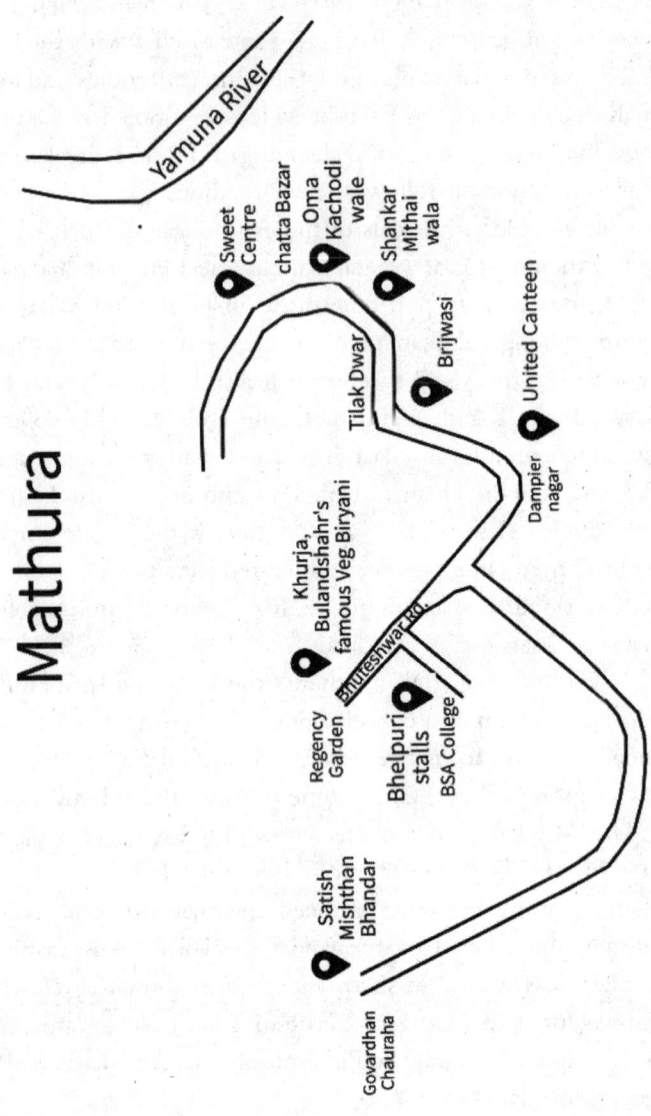

AN ABUNDANCE OF PEDHAS

Mathura–Vrindavan

What could give a town more cachet on the pilgrim trail and tourist circuit than being considered the birthplace of Lord Krishna? Woven into legend and mythology, mentioned in the Ramayana and exalted in the songs of Kalidasa, seat of the Kushana and Gupta empires, its past is unquestionably glorious.

Today, it's a colourful, crowded, chaotic place in the tradition of most Indian pilgrimage towns. The Yamuna flows somewhat sluggishly and is lined with ghats where the devout gather to take dips in the holy water and witness evening aartis with the clanging bells, the blowing of conches and lamps ablaze.

Krishna Janmashtami, the birthday of the presiding deity of Mathura, and Holi are celebrated with much gaiety in the town, with mithai and thandai sweetening the festivities. The pedha of Mathura is famous and visitors don't leave without a box to carry back. Crafted from thickened milk, khoya, and sugar, and scented with cardamom, the pedha is good almost anywhere you eat it in Mathura.

Nearby, Vrindavan lays claim to making an equally delicious if not superior pedha. Sweet-shop owners draw comparisons between the two. As we covered these twin towns, we realized that the battle for pedha supremacy here is not unlike the one for rosogolla between Bengal and Odisha. But these two towns lie just 15 km apart and are bound by the Krishna legend. Vrindavan is revered for its forests and groves where the young Krishna frolicked as a child and for being the place of the raas leela, the divine dance of Krishna and the *gopika*s.

Our Mathura sojourn, though, started not with the town's famed pedha but with the unlikely pure vegetarian biryani that seemed hugely popular here.

Some 500 m from the dusty Mathura bus stand on the main Bhuteshwar Road, near the Regency Garden convention centre, is a street cart with bright-red signage: Khurja, Bulandshahr's famous Veg Biryani. A large handi holds dum-cooked long-grain rice with soya chunks, resembling meat. Munna, manning the stall, is busy dishing out biryanis for customers in foil plates. He weighs out the biryani, about 250 g a portion, tops each plate with a sliced onion, chutneys and even sev. We liked it better unadorned, but locals seemed to love the biryani served chaat-style. Munna also serves soya chaap on a stick, again drizzled with chutney. Several customers order the biryani with a chaap alongside.

Munna, who started this business in 2010, opens for business at 9 a.m. Once his biryani handis are empty, he closes shop. At just ₹30 for the biryani and ₹20 for the chaap, Munna's stall makes it affordable for a large number of people to have a satisfying, protein-rich meal. He told us that there were other biryani stalls like his in Mathura, all run by one or the other of his relatives. 'But,' he claimed, 'mine is the best and customers not only from Mathura, but even from Delhi, come here for my shudh shakahari biryani.' Other street-food vendors of Mathura display a penchant for prefixing their stall names with *mashoor*, 'famous'. Outside BSA college is a line-up of bhelpuri stalls which appeared to be very popular with students and locals. Bhelpuri with paneer is popular, and so is the veg pattice these stalls sell.

Mathura has government-authorized 'bhaang ki dukan', or shops selling edible cannabis preparations. They are small and inconspicuous, but dot the Mathura-Vrindavan road. What you get here is bhaang ki goli, ground cannabis leaves rolled into balls of different sizes. Most of these shops have large vessels holding cold *jal* jeera and you can have your bhang mixed into the cumin-flavoured drink. We had a tumbler and decided we liked the bhaang-infused thandai of Varanasi and Lucknow better. The bhaang jal jeera does leave you with a pleasant headiness.

Nearly every sweet shop here sells *mishri* makhan and the confection, said to be much loved by Krishna, is also served as the prasad in temples. It's simply a mixture of mishri or rock sugar, stirred into freshly churned butter. The ratio of the ingredients and the method of mixing varies between shops. At most places, it's served in a small earthen pot and topped with dry fruit and nuts.

The frozen fruit makhan mishri is a variation on the sweet and you can buy it at street stalls displaying colourful fruit-shaped items in small leaf bowls. Food colour is added to the mishri makhan and it's shaped to resemble fruits like pomegranate, orange and guava before being frozen. We ate a 'pomegranate'. The outer shell was of butter and inside were sugar crystals coloured red to create the seeds. It was surprisingly tasty, though very sweet

Started in 1947, Pandit Dwarka Pedha is currently run by Rajesh Sharma, from the fifth generation of the family. This once small outlet at DK Chowk is now a large shop with a backend factory to make the pedhas. The secret of their pedha is the quality of the khoya, they claim. Fresh mawa, elaichi, semolina, sugar and a few other ingredients which they hesitate to reveal go into making their famous Mathura pedha.

An arch welcomes you to the Chatta Bazaar area, and as you start walking through, you smell the tantalizing aroma of frying. It emerges from Oma Pehelwan Kachodi Wale. The small shop has been around since the late '60s and is reputed for its hing kachori and ghee jalebi. Begun by Chote Lal Pehelwan, the shop is currently run by Manoj Agrawal from the third generation of the family. It is most popular for its breakfast of hing kachori, served with aloo ki sabzi and an assortment of chutneys. The kachori was brilliant, with a flaky crust and flavourful hing masala within. Wandering about Chatta Bazaar, we came across other modest shops serving

similar fare, but Oma Pehelwan is clearly in a league of its own.

Also in Chatta Bazaar is Om Sweet Centre, started by Pandit Chel Vihari in the late '80s and now run by his son Om Prakash. This shop serves kachori, bedai and jalebi. The accompaniments are a unique mix of three dishes: a simple aloo ki sabzi, a sweet and sour sitaphal chutney, and a spiced buttermilk raita.

The Jain Milk Centre in the area has been around since the 1950s, when it was started by Padamchand Jain. They have their own dairy farm and offer a variety of milk-based items, including excellent paneer, yoghurt and sweets, such as milk cake.

Tilak Dwar is where the first Brijwasi store was opened in the 1950s by Keshari Deb. It has grown to become a popular chain in Mathura with eight branches in the area. The new outlets are all sleek and brightly lit and have none of the smoke-stained, small-shop charm we have come to love. Still, the quality of the food here is good and the pedha is outstandingly so. Unsurprisingly, this is where most tourists come to buy sweets to carry back.

Shankar Mithaiwala, established in 1958 by Shankarlal Khandelwal, is another popular sweet shop in this quarter of Mathura. It has been modernized considerably and also serves a hearty puri meal, alongside the range of mithai.

Kalua Chacha Kachori wale, begun by Gullu Kashyap and in its seventieth year, is the most popular breakfast place in Tilak Dwar. This place serves a very light kachori, known as the *halki* kachori. The masala that goes into the kachori is made fresh every day and the flour is chosen and mixed with care. This, says this kachoriwala, is what makes his fare stand apart. Kalua Chacha's kachoris are some of the best we have eaten anywhere.

In Dampier Nagar, we went for snacks to United Canteen, a popular hangout. Begun in the early '90s by Rajendra Prasad Gupta, this place serves freshly made local fare at very reasonable prices. Their kachoris, bread pakodas and onion samosas are gone as soon as they are lifted out of the karhai.

Located at Govardhan Chauraha, Satish Misthaan Bhandar is a popular stop for those travelling via Mathura on the bypass road. Their dal and aloo-pyaaz kachoris are hot sellers and their pedhas are delightful too.

We travelled on to Vrindavan, about an hour's drive from Mathura. The town appears more ancient than Mathura. Its narrow lanes through which pilgrims weave their way are lined with vendors selling chaat and mithai, including the Vrindavan pedha.

Near the main Brijwasi store in Vrindavan is Rupam Chaat Bhandaar. Run by Brij Kishore Saini since the 1990s, this stall serves a fabulous pani puri. You have a choice of sooji or atta puris and these are handmade every day to be served filled with tangy-spicy pani.

At most chaat shops we go to, we almost always start with a plate of pani puri. So, we've eaten a lot of pani puri and Rupam's counts among the really good ones. Saini, who also sells papdi chaat and dahi bhalle, said keeping it simple makes his pani puri what it is.

Bharti Foods began as a small shop in 1957. Raj Kishore Bharti and his wife Asha have grown the business and it's now a full-fledged restaurant. While they only sold pedha initially, they now serve samosa, mathri and other milk sweets. The pedha here is slightly different from the Mathura one. The restaurant manager claimed this was because of the superior quality of the milk in Vrindavan. 'The cows are Lord Krishna's own,' he said.

At Gopalji's lassi stall, too, they said the milk came from cows blessed by Vrindavan's favourite deity. The kesar maakhan lassi was simply outstanding and they claimed that the secret was the milk that came from Vrindavan's cows blessed by Lord Krishna. This place is about two decades old and run by Sandeep, aka Sanju.

The main food hub in Vrindavan is the narrow, crowded road leading to the Banke Bihari Temple. It's an entire stretch of shops selling lassi, pani puri, chaat and more. We were kids in a candy shop, wanting to try everything. At the beginning of Shri Banke Bihari Marg are pani puri vendors, all of whom claim to have been here since the '90s. Here, too, the puris were perfect and the pani came in different flavours.

Then there are the doodh bhandars, milk shops, each with enormous karhais in which milk simmers away and platters of fresh yoghurt are scattered with rose petals, which is turned into lassi. The lassi and milk are served in clay tumblers and are of a superb quality in every shop. Many of these shops such as the Kaalia Doodh Bhandaar have been around since 1970. Most source their milk from trusted small dairy farms in the surrounding villages.

Along this stretch is Premi Chaat Bhandaar, started by Tansigh Saini in the 1980s. He still mans the shop, making a delightful aloo tikki fried in ghee. This chaat bhandar is known for its pani puri, bhalle papdi, dahi bade and aloo tikki, and is hugely popular with the local traders. Like most of the shops here, all the dishes eschew onions and garlic.

It looks like every other shop on this street is a pedha vendor. Many have no signboard or name. Some have grown over time and have acquired an upgraded look. These include Bankey Lal Pede Wale, Agrawal Mithai Bhandaar and Radhe Shyam Agrawal Pede Wale.

BAZAAR BITES

The narrow lane leading to the temple entrance is chock-a-block with pilgrims and you have to inch your way through the crowds. There are more pedha shops here: Rambabu, Radhe Shyam Agrawal, Mohan Lal, Vishnu, Heera Misthaan, Sri Gopalji, to name a few. They are nearly all over half a century old and specialize in making the Vrindavan pedhe.

The place that stood out for us was the Radhe Radhe Pedhe Wale, said to be the very first pedha shop in the Mathura–Vrindavan region. It now offers an array of fresh milk sweets, many of them seasonal such as the malai roll and the khurchan malai, served in a lamp-shaped clay platter. The khurchan malai is a lighter, less sweet version of the rabri and we loved it. The pedha was outstanding, too. Priced at ₹90 for a 250 gm box, it's a hot seller for pilgrims and tourists to take away.

Making what is considered some of the best chaat in Vrindavan is the shop known as Mukesh Sharma Chaat Lassiwale. Started in 1980 by Mukesh Sharma, this shop is known for its aloo tikki, papdi chaat and lassi.

From an adjacent cheela shop, Sharma serves paneer cheela. As business expanded, his three sons, Mayur, Ashok and Dhiraj, have also stepped in. We ate aloo tikki and paneer cheela, washing it down with kesar lassi, and everything was spectacular.

Agrawal Mithai Wala, begun in 2002 by Dhruv and Vishnu Agarwal and housed in a heritage building with loads of atmosphere, is also recommended for its aloo tikki, radhaballabi, the dal-stuffed kachori, and lassi.

The street-food vendors of Banke Bihari Temple lane are too numerous to list here. Do look out for Agrawal Mithai Wala, and the pani puri walas with their multi-coloured puris which, they claim, are tinged with natural vegetable colours.

Stop at Akash Bhel Puri Wale, who has been around since 2010, and serves just one item: a dry bhel puri without onions. It has mix of farsan and fried tidbits and served in a paper cone. It would be great with our evening drink, we agreed.

AN ABUNDANCE OF PEDHAS

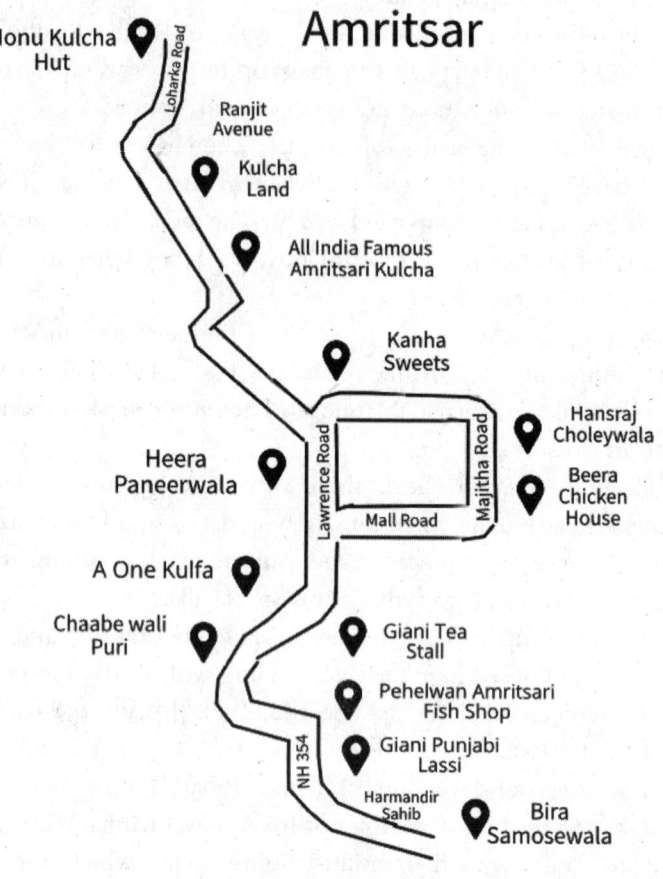

KULCHA LIKE NO PLACE ELSE

Amritsar

Amritsar agrees with our shared love of old cities, chaos and all. Named after the sacred lake, Amrit Sarovar, in the midst of which stands the Harmandir Sahib, the city swirls around the temple, at once dazzling and serene, most sacred among gurudwaras to Sikhs everywhere. The area surrounding it is a riot of colours with phulkari-worked dupattas and sequined salwar kameezes fluttering in front of small shops. Crazy traffic, including cycle rickshaws, weaves through the narrow lanes, piles of papad and vadi seem to spill over on to the streets, and at every turn there's food: samosas, Amritsari fish, the unbeatable kulchas and the famous lassi.

Despite the dusty streets and the chaos, there's definite joie de vivre here, one that belies Amritsar's troubled past. It was in Jallianwala Bagh, not far from the Golden Temple, that the British unleashed the infamous massacre of 1919. Sixty-five years later, the Indian military conducted Operation Blue Star at the temple in an action intended to flush out militants from the complex.

The pleasure Amritsar locals derive from a hearty plate of kulcha, unsparingly doused in butter, or a stop for lassi after a visit to the Golden Temple or a calorie-packed satpura samosa in the middle of a shopping trip in the Chowk area is a remarkable feature of the Punjabi spirit. While the crowded but utterly atmospheric old city is where many of Amritsar's street-food gems are, its upscale areas like Maqbool Road house the most rustic of kulcha businesses. Lawrence Road is also heaven for those seeking a true taste of

Amritsar off the street and in small shops.

You may have eaten Amritsari kulcha in North Indian restaurants elsewhere. Take our word for it—it's nothing like the real thing in the city of its origin. Kulcha is available everywhere in Amritsar, and there are some shops that have stood the test of time. Nearly all of these began in the main market area, but have moved to other parts of the city as the hub got increasingly congested.

One of the most popular of these is the All India Famous Amritsari Kulcha. The place has none of the grandiosity of its name; its original name when it was in Lokhand Chowk in the market area was Chungi di Kulche. The business moved to its current location on Maqbool Road in 1989. Sardar Jaswant Singh began the kulcha business in Lokhand Chowk 80 years ago. His son Samarjeet Singh continued running it and shifted out of the original address. The shop is now run by Kanwalpreet Singh of the third generation.

The kulcha is made with the excellent wheat flour of Punjab and filled with a deliciously spiced potato masala. Expertly rolled out, these are quickly baked in a blazing tandoor and a massive dollop of Amul butter is slapped on, melting on the hot, golden surface. The kulcha here is served with chana masala and a chutney made with spring onions and radish. Kanwalpreet, calmly slicing radishes for the next batch of chutney, told us it was his grandfather who made kulcha famous in Amritsar and beyond. Hence the decision to rename the shop to All India Famous Amritsari Kulcha. Sitting there with the lunch crowd occupying the rickety tables and tucking into the kulche that emerged from the tandoor, we think the place fully deserves to call itself 'All India Famous'.

Pappi di Hatti is another reputed kulcha maker in Amritsar. It was started in the early '80s by Sunil Kumar and his brother Kewal Kishan as a small stall in a residential neighbourhood of Amritsar. Pappi di Hatti lays claim to making the *bheega* or wet kulcha popular here. Pappi, in the tradition of Punjabi families, is Kewal Kishan's nickname. The kulcha here is a *khameeri* or fermented bread and has a spongy texture. The stall served just kulcha chana and mathri

BAZAAR BITES

chana. The chana masala, they say, is the secret of their success. Along with the usual spice mix, it includes also raw mango or amla for souring and a balance of ginger, chilli and coriander.

When you order the kulcha chana, Sunil Kumar, who mans the food counter, takes a kulcha, literally dunks it into the container holding the chana masala, plates it and tops it with more chana masala and a shower of grated radish, and serves it up. It makes a satisfying plate. For the mathri chana, the crisp mathri is roughly broken up and topped with the masala. About 20 years ago, the owners of Pappi di Hatti bought the corner building outside which they started their stall and set up a full-fledged multicuisine restaurant there. But they have been smart enough to retain the kulcha stall outside. It's a crowd-puller, selling several plates of kulcha chana and mathri chana. The stall is open from 11 a.m. to 8 p.m. and is a favourite hangout in this part of Amritsar.

Kulcha Land where we went for more kulcha—we really couldn't have enough of it—is an exceptional example of how a successful street-food vendor can transition to a restaurant-style set-up, still retain the ethos of the original street-food store, and provide the same experience to customers as before. Owned by the same family that began Chungi di Kulche family, Kulcha Land was set up in the 1990s on upmarket Ranjeet Avenue, when the original shop shifted out of the city market area. Run by Samarjit Singh and Sucha Singh (sons of Dewan Singh, who was one of the brothers in the Chungi Di Kulche business), Kulcha Land serves the same tandoor-baked kulche as All India Famous Amritsari Kulcha. A 60-seater restaurant that still feels like a street-food stall with comfortable dhaba-style seating, Kulcha Land has just four items on the menu: Amritsari kulche, masala kulche, paneer kulche and lassi. All the kulchas are served with chhole masala and radish. The place is packed at all hours.

Amritsaris' fondness for kulcha is evident also from Monu Kulcha Hut located in a small alley off the main Loharka Road in a remote corner of Amritsar, beyond the national highway.

Like most North Indian cities, Amritsar has its share of puri shops. Almost all of them serve chhole masala with puri. For an outstanding puri meal experience, head to Chaabe Wali Puri near Hathi Gate. It is a hole in the wall and there is no signboard, but locals throng the place. Set up 50 years ago by Kantraj, a migrant from Himachal Pradesh, everything in this shop is cooked over coal fire. Now run by Kantraj's son Desraj, the shop is open between 7 a.m. and 3 p.m. and serves just one item, puri chhole. The chhole here is light, subtly spiced with a hint of turmeric. The fried puris are piled up in a stack. When a customer orders, the puris are heated over coal, placed on a small sheet of paper and the chhole is served in a leaf katori. For ₹20, you get four puris and a deliciously light chhole. This place is a real gem, serving food of a very high quality at a price that everyone can afford.

On the quest for more puri meals, we went to Kanha Sweets. The 100-year-old shop also relocated from the main city market area to Lawrence Road. The original shop was started by Kanhaya Lal Santram, while the next generation of brothers separated and set

BAZAAR BITES

up their own shops. Kanha Sweets was set up by Amritlal Kamboj and is now run by Samket Kamboj, from the third generation of the family. While this is now a sweet shop, locals and tourists swarm this place in the morning for their famous puri aloo. The puris here are large and served with chhole masala, a slightly sweet potato curry and pickle. Ten years ago, Kanha Sweets took up a space behind the shop which is now a dining hall where customers can sit down to a puri aloo meal. The puris are still made in the shop and carried to the dining hall. Kanha Sweets is also famous for its array of mathris and Punjabi mithai.

At the other end of Lawrence Road, opposite Novelty Chowk, is Heera Paneer Wala, a dairy business that branched out to become a chai shop and eatery. Plastic chairs are scattered in front of the shop and it's a popular adda for locals in this part of Amritsar.

Run by Heera Singh and his son, Daman, the outlet serves paneer pakoda, paneer sandwich and paneer bhurji. One evening in the city, after a day of pounding the streets, we sat down to have a drink when late night hunger pangs hit. We went to Heera and ordered paneer bhurji with bread. We remember it as one of the most satisfying meals we ate in the city.

Located in the Basant Nagar area, Hansraj Choleywala is an interestingly located shop opening on to two main roads. Hansraj makes an excellent chhole masala and you can eat it four ways: with bhatura, kulcha, mathri or rice. While we were there, nearly everyone seemed to be ordering only the chhole-bhatura combo. The chhole is the star here and the breads are either served on top or on another small plate. Here, too, like Chaabe Wale Puri, the bhaturas are fried and stacked. When a customer orders, they are heated over a coal fire and served. Started 30 years ago by Hansraj, this shop is a favourite, especially amongst students who seem to love the small plates and the spicy chhole here.

The satpura samosa is uniquely Amritsari and was made famous by S. Bira Singh. Started 71 years ago in the main city market area, Bira Samose Wale, as the shop is referred to, makes a samosa with a

KULCHA LIKE NO PLACE ELSE

fabulously flaky casing. Run now by Ajeet Pal Singh, S. Bira Singh now has a second larger location on Sultanbin road. The samosa wrapper here is made of dough rolled and folded into seven layers. It's stuffed with a spicy potato mixture. It takes great skill to get it just right. This tiny, oil-stained shop in the vicinity of the Golden Temple also sells a popular bread roll, crumb-fried and filled with a mash of vegetables.

But it's not all kulche, puri and aloo sabzi in Amritsar. The city has a robust non-vegetarian street-food culture as well.

While the Makhan Fish and Chicken Shop is much written about, we went to Pehelwan Fish Shop outside Hall Gate in the old part of town. Singhara from the catfish family and sole are marinated, fried to a crisp, and served with a sprinkling of chaat masala. Yes, that's the Amritsari fish fry that has travelled everywhere. For chicken, Beera Chicken House on Majitha Road wins the popularity vote.

When you are in Amritsar, a lassi—or maybe several if it's hot weather—is de rigueur. We went to Giani Punjabi Lassi, located opposite Regent Cinema in one of the lanes leading to the Golden Temple. It has been serving what is possibly the city's most loved lassi since 1927. They keep it simple here and two lassis are on offer, the normal and the pedha lassi. It's a large stainless-steel tumbler of yoghurt whisked with just enough sugar, served topped with a generous dollop of malai, cream. The pedha lassi is indulgent—a pedha is crushed and whipped till it exudes cardamom-scented makhan, butter, and the lassi is served with this.

Yes, it was an overdose of milk and dairy products, but we could not leave Amritsar without eating its famous *kulfa*. This cold dish is one creamy sweet thing on top of another. A One Kulfa is a small shop at Crystal Chowk. You place your order and a wedge of phirni is placed on old-fashioned ceramic plates. This is topped with kulfi, then strands of falooda, and crowned with rich rabri.

On our last morning in Amritsar, a friendly auto driver told us we could not leave without having chai at Giani Tea Stall. So, off we went to Queen's Road. Giani Gurmeet Singh, seated at the entrance, is an imposing presence and happy to talk about the history of this grimy, crowded tea shop. His grandfather had a tea shop in Lahore. After partition, Gurmeet's father, Kartar Singh, opened this one. Despite its purely functional ambience, it attracts even film stars and celebrities. It could be the chai, boiling away in a brass vessel—the special is flavoured with cardamom and nuts—or the bread omelette or kachori, all of which are very good.

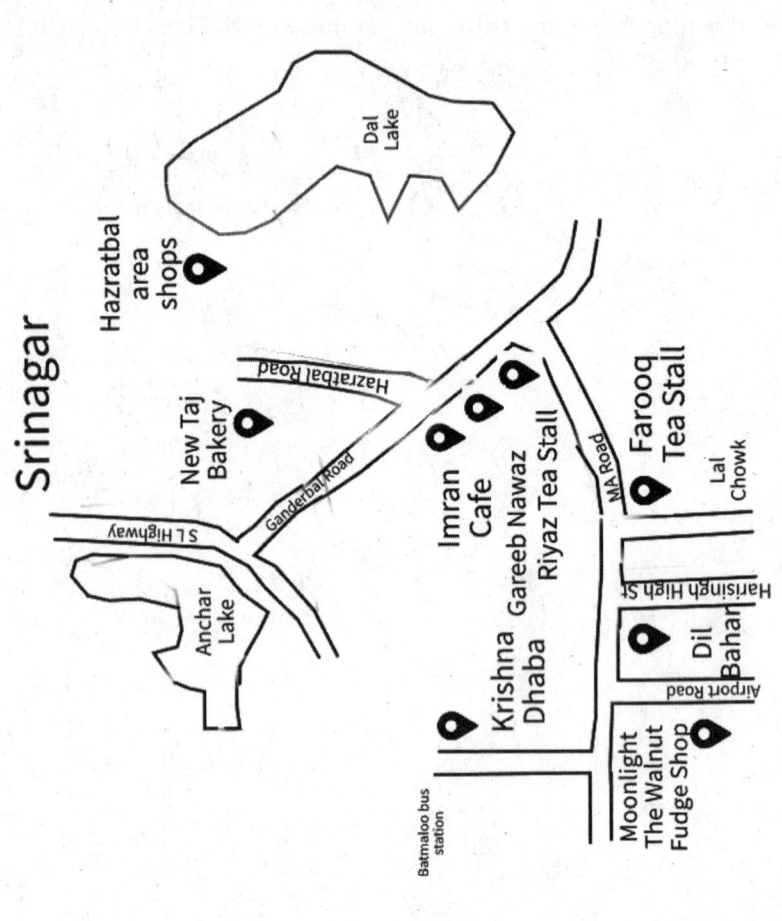

BEGIN THE DAY WITH A GIRDA

Srinagar

The flight into Srinagar skims over mountains, their peaks dusted with the last of the summer snow. It is an uplifting sight. But given the turmoil in Kashmir, trepidation that its beauty is fraught is completely understandable. Armed security personnel are at every turn and there are barbed wire fences to be seen. Yet, as you drive into the centre of Srinagar, the bazaars and chowks are abustle with people going about their everyday lives. The Jhelum flows placidly and houseboats line its banks. The mountains are a constant presence, their majesty providing a backdrop to a city that cast its spell on us. Srinagar is Kashmir's visiting card, promising you that it's a very special place.

On our first afternoon, we went to explore the area around Hazratbal, the sacred shrine that sits in a scenic spot at the northern edge of the Dal Lake. At the entrance to the dargah and along the lakeside lanes leading off it are scores of food vendors. To us, their wares looked new and exciting and we dived in, buying and tasting everything we laid eyes on.

A vendor just outside the main gates of the dargah sold masale *tchot* from a rickety stand. This was a wrap of *lavasa*, one of Kashmir's many traditional breads, filled with a puree of spiced chickpeas, the masale. It was topped with a tangy chutney and served rolled up; it was utterly delicious. Right next was a vendor with two baskets; one held *kaanak* masala, a mixture of boiled wheat and small beans, tossed in a spice mix, and the other a pile of *mongh* masala, the mongh being Kashmir's unique black bean. Other stalls sold an array of fried foods; there was *nadir monje*, strips of lotus stem, dipped in rice flour batter and fried to a crisp, clusters of fried white peas and *lale sangram*, crumbly, fried squares made of semolina and sugar.

We were most fascinated by the halwe-parathe here. An entire street was lined with stalls that specialized in this item. We had eaten combinations of puri-halwa in Kolkata and paratha-halwa in Nagpur. But in Srinagar the making of it is a spectacle. Discs of dough, measuring about three feet across, are slid into oil in a large, flat karahi, and a skilled worker presses and turns with a long spatula until it emerges golden and crisp. This is then served with a vivid yellow halwa and it's something that visitors to Hazratbal seem to love.

Outside the lakeside park with its summer flowers in bloom, vendors sell fruit and the sugar-coated sweets unique to this part. There's *khand gazri*, strips of fried dough tinted pink, dipped in sugar, and *laayeh* which is from the same family of street sweets.

In the lanes leading off this street-food hub are bakeries that are decades old, as also traditional *kandurs*. These smoke-darkened shops have an array of local breads which you won't find anywhere else in the country. We tasted some of these at a landmark bakery near Kashmir University. New Taj Bakery was begun in 1962 by Abdul Salaam and is best known for its Kashmiri breads and bakes. There's sheermal with its ridged surface, nothing like its namesake in Lucknow or Hyderabad, layered *baqarkhani* scattered with sesame seeds, and kulcha, a crisp, crumbly bread to be eaten with *kahwa* or noon chai, the salted tea. One of the traditional delights we discovered here is *basrakh*, a sweet of flour and sugar that takes great skill to get right. These cylindrical confections are enrobed in sugar and studded with dry fruit. Taj Bakery's current owner Ghulam Qader told us it's part of wedding rituals in Kashmir. Another absolutely delicious thing to eat at this old bakery is the chicken puff, piping hot with a creamy filling.

In the same area is a quaint little shop specializing in walnut fudge. It's made up of a mixture of white walnuts from Uri, honey

BAZAAR BITES

from one particular producer, and dates. This sticky, nutty, sweet mixture is then laid atop a crumbly base. Moonlight traces its origins back to 1898. Moonis Mehraj, busy handling orders for gift boxes of the speciality, told us it was begun by his grandfather, Ghulam Mohammed, and they continue to make the fudge in the same way. Moonlight seemed an unusual name for a sweet shop, we said. 'It was named after my grandmother, Joona. It means moonlight in Kashmiri,' Mehraj said.

For nearly all Kashmiris, the day begins with another bread, *girda*, with a cup of tea. We ate this bread, baked by the kandurs in every neighbourhood, at a tea stall near Dalgate and from a grocery store. Its golden surface marked with the fingerprints of the baker is perfect for being slathered with butter.

We also went to Khayam Chowk where the Riyaz Tea Stall, now managed by the third generation of a family, is a popular breakfast destination, serving butter puff, a gorgeous flaky thing, with noon chai. It is at night that Khayam Chowk, known as meat street, truly comes alive. The aroma of grilling meat as the fat drips on to coals fills the air, tempting you to stop and taste the *tujj*. This is probably some of the best kebab you'll eat anywhere in the country.

We stopped at Imran Cafeteria for the mutton tujj. Tender cubes of meat are marinated, skewered and grilled over hot coals. The good-

BEGIN THE DAY WITH A GIRDA

looking owner, Arshad, who was doing the cooking, told us the shop was begun in the 1970s by Mohammad Yusuf. Each skewer is cooked to order. The grilling is done at the shop front and customers can sit in a small room inside. The cooked meat is served atop five types of chutney, including carrot, radish and cucumber, making a colourful base for the cubes of utterly delicious meat. It's served with lavasa.

Gareeb Nawaz and Sher BBQ Cafeteria, begun in the 1940s, are other places to stop for excellent tujj and seekh kebabs.

Khayam Chowk is also home to several tiny eateries serving the famed *wazwan*. Our Kashmir-expert friends, however, warned us to steer clear of these; this traditional meat feast is not at its best on the street. But the rishta—meatballs bobbing in a bright, red gravy and one of the stars of the wazwan—is also a mainstay of the meal stalls near the bustling Batmaloo bus stand. Huge vessels hold rice, rishta and some greens, making an affordable, satisfying lunch for the working class and passers-by.

For vegetarians, especially pilgrims headed to Amarnath, Krishna Dhaba, popular for its rajma-chawal, seemed to be the biggest draw. We ate here, but thought it wasn't deserving of the hype. Something sweet was called for.

We found just the thing at Dil Bahar on Hari Singh High Street. Made by hand, the old-fashioned way, the kulfi here—there's just one kind—is really special. If you are wandering around Lal Chowk on a warm summer evening, try the kulfi at Farooq's stall. In winter, he starts serving gajar ka halwa.

Kashmir's breads, sweets, fried snacks and meats were unique and deliciously satisfying, held together by a distinct culinary tradition. There was another thing to tick off our list before we left. A shikara ride on Dal Lake is wonderfully relaxing, with none of the tackiness of touristy activities. Mid-lake, you can eat paneer pakoras and sip kahwa. A kebab shop in a shikara was an unexpected delight. The vendor deftly cooked trout on coals and we bought a plate. Floating along, watching a golden sun sink behind the high mountains, this really did feel like *jannat*.

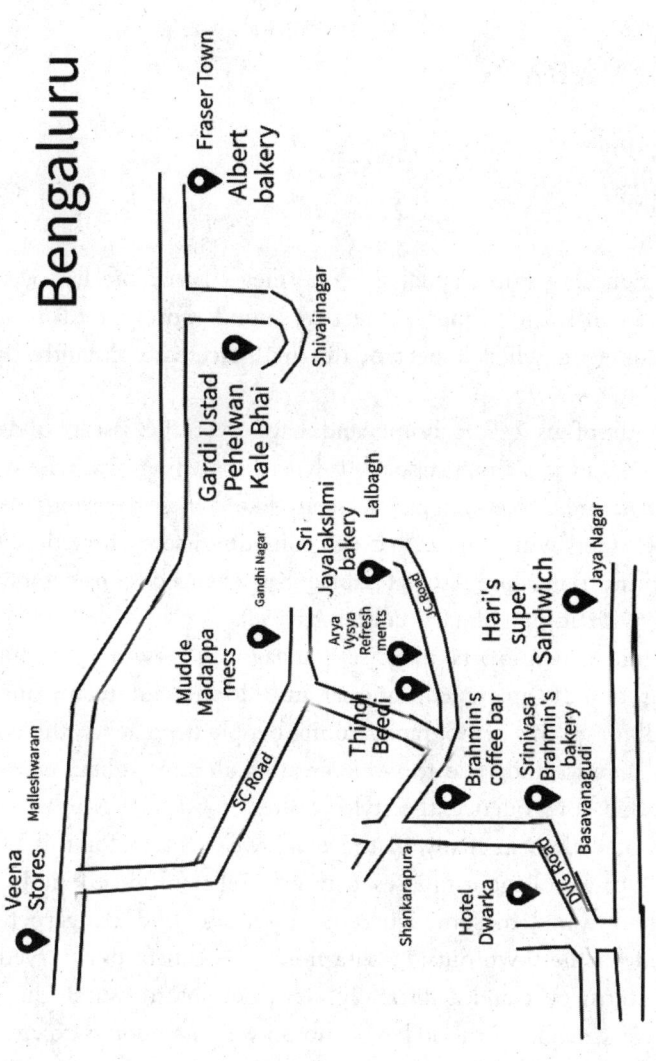

IDLI VADA ICONS

Bangalore

*G*arden City, Pub Capital, Silicon Valley—Bangalore has over time acquired many sobriquets. One may sound more apt than another depending on which aspect of this multifaceted, constantly shifting city you see.

Both of us call it home and have over the last two decades seen it transform from laidback town to sprawling city, where mega infrastructure projects make it seem like a never-ending work in progress, and with a pace that can sometimes seem frenetic. During this time, Bangalore's social fabric has changed considerably and, along with it, its culinary culture as well.

Once a pensioners' paradise, Bangalore is now a predominantly young city. Its many educational institutions and tech companies contribute to this demography. Young people from across the country come here to study and to work, creating a cosmopolitan tapestry. As a possible consequence, the style of street food here is more diverse, less rooted than in many of the cities we went to for this book.

Outside college campuses, pani puri sellers from UP and Odisha ply their wares. In some quarters you'll also find Bangarpet chaat, named for the town outside Bangalore. This is pani puri served filled with warm peas and a distinctly clear, but spiced, water, the pani.

Every neighbourhood has its momo vendors—some exceptionally good—and the Kolkata kathi rolls are a hit everywhere. The 99 varieties dosa cart is also a Bangalore fixture; the number may be an exaggeration, but the offerings that extend from dosas stuffed with

Szechwan noodles to chocolate are a reflection of the diverse nature of those who seek cheap and cheerful meals in this city.

As many of these are ubiquitous and none are what we would describe as iconic, we've chosen here to bring to you some of the long-established street-food shops of our hometown; some are famous, others are little known outside their neighbourhoods.

It is in the multicultural nature of Bangalore that if the hip brewpubs draw crowds that relish IPA and chomp on nachos and cheesy fries, there are also those who begin to mill around Brahmins' Coffee Bar on Ranga Rao Road in Shankarapura a good half an hour before it opens. This is one of our most memorable street-food scenes in Bangalore. The morning service at Brahmins' Coffee Bar is from 6 a.m. to 12 noon; in the evenings it's open from 3 p.m. to 7 p.m. Just after 2.30 p.m., a crowd begins to gather on the street. Inside, staff take their places, as if for a theatrical performance. The coffee-maker at his station, the server of extra chutney behind the two large vats of the stuff, the cashier arranges coins for change—few places handle cash as quickly and deftly as here—and a member of the family joins him. At the stroke of 3 p.m., customers rush in, pay, collect tokens and queue up to pick up their food and coffee or tea. Brahmins' Coffee Bar serves just four food items: idli, vada, *kharabhath*, served with a hugely popular chutney—no sambar—and *kesaribhath*. Fans rate the idli the softest, the vada the crispest, and the chutney the very best in town. We agree that these are of superb quality. This is, to a great extent, the result of this tiny eatery staying steadfastly committed to its original line-up of dishes, eschewing the temptation to add items.

'It would be a big mistake to change anything,' according to current owner Radhakrishna Adiga. Brahmins' Coffee Bar was begun in 1965 by his father K.V. Nagesh Rao, with the support of his wife K.N. Saraswathi, after several unsuccessful forays into the food business. It opened in a narrow strip of space that used to be a garage. And it operated there for decades before a recent expansion. The additional space allows customers to get their idli-vada without being jostled

and having to hold the plates over their heads. Radhakrishna Adiga and his brother Shankar Narayana along with the third generation of the family now look after the business. Brahmins' has a timeless charm about it and we hope it stays that way.

Nearly always spoken in the same breath as Brahmins' is Veena Stores in Malleshwaram. Pradeep Suryanarayn runs the business begun by his father in 1977 and named after his sister, Veena. Originally it sold condiments, hence the name 'Stores', and idli and coffee on the side. Over time, the idli earned a reputation for itself and now there's also a famous vada, which is gorgeously crisp and delicious. Veena Stores also serves *shavige bhath*, savoury vermicelli, *puliogare*, *bisibelebhath* and sweets like kesaribhath. Once a hole in the wall on Margosa Road, Veena Stores has undergone a makeover and expansion overseen by Pradeep. You no longer have to stand on the pavement, balancing your plate of idli-vade in your hand, but the taste and satisfaction have remained unchanged. We order a plate and nearly always end up succumbing to the temptation to have another idli or vada. They are that good. And so is the coffee.

Tucked into the Kalyan Trust in Gandhinagar, the bustling commercial hub of Bangalore, is an old eatery specializing in the uniquely Karnataka staple of ragi *mudde*, a ball of cooked millet flour. This is the Mudde Madappa Mess that has been around since the late 1950s. Begun by H.S. Basavanna, a government officer, it is now managed by his brother and cousin Somshekar and Puttanna Basappa. The family is from Mandya and the cooking at this mess reflects the rustic cooking traditions of this agricultural belt.

The core dish at this basic but spanking clean eatery is the mudde, made by cooking ragi flour into a thick paste and then forming it into a ball. 'It has to be cooked properly or the mudde will give you indigestion,' Basappa told us, adding that they buy and grind the flour in-house, not buying readymade. Customers buy a token for ₹120 for a mudde meal and sit down to it. A server comes around with a jug of hot water and a basin and you wash your plate. On the table are water bottle caps. You place one under one edge of the plate, so it's atilt. This allows the sambar or the saaru to slide to the lower side of the plate and the mudde sits away, dry. It's uncouth to let the mudde sit and disintegrate into the sambar. You break off a small lump, dip into the sambar and then swallow it. No chewing. Along with the sambar, a vegetable of the day and pickle, plus papad, are served. This is followed by rice with sambar, rasam, buttermilk and pickle. All of it makes for a satisfying, nourishing meal. The mudde is also recommended for managing diabetes. 'Eat here every day for two weeks and see your health improve,' Basappa said.

Another old-world eatery in South Bangalore we recommend is Hotel Dwarka in NR Colony. This no-frills shop sits under a sprawling and ancient tree. Dwarka was begun by Sridhar S. Holla in 1972 and was then on Bull Temple Road. In 2006, it moved to the current location, an area with lots of old-world charm. It's best known for its *khali* dose, soft and fluffy, served with butter. Besides the khali dose, the rava vada and carrot halwa are much-loved signature items here.

Ask South Bangaloreans about their favourite street-food shops and most are likely to include Hari's Super Sandwich on the list. Beginning in 1987 with a single store serving vegetarian sandwiches in Jayanagar 3rd Block, Shivanna, an unassuming entrepreneur, has grown the business to 15 outlets spread across the area. Sandwiches—Mumbai-style veg, corn and cheese, even chocolate—are the mainstay of the menu. Hari's now also serves chaat and tava pulao, which seem to be a hit with college students and office-goers in the area. What's the secret to a simple sandwich operation becoming so big and popular, we asked Shivanna. 'I've done nothing extraordinary, I've just earned the trust and loyalty of my customers,' says the soft-spoken Shivanna.

The Thindi Beedi, Food Street, in VV Puram is possibly Bangalore's best-known hub for street food. It's only about 150 metres of road and is lined with food shops and stalls. Having travelled to so many cities, we can say with some assurance that Thindi Beedi enjoys more hype than it merits; the lockdowns also robbed it of some of its earlier vibrancy. You'll find here a stall selling 99 types of dosa; think cheese sweet-corn paneer dosa, cheese pasta dosa, Szechwan Kerala dosa and other combinations or innovations, depending how you enjoy these creations. There are ice cream, juice and milkshake vendors. *Holige*, the *puran poli* of Karnataka, is also available. The potato twister, finished with peri peri sauce and mayo, seemed to be a hot seller on our last visit.

For traditional dishes, we recommend Arya Vysya Refreshments for its *mosaru kodubale*, a deep-fried ring of rice flour and yoghurt that has a lovely crisp-chewy texture. Begun in 1962, this is one of the oldest businesses in Thindi Beedi.

Another street-food experience which too has lost some of its charm is Mosque Road during the month of Ramazan. The eateries here put out stalls that serve an array of kebabs, fried fish, beef samosa, juice and falooda. A mashawi stall that caught our attention on our most recent stroll here had portions of whole lamb on a bed of pilaf. There were also camel meat dishes being sold under a tent. One of our picks here would be the *haleem* vendors many of whom, probably on account of the rising cost of mutton, have begun to serve chicken haleem.

For a unique non-vegetarian meal, we'd recommend Shivajinagar

Gardi Ustad Pehelwan Kale Bhai. This is a wrestling pit, opened in the 1930s by Kale Bhai. The wrestling tradition goes back to the time of Ranadhira Kanteerava Narasaraja Wodeyar, then Maharaja of Mysore, who encouraged his male subjects to build body strength. Wrestling flourished in spaces such as this. In the late '90s, when maintenance of the space became a struggle, it was decided to open the kitchen to customers. Now managed by Khader Bhai, the akhada serves a fragrant biryani, mutton chops and kebabs. Go prepared to rough it out—you'll be sitting on rickety benches in the wrestling pit, but you'll be assured of a memorable meal experience.

Here we thought of paying tribute to the uniquely Bangalore institution, the Iyengar Bakery. Every neighbourhood has one and those in the old parts of the city trace their origins back to several decades. These bakeries with their vegetarian offerings—some do include eggs in some of the bakes—serve entire swathes of the population with fresh, affordable snacks. Many a school kid or salesman can grab a capsicum bun or vegetable puff and have their hunger sated.

Sri Jayalakshmi Bakery near Lalbagh began in the 1960s and has branched out to include a second outlet nearby. We went there on a rainy afternoon and it was packed with customers lining up for *khara* bun and biscuits. Our pick would be the syrup-moist honey cake.

Then, there's Srinivasa Brahmins Bakery in Basavanagudi. It was begun in the 1950s by Ramaswamy Iyengar. The original outlet is on DVG Road and a newer one is on Bull Temple Road. Like most Iyengar bakeries, the owners hail from Hassan district in Karnataka. SBB, now run by Ram Prasad, is best known for its Congress *kadalekai*, a spiced peanut mixture. It's carried away by NRIs longing for a taste of Bangalore and home, and can also be served in a bun. The coconut-filled *dil pasand* here is also a top seller. The manufacturing is mechanized now and scores of different types of eggless cookies are also produced here.

If we were to choose a local bakery, it would be Albert Bakery in Frazer Town. This isn't an Iyengar Bakery, being famous for its *bheja* and mutton puffs. Begun in the year 1902 by Mohammed Yacoob, it was originally a godown near Kamaraj Road. It was the time of British rule and Yacoob thought it would be a good idea to give it an English name, hence Albert Bakery it was. He peddled buns and breads in the neighbourhood, going on to open the store in Frazer Town. Mohammed Sabir Faizan of the fourth generation now manages the store with his father Nawab Jan. It's a quirky business, opening only at 3 p.m., when crowds throng the place and chaos reigns. You consider yourself fortunate if you catch the eye of the staff, place your order, pay and pick up your goodies. But one bite of the khova naan and all the trouble is absolutely worth it. Imagine molten khova in a warm puff, fresh from the oven. Yes, it's sinful and delightful, and a perfect way to end a day on the street-food trail in our city.

ACKNOWLEDGEMENTS

We are deeply grateful to Sangeeta Prabhu Mahendran for her generosity and unstinting support that made this book possible. She both enabled the project and filled it with her special brand of positive energy.

Neel Sharma, friend who is family, planned itineraries, travelled alongside, tasted and captured the food and vendors in photographs and videos. A huge thank you is owed to him.

Chef Anumitra Ghosh-Dastidar guided us through Kolkata's iconic eateries. Sohini Sengupta, also from the city, helped us navigate its chaos.

In Madurai, Padmini and R. Sivarajah played host and helped us make connections with street-food vendors.

Elsewhere, our friends, colleagues and food lovers came forward and shared a wealth of information about the street food in their cities. Sabyasachi Ray Chaudhuri in Hyderabad, Jayesh Paranjape in Pune, Satya Behera in Orissa, Arvind Nadig in Bangalore, Anil Mulchandani in Ahmedabad, where Parvez Malik guided us through the old city, and Nickey Christie who took time off to show us the hidden corners of Surat. A big thank you to Soumya Gopi, who diligently researched Kerala and helped us discover the street food of the state, and Dev Ramanathan who planned itineraries for Jaipur and made walking through the city a breeze. Thanks are also due to Chef Prateek Sadhu, for his insights for Srinagar, and Chef Vikas Seth who did the same for his home town, Amritsar.

Kumar Ravichandran and Pratiksha Roy worked on the maps and drawings that illustrate the chapters.

This book is also a tribute to the countless street-food vendors of this country and we are grateful to them for the food they served us, the stories they shared, and their largeness of heart; many had to be forced to accept payment for the kachoris, pani puri and parotta we sampled. 'You are our guests,' they said. Little do they know that it is we who owe them a debt of gratitude for what they do.

What began merely as a nebulous idea of ours has become this book thanks only to the expert team at Rupa Publications. Thank you, Rudra Sharma, for your guidance and your patience as you stayed with a project that felt the full impact of the pandemic.

GLOSSARY

Aam	Mango
Aam barfi	Mango-flavoured fudge-like sweet
Aamiri khaman	Spicy snack of crumbled steamed lentil cakes topped with condiments
Aamras	Mango pulp
Aarti	Prayer ritual involving lamps
Adda	Gathering place for conversations
Ajwain	Carom seed
Akhada	Wrestling ring
Akuri	Parsi-style scrambled eggs
Aloo	Potato
Aloo palya	Dish of boiled and spiced potatoes
Aloo thukpa	Soup with potatoes and noodles
Aloo tikki	Potato croquette
Amla	Gooseberry
Amrit	Nectar
Amritsari kulcha	Stuffed Indian flat bread of Amritsar
Anarsa	Deep-fried oil cakes made of rice flour
Anda Bada	Egg fritters
Anna	Lowest denomination of ancient currency
Appam	Kerala staple of rice-flour batter cooked in shallow pan
Atta	Wheat flour
Aval	Flattened rice
Avil milk	Drink with milk, flattened rice and banana
Awadh	Historical region in North India, ruled by the Mughals
Azaadi	Freedom
Bada	Deep-fried savoury doughnuts made from lentil; same as vada, vadai, vade, bora
Bade miya	Old man
Baida roti	Flatbread stuffed with egg and/or meat

Bajra	Pearl millet
Balushahi	Flaky, deep-fried pastry coated in sugar syrup
Bandhini	Fabric with tie-and-dye pattern
Bandi	Cart
Baqarkhani	Thick, spiced flatbread of Mughlai cuisine
Barfi	Fudge-like sweet made from thickened milk
Barish mein toh majha hi majha hai	What fun it is in the rains!
Basrakh	Traditional Kashmiri winter sweet made of sugar, ghee and flour topped with dry fruit
Batata vada	Boiled and spiced potato balls that are batter-fried
Batla kachori	Deep-fried snack made with refined flour and stuffed with spicy green peas
Batla pattice	Spiced and mashed potato croquette with a filling of spiced peas
Bawaji	Father figure
Bazaar	Market
Bebinca	Many-layered baked sweet
Bedai or Bedmi puri	Deep-fried puffed bread stuffed with a lentil mix
Beegha kulcha	Indian flat bread dunked into a spicy chickpea curry
Begum	Muslim woman of high rank
Beguni	Batter-fried eggplant
Benne dose	Fermented batter pancake cooked to a crisp with liberal amounts of white butter
Besan	Chickpea flour
Bhaang	Preparation made from cannabis leaf
Bhaath	Flavoured rice
Bhai	Brother
Bhajia	Fritters
Bhalle papdi	Soft lentil dumplings soaked in yogurt, topped with spicy crackers and chutneys
Bhandar	Shop or store
Bhatura	Large deep-fried bread made with leavened dough
Bhelpuri	Snack of puffed rice, spices and chutney tossed together
Bhojanalay	Eating place
Bhujia	Light, crunchy snack made with gram flour and spices
Bhul bhulaya	Name given to Surat's layered omelette
Bhuna gosht	Mutton slow-cooked with a variety of spices
Bhunja	Roasted ingredients like rice and gram tossed together
Bhurji	Scramble

Bhutte ke khees	Fresh corn grated and cooked in milk with ghee
Biryani	Elegant, aromatic dish of rice cooked with meat
Bisibelebhath	Rice cooked with lentils and vegetables
Boi para	Book-selling neighbourhood
Bolinhas	Coconut cookies
Bolo de batica	Semolina and coconut cake
Bonda	Deep-fried dumpling
Boondi	Deep-fried droplets of batter soaked in sugar syrup
Bread bada	Bread stuffed with spiced potatoes and batter-fried; same as bread pakora
Bun maska	Bun slathered with butter
Bun parotta	Small, layered bread
Bun samosa	Samosa in a bun
Bun tikki	Potato croquette in a bun
Bundiya	Deep-fried droplets of batter soaked in sugar syrup; same as boondi, bunia
Bunia	Deep-fried droplets of batter soaked in sugar syrup, same as boondi, bundiya
Burqa	Long garment worn by Muslim women
Carrot halwa	Sweet dish made with grated carrots; same as gajar ka halwa
Cha	Tea in Bengal
Chaamp	Chop
Chaat	A star genre in street food, a family of savoury snacks that are a medley of textures and temperatures, finished with sweet, spicy, tangy sauces
Chaat masala	Spice mix containing cumin, dried mango, black salt and other ingredients
Chacha	Uncle
Chai	Tea
Chaiwala	Tea seller
Chakuli	Batter steamed to make thin, light breads
Chamanthi podi	Powder of chilli, lentils and coconut
Chana masala	Chickpea cooked in a spicy gravy
Chanawala	Seller of chickpea dishes
Chappan bhog	Offering to Lord Jagannath of Puri comprising 56 dishes
Chappan dukan	56 shops
Chatpata	Tangy
Chaura Rasta	Four-road junction
Chawal	Rice
Chawl	Neighbourhood comprising modest housing

GLOSSARY

Cheela	Lentil flour pancake
Chemmeen	Prawn/shrimp in Malayalam
Chenna poda	Sweet baked cottage cheese
Chhana	Cottage cheese
Chhanar Pulao	Sweet dish of cottage-cheese grains
Chhena jhilli	Fried cottage cheese, soaked in sugar syrup
Chhole	Spicy chickpea dish
Chhole masala	Chickpea cooked in a spicy gravy
Chicken 65	Chicken pieces, coated in spices and deep-fried
Chikan	Hand embroidery of Lucknow
Chikki	Nut brittle
Chivda	Savory snack of flattened rice flakes
Chokha	Mash, frequently made with potatoes and/or eggplant
Cholar dal	Mildly flavoured dal with coconut chips
Choora kadamb	Soaked beaten rice served with cottage cheese and sweetened, reduced milk
Choora matar	Flattened rice and fresh peas tossed together
Chooran	Digestive paste or powder
Chop	Croquette
Chorafali	Deep-fried snack made with lentil flour
Chori ka maal	Cheap goods, being sold as if they were stolen
Choris pao	Goan pork sausage cured with vinegar and spices served between bread
Chorizo	Goan pork sausage cured with vinegar and spices
Chote	Small
Chowk	Open market area at a street junction
Chowmein	Noodles tossed with vegetables and meat
Churma	Fried or roasted dough dumplings, crushed and sweetened
Churmura	Puffed rice
Churpi	Hard cheese from the Himalayan region
Chutney	A term encompassing an entire world of condiments to accompany any snack or meal
Congress kadalekai	Roasted peanuts tossed with spices
Curd vada	Lentil fritters immersed in yogurt
Dada	Grandfather
Dahi	Yogurt
Dahi bada	Deep fried lentil dumplings soaked in spiced yogurt and topped with chutney; same as dahi bhalle
Dahi bara aloo dum	Lentil fritters soaked in buttermilk, served with potato curry

BAZAAR BITES

Dahi bhalle	Deep-fried lentil dumplings soaked in yogurt and topped with chutneys; same as dahi bada
Dal baati	Baked balls wheat dough, served with a lentil curry
Dal bada	Lentil fritter; same as dal vada
Dal makhani	Slow-cooked black lentils enriched with butter
Dal moth	Mixture of fried dal and crunchy bits
Dal pakwan	A crisp fried bread served with dal
Dal puri	Deep-fried flatbread with a lentil filling
Dal Vada	Lentil fritter
Dalda	Hydrogenated vegetable oil
Dalma	Odisha staple of lentils cooked with seasonal vegetables
Dargah	Tomb of Muslim saint
Dasara	Indian festival dedicated to Goddess Durga
Deg	Larg, deep vessel
Desi	Native
Dhoka	Steamed and fried cakes of lentil paste
Dhokla	Steamed lentil flour squares
Dil pasand	Indian pie stuffed with sweetened coconut
Dilli	Delhi
Diwali	Indian festival of lights
Doce de grao	A fudge made with lentils and sugar
Dona	Cup crafted from leaves
Doodh	Milk
Dosa	Fermented batter pancake; same as dosai, dose
Dukan	Shop
Egg benjo	Indore name for omelette in a bun
Egg kachu	Egg cooked in spicy gravy
Ela ada	Batter steamed in leaves with sweet filling
Elanchi	Sweet pancake with coconut stuffing
Fafda	Deep-fried strips of chickpea flour
Falooda	Layered drink-cum-dessert of milk, syrup, Indian basil seeds and vermicelli
Farsan	Collective term for savoury snacks, typically deep-fried
Farsi puri	Crisp-fried snack
Filter coffee	Coffee extracted in metal filter, served with milk and sugar
Fulori	Gram-flour fritters
Gaddos	Street carts of Goa
Gadi	Cart or food truck
Gajak	Sesame sweet
Gajar ka halwa	Sweet dish of grated carrots

GLOSSARY

Galawati kebab	Kebabs shaped from minced mutton pounded with an array of spices and aromatics
Gali ki sabse purani dukan	Oldest shop in the street/lane
Galli	Lane/Street
Gamcha	Cotton towel
Garadu	Purple yam or taro
Garam masala	A combination of key spices like cardamom, cloves and cinnamon
Gathiya	Crisp-fried strands of gram-flour dough
Gatte ki sabzi	Chickpea flour dumplings cooked in a yogurt gravy
Ghanta ghar	Clock tower
Ghar	House
Ghari	Sweet made from wheat-flour batter, thickened milk, ghee and sugar
Ghat	Bank
Ghevar	A disc-shaped Rajasthani sweet with a honeycomb texture
Ghirmit	North Karnataka snack of puffed rice tossed with spices
Goda masala	Aromatic spice blend from Maharashtra
Ghotala	Medley of boiled and scrambled eggs
Ghujia	Pastry crescents with a sweet filling
Ghulamon ka koi naam nahi hota	Servants do not have names
Girda	Kashmiri tandoor-baked bread made with fermented dough
Gobhi manchurian	Spiced and batter-fried cauliflower florets
Gol gappa	Crisp shells, filled with spiced potato and topped with cold, spiced water; same as gupchup, pani puri, puchka, patashe
Goli	Small balls
Gondh	Edible gum with medicinal properties
Gopika	Woman who tends to cows
Gopuram	Temple tower
Gughni	Gravy made with peas
Gulab jamun	Sugar syrup-soaked dumplings
Gulkand	Rose-petal jam
Gupchup	Crisp shells, filled with spiced potato and topped with spiced water; same as gol gappa, pani puri, puchka, patashe
Gurda-kaleji	A spicy dish of kidneys and liver
Guru	Teacher
Hakim	Medicine man in the Islamic tradition
Haleem	Wheat, lentils and meat cooked to a puree
Halki	Light

Halve-parathe	Large deep-fried breads served with a sweet dish made of wheat flour or semolina
Halwa	Fudge made of flour, nuts or fruit
Halwai	Sweet maker
Handi	Cooking vessel
Hara chana	Fresh, green chickpeas
Haveli	Mansion
Hing kachori	Deep-fried breads filled with lentils flavoured with asafoetida
Hing	Asafoetida
Holige	Flat bread stuffed with sweetened lentils or coconut; same as puran poli
Ice orathi	Calicut beach special of shaved ice, syrup and toppings
Idiappam	Steamed rice noodles
Idli	Steamed cake of fermented rice and lentil batter
Imarti	Spirals of lentil batter soaked in sugar syrup
Ittar	Fragrance
Iyengar	People belonging to a South Indian caste
Jadoh	Rice cooked in pork fat, topped with curries and salads
Jal jeera	Digestive drink flavoured with cumin
Jaleba	A large version of the Jalebi
Jalebi	Deep-fried batter spirals soaked in sugar syrup; same as jilebi
Jamun	Purple fruit that is sweet and astringent
Janmashtami	Lord Krishna's birthday
Jannat	Paradise
Jeera	Cumin
Jhalmuri	Puffed rice tossed with mustard oil and spices
Jharoka	Carved window frame
Jhula	Swing
Jigarthanda	Cooling drink of reduced milk, almond resin and ice cream
Jil jil	Cold or cooling
Jilla	District
Jirem-mirem	Goan and Mangalorean spice blend of cumin seeds and black pepper
Kaanak masal	Boiled wheat and small beans, tossed in a spice mix
Kabiraji	Deep-fried dish of chicken or seafood with a lacy egg coating
Kachaloo	Taro
Kachori	Deep-fried bread with a spicy filling
Kachri	Family of fried snacks
Kadhai	Iron pan, used for deep frying; same as karhai
Kadhi	Yogurt gravy thickened with chickpea flour

GLOSSARY

Kahwa	Kashmiri tea flavoured with saffron
Kakdi	Condiment of grated cucumber and yogurt
Kalakhand	Milk sweet
Kandoi	Confectioner
Kandur	Baker in Kashmir
Kanji vada	Moong-bean fritters soaked in mustard water
Kappa	Tapioca
Karam podi	Hot spice powder
Karela paapdi chaat	Layered pastry that is deep-fried, served with chutneys
Karhai	Iron pan, used for deep frying; same as kadhai
Kari dosai	Fermented batter pancakes topped with mutton
Karighar	Skilled artisan
Karkhana	Factory
Kasuri methi	Dried fenugreek leaves
Kathi roll	Flatbread roll wrapped around vegetables, egg or meat
Katori	Small cup-like container
Kebabs	Grilled meats or veggies
Kesar	Saffron
Kesaribhath	Sweet dish made with semolina and ghee
Khaja	Sweet of layered dough, coated in sugar syrup
Khajur	Dates
Khali dose	Fermented batter pancake
Khaman	Spongy snack made from a steamed batter
Khameeri roti	Leavened Indian bread
Khand gazri	Strips of fried dough dipped in sugar syrup
Khara bun	Savoury bun
Kharabhath	Soft-cooked savoury dish made with semolina; same as upma
Khari	Flaky, savoury biscuit
Khau galli	Food street
Kheema	Minced meat
Kheer	Rice pudding
Khichdi	Rice and lentil cooked together
Khomcha	Makeshift, moveable food stand
Khova naan	Puff pastry stuffed with reduced milk
Khoya	Reduced milk
Khurchan	Sweet made from reduced milk
Kofta	Roundels of meat, cottage cheese or vegetables
Kola urundai	Deep-fried roundels of minced meat and spices
Kopra	Dried coconut
Korma	Gravy, often enriched with nuts

Kosha mangsho	Rich, slow-cooked mutton dish
Kothimbir vada	Savoury snack made with gram flour and coriander leaves
Kovil	Temple
Kulcha/Kulche	Type of bread
Kulfa	Cold sweet of rice pudding and Indian ice cream
Kulfi	Indian ice cream
Kulhad	Terracotta cup
Kurta	A loose collarless shirt
Laayeh	Coloured puffs made from rice and sugar
Laccha aloo tikki	Hashbrown-like potato crisp
Ladoo	Sweet balls made from any one of many ingredients
Lai	Sweet made from amaranth seed-like grain
Lassi	Sweet yogurt drink
Lassiwale	Lassi seller
Laung lata	Deep-fried pastry triangles pinned with a clove, soaked in sugar syrup
Laung sev	Savoury deep-fried strands spiced with cloves
Lavasa	Thin flatbread of Kashmir
Litti	Coal-roasted dough balls stuffed with lentil powder
Locho	Snack of steamed gram flour, topped with condiments
Luchi	Puffed deep-fried breads made with refined flour
Maalu ka patta	A leaf with medicinal properties used as a plate
Maidan	Open green space
Makhan	White butter
Makkai ki atta	Maize flour
Malai	Cream of milk
Malai makhan	Winter speciality of whipped top of milk; same as nimish, malaiyo
Malai puri	Sweet made from top of the milk
Malaiyo	Winter speciality of whipped top of milk; same as nimish, malai makhan
Malpua	Sweet pancakes
Marg	Street
Masal dose	Fermented batter pancake with a spiced potato filling
Masal vade	Crisp, deep-fried lentil fritters
Masala	Any combination of spices or aromatics, can be whole, ground or powdered
Masala tak	Salted yogurt drink topped with crisp bits
Masale tchot	Kashmiri flatbread roll stuffed with yellow peas and chutney
Mashawi	Arabic for grilled meat or vegetables
Masjid	Mosque

GLOSSARY

Mastani	Ice cream blended with milk and fruit pulp
Matar	Peas
Matar ka pani	Soupy dish of green peas
Mathri	Crisp discs spiked with pepper
Mausi	Aunt
Mawa	Milk solids
Mawa bati	Syrup-soaked dumplings stuffed with dry fruit
Mawa kachori	Crisp, deep-fried bread stuffed with milk solids and soaked in sugar syrup
Mazaa	Fun
Mehendi	Art of decorating hands and feet with the orange tint of henna leaves
Mess	No-frills eatery
Minar	Tower
Mirchi bada	Stuffed chilli fritters that are batter-coated and deep-fried; same as mirchi vada
Mirchi bhajji	Batter-fried chillies
Misal	Lentil curry topped with crunchy bits and onions
Mishri	Rock sugar
Mishtaan	Sweet
Mishti	Sweet
Mitha	Sweet
Mithai	Sweet
Mithaiwala	Seller of sweets
Mogar kachori	Crisp, deep-fried bread stuffed with moong dal
Moghlai or Mughlai	Of the Mughals
Moghlai paratha	Griddle-cooked bread stuffed with egg, meat and spices
Mohantal	Fudge made with gram flour, ghee and sugar
Mojri	Handcrafted footwear
Momo	Tibetan steamed dumplings, stuffed with meat or vegetables
Mongh masalah	Steamed Kashmiri black bean with salt and chillies
Moong	Green gram
Mosaru kodubale	Deep-fried rings of rice flour and yogurt dough
Motichoor ladoo	Roundels formed with syrup-soaked gram-flour droplets
Muri	Puffed rice
Mysore pak	South Indian sweet crafted from lentil flour, sugar and ghee
Naan	Type of flatbread
Naariyal	Coconut
Nadir monje	Lotus stem, dipped in rice-flour batter and fried to a crisp

BAZAAR BITES

Nagori halwa	Deep-fried breads served with semolina sweet
Nalli	Bone marrow
Namak para	Savoury snack of small, flaky pastry squares
Namakwali chai	Salty tea
Namkeen	Term referring to a family of savoury snacks
Nankhatai	Buttery, shortbread-like biscuits
Nargisi kofta	Spiced minced meat croquette with a piece of boiled egg inside
Narkol	Coconut
Nashta	Breakfast or snacky meal
Nawab	Erstwhile ruler of the Awadh region
Neichoru	Ghee rice
Nendran banana	Banana variety, common in Kerala
Nihari	Lamb shank and dish using this part
Nimish	Winter speciality of whipped top of the milk; same as malaiyo, malai makhan
Niwas	Residential building
Nizam	Erstwhile rulers of the Hyderabad region
Noogre	Crisp little balls of gram flour
Paan	Betel leaf
Pakoda	Deep-fried fritters made with vegetables dipped in gram-flour batter; same as pakora
Pakodewale	Seller of pakoda
Palav	Rice cooked with spices, vegetables or meat; same as pulav, pulao
Paneer	Cottage cheese
Paneer bhurji	Cottage-cheese scramble
Pani	Water
Pani ke patashe	Crisp shells, filled with spiced potato and topped with cool, spiced water; same as gol gappa, gupchup, puchka, pani puri
Pani puri	Crisp shells, filled with spiced potato and topped with cool, spiced water; same as gol gappa, gupchup, puchka, patashe
Pao	Small soft breads; same as pav
Papad	Lentil crisps served roasted or fried
Papdi chaat	Crisp flour discs topped with chutneys
Parantha	Griddle-cooked bread stuffed with vegetables or meat; same as paratha
Parotta	Many-layered bread cooked on griddle
Paruthi paal	Cottonseed milk
Patodi	A deep-fried envelope of dough stuffed with a mixture of gram flour, lentils and fresh coriander

GLOSSARY

Patra	Rolls of Colocasia leaves with a spiced lentil filling
Patthar ka gosht	Meat cooked on a hot stone
Pattice	Croquette
Pav bhaji	Meal comprising dish of mixed vegetables cooked down to a puree, served with small breads
Paya	Trotters; also dish made with trotters
Pazham pori	Batter-fried ripe banana
Peda	Sweet crafted from milk solids
Perad	Guava cheese
Permal	Type of rice
Petha	Candied squares of gourd
Phing	Mung bean jelly
Phirni	Rice pudding
Phoolwari	Abode of flowers
Phulkari	Type of embroidery
Phumbi	Mung-bean noodles from Kalimpong
Piaji	Fritter of onions and lentil flour
Pinaca	Sweet made with rice and jaggery
Pithe	Family of steamed and fried dishes crafted from rice flour
Poders	Traditional Goan bakers
Podi	Spice powder
Poha	Flattened rice
Poi	Goan bread
Pongal	Dish of soft-cooked rice and lentils
Prawn rissois	Seafood encased in a soft, crumb-fried crescent
Puchka	Small crisp shells filled with spiced potato and topped with cold, spicy water; same as gol gappa, gupchup, pani puri, patashe
Pudina	Mint
Puja	Prayer ritual
Puliodharai	Rice mixed with tamarind paste; same as puliogare
Puliogare	Rice mixed with tamarind paste; same as puliodharai
Pumaloi	Steamed powdered rice cake with sweet filling
Puran poli	Flat bread stuffed with a variety of sweet fillings like lentils or coconut; same as holige
Purani Dilli	Old Delhi
Puri	Deep-fried puffed bread; same as poori
Puriwale	Puri seller
Puttu	Steamed rice and coconut crumble
Pyaaji	Onion fritters
Pyaaz	Onion

Raas leela	Divine dance
Rabri	Sweetened reduced milk; same as rabdi
Radhaballabi	Small fried breads with a lentil filling
Ragi	Type of millet
Ragi mudde	Millet-flour balls
Raita	Yogurt accompaniment
Raj bhog	Syrup-soaked, cottage-cheese balls stuffed with nuts
Rajma	Red kidney beans
Ram naam satya hai	Chant accompanying the bearing of corpses to burning ghat or crematorium
Ramzan	Ninth month of the Muslim calendar; same as Ramadan
Rasam	Thin, sour, spicy broth
Rasmalai	Cottage-cheese balls, immersed in thickened milk
Rassa	Gravy
Raswala	Juicy
Ratalu	Purple yam
Rava	Semolina
Rava vada	Crisp semolina cakes
Rishta	Relation
Ros omelette	Omelette served with gravy
Rosogolla	Cottage-cheese balls cooked in sugar syrup
Roti	Flatbread
Rudraksha	Dried seeds of the fruit of the Elaeocarpus ganitrus tree
Saada	Normal
Saaru	A thin soupy dish of meat or vegetables
Sab ghuzaaron ke ashirwad	The blessings of ancestors
Sabja seeds	Basil seeds
Sabudana	Sago
Sagla bagla	Filo-like pastry enfolding milk solids and dry fruit
Sagu	Vegetable gravy
Sali boti	Parsi mutton dish topped with crispy fried potato sticks
Salna	Thin gravy, often with a meat broth base
Salwar	Loose trousers
Salwar kameez	Ethnic wear of loose trousers and long tunic
Sambar	Dish of lentils and vegetables
Samosa	Crisp triangles, filled with spiced potatoes or meat
Samrat	Emperor
Sandesh	Sweet shaped from fresh cottage cheese and sugar or jaggery
Santra	Orange

GLOSSARY

Sarovar	Lake
Satpura samosa	Spiced potato filling in a puff pastry
Sattu	Gram flour
Sattwik/Sattvik	Clean, fresh food, typically without the use of onion and garlic
Seekh kabab	Minced meat cooked on a skewer
Segari	Water chestnut
Sev	Noodle-like crisps; same as shev
Shab-e-malwa	The evenings of Malwa
Shahi samosa	Royal version of the samosa with nuts
Shahi sheermal	Sweet flatbread brushed with saffron milk
Shakarkand	Sweet potato
Shapaley	Tibetan dish of meat-filled pastries
Sharva	Thin meat gravy that accompanies, say, biryani
Shavige bhath	Savoury dish made with thin rice noodles
Sheera	Sweet made with semolina, ghee and sugar
Sheermal	A slightly sweet flatbread
Sherbet	Sweet cold drink
Shikanjvi	Thickened milk blended with yogurt, spices and nuts
Shivroli	Rice-flour strands topped with jaggery
Shudh shakahari	Pure vegetarian
Silli gosht	Mutton cooked on skewers
Singhara	Name for samosa in West Bengal and Odisha
Sitaphal	Custard apple
Sohan halwa	Dense fudge-like sweet
Sonth ke ladoo	Sweets flavoured with dry ginger
Sooji	Semolina; same as rava
Sorpotel	Pork dish using offal
Soya chaap	Nuggets made from soybean and processed to resemble the texture of meat
Sukiyan	Sweetened green lentil balls, batter-fried
Surti khaman	Steamed snack made with a lentil-flour batter
Sussegad	The laidback attitude of Goa
Swadisht	Tasty
Taipo	Mega-sized steamed dumplings
Tam tam khaman	Steamed snack made with lentil batter
Tamatar chaat	A medley of tomatoes and potatoes, topped with crunchy bits and chutney
Tandoor	Clay oven
Tapri	Tea stall
Tarri	Dark, spicy brown-chickpea gravy

Tava pulao	Rice tossed on a griddle with vegetables and spices
Tava	Griddle Tele Bhaja Any dish from a family of deep-fried snacks
Thali	Platter or meal served on platter
Thalipeeth	Multigrain flatbread of Maharashtra
Thandai	Drink of milk enriched with nuts and spices
Thatte idli	Larger and softer than regular idli
Thattukada	Street cart
Theeka	Spicy
Thela	Cart
Thindi beedi	Food street
Thukpa	Tibetan-style broth with noodles and meat
Tiffin	Light meal
Tikki	Croquette
Tikki chaat	Potato croquette topped with chutney
Tilgud	Sweet made with sesame and jaggery
Tonga	Horse cart
Tujj	Grilled meat
Tungrymbai	Soybean condiment unique to Meghalaya
Tungtap	Fermented fish condiment
Uddin vade	Deep-fried, doughnut-shaped lentil fritters
Undiyo	Medley of seasonal greens, beans and vegetables
Unnakkaya	Deep-fried banana with sweet stuffing
Unniappam	Small, pan-fried sweet dumplings
Upahar gruh	Eating house
Upma	Savoury dish of soft-cooked semolina; same as kharabhath
Urad	Black lentil
Urs	Death anniversary of Sufi saint
Vada	Deep-fried lentil fritter; same as vade, bada, bara, bora
Vada pav	Batter-fried mashed potato balls in a bun
Vadai	Deep-fried lentil fritter; same as vada, vade, bada, bara, bora
Vadi	Spiced lentil dumplings that are sun-dried; same as wadi
Vanaspati	Hydrogenated vegetable cooking oil
Vanela gathiya	Deep-fried snack made of gram flour
Vatthal kuzhambu	Sour curry
Vel muri	Puffed rice, tossed with spices and drizzled with mustard oil; same as bhelpuri
Wadi	Spiced lentil dumplings that are sun-dried; same as vadi
Warq	Silver foil
Wazwan	Traditional Kashmiri meal of meat dishes
Xacuti	Goan curry

GLOSSARY